THE GREAT ANARCHISTS
Ideas and Teachings of
Seven Major Thinkers

PAUL ELTZBACHER
Translated by Steven T. Byington

DOVER PUBLICATIONS INC.
Mineola, New York

Bibliographical Note

This Dover edition, first published in 2004, is a republication of *Anarchism,* originally published by Benjamin R. Tucker, New York, in 1908. The Translator's Preface and the plates have been omitted from this edition.

Library of Congress Cataloging-in-Publication Data

Eltzbacher, Paul, 1868–1928.
   [Anarchismus. English]
   The great anarchists : ideas and teachings of seven major thinkers / Paul Eltzbacher ; translated by Steven T. Byington.
     p. cm.
   Originally published: Anarchism. New York : B.R. Tucker, 1908.
   Includes bibliographical references and index.
   ISBN 0-486-43632-2 (pbk.)
    1. Anarchism. 2. Anarchists. I. Title.

HX828.E5413 2004
335'.83'0922—dc22

                                     2004056028

Manufactured in the United States of America
Dover Publications, Inc., 31 East 2nd Street, Mineola, N.Y. 11501

CONTENTS

THE GREAT ANARCHISTS
Ideas and Teachings of Seven Major Thinkers

INTRODUCTION

1. We want to know Anarchism scientifically, for reasons both personal and external.

We wish to penetrate the essence of a movement that dares to question what is undoubted and to deny what is venerable, and nevertheless takes hold of wider and wider circles. Besides, we wish to make up our minds whether it is not necessary to meet such a movement with force, to protect the established order or at least its quiet progressive development, and, by ruthless measures, to guard against greater evils.

2. At present there is the greatest lack of clear ideas about Anarchism, and that not only among the masses but among scholars and statesmen.

Now it is a historic law of evolution* that is decribed as the supreme law of Anarchism, now it is the happiness of the individual,† now justice.‡

Now they say that Anarchism culminates in the negation of every programme,§ that it has only a negative aim; ‖ now, again, that its negating and destroying side is balanced by a side that is affirmative and creative; ¶ now, to conclude, that what is original in Anarchism is to be found exclusively in its utterances about the ideal society,** that its real, true essence consists in its positive efforts.††

---

* "*Der Anarchismus und seine Traeger*" pp. 124, 125, 127; Reichesberg p. 27.
† Lenz p. 3. ‡ Bernatzik pp. 2, 3. § Lenz p. 5. ‖ Crispi.
¶ Van Hamel p. 112. ** Adler p. 321. †† Reichesberg. p. 13.

Now it is said that Anarchism rejects law,* now
that it rejects society,† now that it rejects only the
State.‡
    Now it is declared that in the future society of An-
archism there is no tie of contract binding persons
together; § now, again, that Anarchism aims to have
all public affairs arranged for by còntracts between
federally constituted communes and societies.‖
    Now it is said in general that Anarchism rejects
property,¶ or at least private property; ** now a distinction is made between Communistic and Individualistic,†† or even between Communistic, Collectivistic,
and Individualistic Anarchism.‡‡
    Now it is asserted that Anarchism conceives of its
realization as taking place through crime,§§ especially
through a violent revolution‖‖ and by the help of the
propaganda of deed; ¶¶ now, again, that Anarchism
rejects violent tactics and the propaganda of deed,***
or that these are at least not necessary constituents of
Anarchism.†††
    3. Two demands must be made of everybody who
undertakes to produce a scientific work on Anarchism.
    First, he must be acquainted with the most impor-
tant Anarchistic writings.   Here, to be sure, one

---

* Stammler pp. 2, 4, 34, 36; Lenz pp. 1, 4.
† Silió p, 145; Garraud p. 12; Reichesberg p. 16; Tripels p. 253.
‡ Bernstein p. 359; Bernatzik p. 3.   § Reichesberg p. 30.
‖ Lombroso p. 31.   ¶ Silió p. 145; Dubois p. 213.
** Lombroso p. 31; Proal p. 50.
†† Rienzi p. 9; Stammler pp. 28-31; Merlino pp. 18, 27; Shaw p. 23.
‡‡ "Die historische Entwickelung des Anarchismus" p. 16; Zenker p. 161.
§§ Garraud p. 6; Lenz p. 5.
‖‖ Sernicoli vol. 2 p. 116; Garraud p. 2; Reichesberg p. 38; Van Hamel
p, 113.
¶¶ Garraud pp. 10, 11; Lombroso p. 34; Ferri p. 257,
*** Mackay " Magazin " pp. 913-915; " Anarchisten " pp. 239-243.
††† Zenker pp. 203, 204.

meets great difficulties. Anarchistic writings are very scantily represented in our public libraries. They are in part so rare that it is extremely difficult for an individual to acquire even the most prominent of them. So it is not strange that of all works on Anarchism only one is based on a comprehensive knowledge of the sources. This is a pamphlet which appeared anonymously in New York in 1894, "*Die historische Entwickelung des Anarchismus*," which in sixteen pages gives a concise presentation that attests an astonishing acquaintance with the most various Anarchistic writings. The two large works, "*L' anarchia e gli anarchici, studio storico e politico di E. Sernicoli*," 2 vol., Milano, 1894, and "*Der Anarchismus, kritische Geschichte der anarchistischen Theorie von E. V. Zenker*," Jena, 1895, are at least in part founded on a knowledge of Anarchistic writings.

Second, he who would produce a scientific work on Anarchism must be equally at home in jurisprudence, in economics, and in philosophy. Anarchism judges juridical institutions with reference to their economic effects, and from the standpoint of some philosophy or other. Therefore, to penetrate its essence and not fall a victim to all possible misunderstandings, one must be familiar with those concepts of philosophy, jurisprudence, and economics which it applies or has a relation to. This demand is best met, among all works on Anarchism, by Rudolf Stammler's pamphlet, "*Die Theorie des Anarchismus*," Berlin, 1894.

CHAPTER I

THE PROBLEM

1.—GENERAL

The problem for our study is, to get determinate concepts of Anarchism and its species. As soon as such determinate concepts are attained, Anarchism is scientifically known. For their determination is not only conditioned on a comprehensive view of all the individual phenomena of Anarchism; it also brings together the results of this comprehensive view, and assigns to them a place in the totality of our knowledge.

The problem of getting determinate concepts of Anarchism and its species seems at a first glance perfectly clear. But the apparent clearness vanishes on closer examination.

For there rises first the question, what shall be the starting-point of our study? The answer will be given, " Anarchistic teachings." But there is by no means an agreement as to what teachings are Anarchistic; one man designates as " Anarchistic " these teachings, another those; and of the teachings themselves a part designate themselves as Anarchistic, a part do not. How can one take any of them as Anarchistic teachings for a starting-point, without applying that very concept of Anarchism which he has yet to determine?

Then rises the further question, what is the goal of the study? The answer will be given, " the concepts of Anarchism and its species." But we see daily that different men define in quite different ways the concept of an object which they yet conceive in the same way. One says that law is the general will; another, that it is a mass of precepts which limit a man's natural liberty for other men's sake; a third, that it is the ordering of the life of the nation (or of the community of nations) to maintain God's order of the world. They all know that a definition should state the proximate genus and the distinctive marks of the species, but this knowledge does them little good. So it seems that the goal of the study does still require elucidation.

Lastly rises the question, what is the way to this goal? Any one who has ever observed the conflict of opinions in the intellectual sciences knows well, on the one hand, how utterly we lack a recognized method for the solution of problems; and, on the other hand, how necessary it is in any study to get clearly in mind the method that is to be used.

2. Our study can come to a more precise specification of its problem. The problem is to put concepts in the place of non-conceptual notions of Anarchism and its species.

Every concept-determining study faces the problem of comprehending conceptually an object that was first comprehended non-conceptually, and therefore of putting a concept in the place of non-conceptual notions of an object. This problem finds a specially clear expression in the concept-determining judgment (the definition), which puts in immediate juxtaposition, in its subject some non-conceptual notion of an object, and in its predicate a conceptual notion of the same object.

Accordingly, the study that is to determine the concepts of Anarchism and its species has for its problem to comprehend conceptually objects that are first comprehended in non-conceptual notions of Anarchism and its species; and therefore, to put concepts in the place of these non-conceptual notions.

3. But our study may specify its problem still more precisely, though at first only on the negative side. The problem is not to put concepts in the place of all notions that appear as non-conceptual notions of Anarchism and its species.

Any concept can comprehend conceptually only one object, not another object together with this. The concept of health cannot be at the same time the concept of life, nor the concept of the horse that of the mammal.

But in the non-conceptual notions that appear as notions of Anarchism and its species there are comprehended very different objects. To be sure, the object of all these notions is on the one hand a genus that is formed by the common qualities of certain teachings, and on the other hand the species of this genus, which are formed by the addition of sundry peculiarities to these common qualities. But still these notions have in view very different groups of teachings with their common and special qualities, some perhaps only the teachings of Kropotkin and Most, others only the teachings of Stirner, Tucker, and Mackay, others again the teachings of both sets of authors.

If one proposed to put concepts in the place of all the non-conceptual notions which appear as notions of Anarchism and its species, these concepts would have to comprehend at once the common and special qualities of quite different groups of teachings, of which groups one might embrace only the teachings of Kropotkin and Most, another only those of Stirner, Tucker, and Mackay, a third both. But this is impossible: the concepts of Anarchism and its species can comprehend only the common and special qualities of a single group of teachings; therefore our study cannot put concepts in the place of all the notions that appear as notions of Anarchism and its species.

4. By completing on the affirmative side this negative specification of its problem, our study can arrive at a still more precise specification of this problem. The problem is to put concepts in the place of those non-conceptual notions of Anarchism and its species, having in view one and the same group of teachings, which are most widely diffused among the men who at present are scientifically concerned with Anarchism.

Because the only possible problem for our study is to put concepts in the place of part of the notions that appear as non-conceptual notions of Anarchism and its species,—to wit, only in the place of such notions as have in view one and the same group of teachings with its common and special qualities,— therefore we must divide into classes, according to the groups of teachings that they severally have in view, the notions that appear as notions of Anarchism and its species, and we must choose the class whose notions are to be replaced by concepts.

The choice of the class must depend on the kind of men for whom the study is meant.   For the study of a concept is of value only for those who non-conceptually apprehend the object of the concept, since the concept takes the place of their notions only.   For those who form a non-conceptual notion of space, the concept of morality is so far meaningless; and just as meaningless, for those who mean by Anarchism what the teachings of Proudhon and Stirner have in common, is the concept of what is common to the teachings of Proudhon, Stirner, Bakunin, and Kropotkin.

But the men for whom this study is meant are those who at present are scientifically concerned with Anarchism.   If all these, in their notions of Anarchism and its species, had in view one and the same group of teachings, then the problem for our study would be to put concepts in the place of this set of notions.   Since this is not the case, the only possible problem for our study is to put concepts in the place of that set of notions which has in view a group of teachings that the greatest possible number of the men at present scientifically concerned with Anarchism have in view in their non-conceptual notions of Anarchism and its species.

2.—THE STARTING-POINT

In accordance with what has been said, the starting-point of our study must be those non-conceptual notions of Anarchism and its species, having in view one and the same group of teachings, which are most widely diffused among the men who at present are scientifically concerned with Anarchism.

1. How can it be known what group of teachings the non-conceptual notions of Anarchism and its species most widely diffused among the men at present scientifically concerned with Anarchism have in view? First and foremost, this may be seen from utterances regarding particular Anarchistic teachings, and from lists and descriptions of such teachings.

We may assume that a man regards as Anarchistic those teachings which he designates as Anarchistic, and, further, those teachings which are likewise characterized by the common qualities of these. We may further assume that a man does not regard as Anarchistic those teachings which he in any form contrasts with the Anarchistic teachings, nor, if he undertakes to catalogue or describe the whole body of Anarchistic teachings, those teachings unknown to him which are not characterized by the common qualities of the teachings he catalogues or describes.

What group of teachings those non-conceptual notions of Anarchism and its species which are most widely diffused among the men at present scientifically concerned with Anarchism have in view, may be seen secondly from the definitions of Anarchism and from other utterances about it. We may doubtingly assume that a man regards as Anarchistic those teachings which come under his definition of Anarchism, or for which his utterances about Anarchism hold good; and, on the contrary, that he does not regard as Anarchistic those teachings which do not come under that definition, or for which these utterances do not hold good.

When these two means of knowledge lead to contradictions, the former must be decisive. For, if a man so defines Anarchism, or so speaks of Anarchism, that on this basis teachings which he declares non-Anarchistic manifest themselves to be Anarchistic,—and perhaps other teachings, which he counts among the Anarchistic, to be non-Anarchistic,—this can be due only to his not being conscious of the scope of his general pronouncements; therefore it is only from his treatment of the individual teachings that one can find out his opinion of these.

2. These means of knowledge inform us what group of teachings the non-conceptual notions of Anarchism and its species most widely diffused among the men at present scientifically concerned with Anarchism have in view.

We learn, first, that the teachings of certain particular men are recognized as Anarchistic teachings by the greater part of those who at present are scientifically concerned with Anarchism.

We learn, second, that by the greater part of those who at present are scientifically concerned with Anarchism the teachings of these men are recognized as Anarchistic teachings only in so far as they relate to law, the State, and property; but not in so far as they may be concerned with the law, State, or property of a particular legal system or a particular group of legal systems, nor in so far as they regard other objects, such as religion, the family, art.

Among the recognized Anarchistic teachings seven are particularly prominent: to wit, the teachings of Godwin, Proudhon, Stirner, Bakunin, Kropotkin,

Tucker, and Tolstoi. They all manifest themselves to be Anarchistic teachings according to the greater part of the definitions of Anarchism, and of other scientific utterances about it. They all display the qualities that are common to the doctrines treated of in most descriptions of Anarchism. Some of them, be it one or another, are put in the foreground in almost every work on Anarchism. Of no one of them is it denied, to an extent worth mentioning, that it is an Anarchistic teaching.

3.—THE GOAL

In accordance with what has been said, the goal of our study must be to determine, first, the concept of the genus which is constituted by the common qualities of those teachings which the greater part of the men at present scientifically concerned with Anarchism recognize as Anarchistic teachings; second, the concepts of the species of this genus, which are formed by the accession of any specialties to those common qualities.

1. The first thing toward a concept is that an object be apprehended as clearly and purely as possible.

In non-conceptual notions an object is not apprehended with all possible clearness. In our non-conceptual notions of gold we most commonly make clear to ourselves only a few qualities of gold; one of us, perhaps, thinks mainly of the color and the lustre, another of the color and malleability, a third of some other qualities. But in the concept of gold color, lustre, malleability, hardness, solubility, fusibility, specific gravity, atomic weight, and all other qualities of gold, must be apprehended as clearly as possible.

Nor is an object apprehended in all possible purity in our non-conceptual notions. We introduce into our non-conceptual notions of gold many things that do not belong among the qualities of gold; one, perhaps, thinks of the present value of gold, another of golden dishes, a third of some sort of gold coin. But all these alien adjuncts must be kept away from the concept of gold.

So the first goal of our study is to describe as clearly as possible on the one side, and as purely as possible on the other, the common qualities of those teachings which the greater part of the men at present scientifically concerned with Anarchism recognize as Anarchistic teachings, and the specialties of all the teachings which display these common qualities.

2. It is further requisite for a concept that an object should have its place assigned as well as possible in the total realm of our experience,—that is, in a system of species and genera which embraces our total experience.

In non-conceptual notions an object does not have its place assigned in the total realm of our experience, but arbitrarily in one of the many genera in which it can be placed according to its various qualities. One of us, perhaps, thinks of gold as a species of the genus "yellow bodies," another as a species of the genus "malleable bodies," a third as a species of some other genus. But the concept of gold must assign it a place in a system of species and genera that embraces our whole experience,—a place in the genus "metals."

So a further goal of our study is to assign a place as well as possible in the total realm of our experience (that is, in a system of species and genera which embraces our total experience) for the common qualities of those teachings which the greater part of the men at present scientifically concerned with Anarchism recognize as Anarchistic teachings, and for the specialties of all the teachings that display these common qualities.

4.—THE WAY TO THE GOAL

In accordance with what has been said, the way that our study must take to go from its starting-point to its goal will be in three parts. First, the concepts of law, the State, and property must be determined. Next, it must be ascertained what the Anarchistic teachings assert about law, the State, and property. Finally, after removing some errors, we must get determinate concepts of Anarchism and its species.

1. First, we must get determinate concepts of law, the State, and property; and this must be of law, the State, and property in general, not of the law, State, or property of a particular legal system or a particular family of legal systems.

Law, the State, and property, in this sense, are the objects about which the doctrines which are to be examined in their common and special qualities make assertions. Before the fact of any assertions about an object can be ascertained,—not to say, before the common and special qualities of these assertions can be brought out and assigned to a place in the total realm of our experience,—we must get a determinate concept of this object itself. Hence the first thing that must be done is to determine the concepts of law, the State, and property (chapter II).

2. Next, it must be ascertained what the Anarchistic teachings assert about law, the State, and property; —that is, the recognized Anarchistic teachings, and also those teachings which likewise display the qualities common to these. What the recognized Anarchistic teachings say, must be ascertained in order to determine the concept of Anarchism. What all the teachings that display the common qualities of the recognized Anarchistic teachings say, must be ascertained in order that we may get determinate concepts of the species of Anarchism.

So each of these teachings must be questioned regarding its relation to law, the State, and property. These questions must be preceded by the question on what foundation the teaching rests, and must be followed by the question how it conceives the process of its realization.

It is impossible to present here all recognized Anarchistic teachings, not to say all Anarchistic teachings. Therefore our study limits itself to the presentation of seven especially prominent teachings (chapters III to IX), and then, from this standpoint, seeks to get a view of the totality of recognized Anarchistic teachings and of all Anarchistic teachings (chapter X).

The teachings presented are presented in their own words,* but according to a uniform system: the first, for security against the importation of alien thoughts; the second, to avoid the uncomparable juxtaposition

---

* Russian writings are cited from translations, which are cautiously revised where they seem too harsh.

of fundamentally different courses of thought. They have been compelled to give definite replies to definite questions; it was indeed necessary in many cases to bring the answers together in tiny fragments from the most various writings, to sift them so far as they contradicted each other, and to explain them so far as they deviated from ordinary language. Thus Tolstoi's strictly logical structure of thought and Bakunin's confused talk, Kropotkin's discussions full of glowing philanthropy and Stirner's self-pleasing smartness, come before our eyes directly and yet in comparable form.

3. Finally, after removing widely diffused errors, we are to get determinate concepts of Anarchism and its species.

We must, therefore, on the basis of that knowledge of the Anarchistic teachings which we have acquired, clear away the most important errors about Anarchism and its species; and then we must determine what the Anarchistic teachings have in common, and what specialties are represented among them, and assign to both a place in the total realm of our experience. Then we have the concepts of Anarchism and its species (chapter XI).

CHAPTER II

LAW, THE STATE, PROPERTY

1.—GENERAL

In this discussion we are to get determinate concepts of law, the State, and property in general, not of the law, State, and property of a particular legal system or of a particular family of legal systems. The concepts of law, State, and property are therefore to be determined as concepts of general jurisprudence, not as concepts of any particular jurisprudence.

1. By the concepts of law, State, and property one may understand, first, the concepts of law, State, and property in the science of a particular legal system.

These concepts of law, State, and property contain all the characteristics that belong to the substance of a particular legal system. They embrace only the substance of this system. They may, therefore, be called concepts of the science of this system. For we may designate as the science of a particular legal system that part of jurisprudence which concerns itself exclusively with the norms of a particular legal system.

The concepts of law, State, and property in the science of a legal system are distinguished from the concepts of law, State, and property in the sciences of other legal systems by this characteristic,—that they are concepts of norms of this particular system. From this characteristic we may deduce all the characteristics that result from the special substance of this system of law in contrast to other such systems. The concepts of property in the present laws of the German empire, of France, and of England are distinguished by the fact that they are concepts of norms of these three different legal systems. Consequently they are as different as are the norms of the present imperial-German, French, and English law on the subject of property. The concepts of law, State, and property in different legal systems are to each other as species-concepts which are subordinate to one and the same generic concept.

2. Second, one may understand by the concepts of law, State, and property the concepts of law, State, and property in the science of a particular family of laws.

These concepts of law, State, and property contain all the characteristics that belong to the common substance of the different legal systems of this family. They embrace only the common substance of the different systems of this family. They may, therefore, be called concepts of the science of this family of laws. For we may designate as the science of a particular family of laws that part of jurisprudence which deals exclusively with the norms of a particular family of legal systems, so far as these are not already dealt with by the sciences of the particular legal systems of this family.

The concepts of law, State, and property in the science of a family of laws are distinguished from the concepts of law, State, and property in the sciences of the legal systems that form the family by lacking the characteristic of being concepts of norms of these systems, and consequently lacking also all the characteristics which may be deduced from this characteristic according to the special substance of one or another legal system. The concept of the State in the science of present European law is distinguished from the concepts of the State in the sciences of present German, Russian, and Belgian law by not being a concept of norms of any one of these systems, and consequently by lacking all the characteristics that result from the special substance of the constitutional norms in force in Germany, Russia, and Belgium. Its relation to the concepts of the State in the science of these systems is that of a generic concept to subordinate species-concepts.

The concepts of law, State, and property in the science of a family of laws are distinguished from the concepts of law, State, and property in the sciences of other such families by this characteristic,—that they are concepts of norms of this particular family. From this characteristic we may deduce all the characteristics that are peculiar to the common substance of the different legal systems of this family in contrast to the common substance of the different legal systems of other families. The concept of the State in the science of present European law and the concept of the State in the science of European law in the year 1000 are distinguished by the fact that the one is a concept of constitutional norms that are in force in Europe to-day, the other of such as were in force in Europe then; consequently they are different in the same way as what the constitutional norms in force in Europe to-day have in common is different from what was common to the constitutional norms in force in

Europe then. These concepts are to each other as species-concepts which are subordinate to one and the same generic concept.

3. Third, one may understand by the concepts of law, State, and property the concepts of law, State, and property in general jurisprudence.

These concepts of law, State, and property contain all the characteristics that belong to the common substance of the most different systems and families of laws. They embrace only what the norms of the most different systems and families of laws have in common. They may, therefore, be called concepts of general jurisprudence. For that part of jurisprudence which treats of legal norms without limitation to any particular system or family of laws, so far as these norms are not already treated by the sciences of the particular systems and families, may be designated as general jurisprudence.

The concepts of law, State, and property in general jurisprudence are distinguished from the concepts of law, State, and property in the particular jurisprudences by lacking the characteristic of being concepts of norms of one of these systems or at least one of these families of systems, and consequently lacking also all the characteristics which may be deduced from this characteristic according to the special substance of some system or family of laws. The concept of law *per se* is distinguished from the concept of law in present European law and from the concept of law in the present law of the German empire by not being a concept of norms of that family of laws, not to say that particular system, and consequently by lacking all the characteristics that might belong to any peculiarities which might be common to all legal norms at present in force in Europe or in Germany. Its relation to the concepts of law in these particular jurisprudences is that of a generic concept to subordinate species-concepts.

4. In which of the senses here distinguished the concepts of law, State, and property should be defined in a particular case, and what matters should accordingly be taken into consideration in defining them, depends on the purpose of one's study.

If, for example, the point is to describe scientifically the constitutional norms of the present law of the German empire, then the concept of the State as defined on this occasion must be a concept of the science of this particular legal system. For scientific work on the norms of a particular legal system requires that concepts be formed of the norms of just this system. Consequently the material to be taken into consideration will be only the constitutional norms of the present law of the German empire.—That the concepts defined in the scientific description of a system of law are in fact concepts of the science of this system may indeed seem obscure. For every concept of the science of any particular system of law may be defined as the concept of a species under the corresponding generic concept of general jurisprudence. We define this generic concept, say the concept of the State in general jurisprudence, and add the distinctive characteristic of the species-concept, that it is a concept of norms of this particular system of law, say of the present law of the German empire. And then we often leave this additional characteristic unexpressed, where we think we may assume (as is the case in the scientific description of the norms of any particular system of law) that everybody will regard it as tacitly added. The consequence is that the definition given in the scientific description of a particular system of law looks, at a superficial glance, like the definition of a concept of general jurisprudence.

Or, if the point is to compare scientifically the norms of present European law regarding property, the concept of property as defined on this occasion must be a concept of the science of this particular family of laws. For the scientific comparison of norms of different legal systems demands that concepts of the sciences of these different legal systems be subordinately arranged under the corresponding concept of the science of the family of laws which is made up of these systems. Consequently the material to be taken into consideration will be only the norms of this family of laws.—Here again, indeed, it may seem obscure that the concepts defined are really concepts of the science of this family of laws. For the concepts that belong to the science of a family of laws may likewise be defined by defining the corresponding concepts of general jurisprudence and tacitly adding the characteristic of being concepts of norms of this particular family of laws.

Finally, if it comes to pass that the point is to compare scientifically what the norms of the most diverse systems of law have in common, the concept of law as defined on this occasion must be a concept of general jurisprudence. For the scientific comparison

of norms of the most diverse systems and families of
laws demands that concepts which belong to the
sciences of the most diverse systems and families of
laws be subordinately arranged under the corresponding concept of general jurisprudence. Consequently
the material to be taken into consideration will be the
norms of the most diverse systems and families of
laws.

Here,—where the point is to take the first step
toward a scientific comprehension of teachings which
pass judgment on law, the State, and property in general, not only on the law, State, or property of a particular system or family of laws,—the concepts of law,
State, and property must necessarily be defined as
concepts of general jurisprudence. For a scientific
comprehension of teachings which deal with the
common substance of the most diverse systems and
families of laws demands that concepts of this common substance—consequently concepts belonging to
general jurisprudence—be formed. Therefore we have
to take into consideration, as our material, the norms
(especially regarding the State and property) of the
most diverse systems and families of laws.

2.—LAW

*Law is the body of legal norms. A legal norm is
a norm which is based on the fact that men have the
will to see a certain procedure generally observed
within a circle which includes themselves.*

1. A legal norm is a norm.

A norm is the idea of a correct procedure. A correct procedure means one that corresponds either to

the final purpose of all human procedure (unconditionally correct procedure,—for instance, respect for another's life), or at any rate to some accidental purpose (conditionally correct procedure,—for instance, the skilled handling of a picklock). And the idea of a correct procedure means that the unconditionally or conditionally correct procedure is to be thought of not as a fact but as a task, not as something real but as something to be realized; it does not mean that I shall in fact spare my enemy's life, but that I am to spare it—not how the thief really did use the picklock, but how he should have used it. The idea of a correct procedure is what we designate as an "ought": when I think of an "ought," I think of what has to be done in order to realize either the final purpose of all human procedure or some accidental personal purpose. All passing of judgment on past procedure is conditioned upon the idea of a correct procedure—only with regard to this idea can past procedure be described as good or bad, expedient or inexpedient; and so is all deliberation on future procedure—only with regard to this idea does one inquire whether it will be right, or at any rate expedient, to proceed in a given manner.

Every legal norm represents a procedure as correct, declares that it corresponds to a particular purpose. And it represents this correct procedure as an idea, designates it not as a fact but as a task, does not say that any one does proceed so but that one is to proceed so. Hence a legal norm is a norm.

2. A legal norm is a norm based on a human will. A norm based on a human will is a norm by virtue

of which one must proceed in a certain way in order
that he may not put himself in opposition to the will
of some particular men, and so be apprehended by the
power which is at the service of these men. Such a
norm, therefore, represents a procedure only as conditionally correct; to wit, as a means to the end (which
we are perhaps pursuing or perhaps despising) of remaining in harmony with the will of certain men, and
so being spared by the power which serves this will.

Every legal norm tells us that we must proceed in
a certain way in order that we may not contravene the
will of some particular men and then suffer under
their power. Therefore it represents a procedure only
as conditionally correct, and instructs us not as to
what is good but only as to what is prescribed.
Hence a legal norm is a norm based on a human will.

3. A legal norm is a norm based on the fact that
men will to have a certain procedure for themselves
and others.

A norm is based on the fact that men will to have
a certain procedure for themselves and others when
the will on which the norm is based has reference not
only to others who do not will, but also, at the same
time, to the willers themselves also; when, therefore,
these not only will that others be subject to the norm
but also will to be subject to it themselves.

Every legal norm, and of all norms only the legal
norm, has the characteristic that the will on which it
is based reaches beyond those whose will it is, and yet
embraces them too. The rule, " Whoever takes from
another a movable thing that is not his own, with the
intent to appropriate it illegally, is punished with im-

prisonment for theft," is not only based on the will of men, but each of these men is also conscious that, while on the one hand the rule applies to other men, on the other hand it applies to himself.

Here it might be alleged that, after all, the mere fact of men's will to have a certain procedure for themselves and others does not always establish law; for example, the efforts of the Bonapartists do not establish the empire in France. But it is not when this bare will exists that law is established, but only when a norm is based on this will; that is, when it has in its service so great a power that it is competent to affect the behavior of the men to whom it relates. As soon as Bonapartism spreads so widely and in such circles that this takes place, the republic will fall and the empire will indeed become law in France.

One might further appeal to the fact that in unlimited monarchies (in Russia, for instance) the law is based solely on the will of one man, who is not himself subject to it. But Russian law is not based on the czar's will at all; the czar is a weak individual man, and his will in itself is totally unqualified to affect many millions of Russians in their procedure. Russian law is based rather on the will of all those Russians—peasants, soldiers, officials—who, for the most various reasons—patriotism, self-interest, superstition—will that what the czar wills shall be law in Russia. Their will is qualified to affect the procedure of the Russians; and, if they should ever grow so few that it would no longer have this qualification, then the czar's will would no longer be law in Russia, as the history of revolutions proves.

4. It has been asserted that legal norms have still other qualities.

It has been said, first, that it belongs to the essence of a legal norm to be enforceable, or even to be enforceable in a particular way, by judicial procedure, governmental force.

If by this we are to understand that conformity can always be enforced, we are met at once by the great number of cases in which this cannot be done. When a debtor is insolvent, or a murder has been committed, conformity to the violated legal norms cannot now be enforced after the fact, but their validity is not impaired by this.

If by enforceability we mean that conformity to a legal norm must be insured by other legal norms providing for the case of its violation, we need only go on from the insured to the insuring norms for a while, to come to norms for which conformity is not insured by any further legal norms. If one refuses to recognize these norms as legal norms, then neither can the norms which are insured by them rank as legal norms, and so, going back along the series, one has at last no legal norms left.

Only if one would understand by the enforceability of the legal norm that a will must have at its disposal a certain power in order that a legal norm may be based on it, one might certainly say in this sense that enforceability belongs to the essence of a legal norm. But this quality of the legal norm would be only such a quality as would be derivable from its quality of being a norm, and would therefore have no claim to be added as a further quality.

Again, it has been named an an essential quality of a legal norm that it should be based on the will of a State. But even where we cannot speak of a State at all, among nomads for instance, there are yet legal norms. Besides, every State is itself a legal relation, established by legal norms, which consequently cannot be based on its will. And lastly, the norms of international law, which are intended to bind the will of States, cannot be based on the will of a State.

Finally, it has been asserted that it was essential to a legal norm that it should correspond to the moral law. If this were so, then among the different legal norms which to-day are in force one directly after the other in the same territory, or at the same time in different territories under the same circumstances, only one could in each case be regarded as a legal norm; for under the same circumstances there is only one moral right. Nor could one speak then of unrighteous legal norms, for if they were unrighteous they would not be legal norms. But in reality, even when legal norms determine conduct quite differently under the same circumstances, they are all nevertheless recognized as legal norms; nor is it doubted that there are bad legal norms as well as good.

5. As a norm based on the fact that men have the will to see a certain procedure generally observed within a circle which includes themselves, the legal norm is distinguished from all other objects, even from those that most resemble it.

By being based on the will of men it is distinguished from the moral law (the commandment of morality); this is not based on men's willing a certain procedure, but on the fact that this procedure corresponds to the final purpose of all human procedure. The maxim, " Love your enemies, bless those who curse you, do good to those who hate you, pray for those who abuse and persecute you," is a moral law; so is the maxim, " Act so that the maxims of your will might at all times serve as the principles of a general legislation." For the correctness of such a procedure is not founded on the fact that other men will have it, but on the fact that it corresponds to the final purpose of all human procedure.

By being based on the will of men the legal norm is distinguished also from good manners; these are not based on the fact that men will a certain procedure, but on the fact that they themselves proceed in a certain way. It is manners that one goes to a ball in a dress coat and white gloves, uses his knife at table only for cutting, begs the daughter of the house for a dance or at least one round, takes leave of the master and mistress of the house, and lastly presses a tip into the servant's hand; for the correctness of such a behavior is not based on the fact that other men ask this of us,—to those who start a new fashion it is often actually unpleasant to find that the fashion is spreading to more extensive circles,—but solely on the fact that other men themselves behave so, and that we want " not to be peculiar," " not to make ourselves conspicuous," " to do like the rest," etc.

By being based on a will which relates at once to those whose will it is and to others whose will it is not, it is distinguished on the one hand from an arbitrary command, in which one's will applies only to others, and on the other from a resolution, in which it applies only to himself.   It is an arbitrary command when Cortes with his Spaniards commands the Mexicans to bring out their gold, or when a band of robbers forbids a frightened peasantry to betray their hiding-place; here a human will decides, indeed, but a will that relates only to other men, and not at the same time to those whose will it is.   A resolution is presented when I have decided to get up at six every morning, or to leave off smoking, or to finish a piece of work within a specified time—here a human will is indeed the standard, but it relates only to him whose will it is, not at all to others.

6.   What is briefly summed up in the definition of the legal norm may, if one takes into account the explanations which have been given with this definition, be expanded as follows:

Men will that a given procedure be generally observed within a circle which includes themselves, and their power is so great that their will is competent to affect the men of this circle in their procedure. When such is the condition of things, a legal norm exists.

3.—THE STATE

The State is a legal relation by virtue of which a supreme authority exists in a certain territory.

1.   The State is a legal relation.

A legal relation is the relation, determined by legal norms, of an obligated party, one to whom a procedure is prescribed, to an entitled party, one for whose sake it is prescribed.   Thus, for instance, the legal relation of a loan is a relation of the borrower, who is bound by the legal norms concerning loans, to the lender, for whose sake he is bound.

The State is the legal relation of all the men who by legal norms are subjected to a supreme territorial authority, to all those for whose sake they are subjected to it. Here the circle of the entitled and the obligated is one and the same; the State is a bond upon all in favor of all.

To this it might perhaps be objected that the State is not a legal relation but a person. But the two propositions, that an association of men is a person in the legal sense and that it is a legal relation, are quite compatible; nay, its attribute of personality is based mainly on its attribute of being a legal relation of a particular kind; law, in viewing the association in its outward relationships as a person, starts from the fact that men are bound together by a particular legal relation. A joint-stock corporation is a person not although, but because, it is a legal relation of a peculiar kind. And similarly, the fact that the State is a person is not only reconcilable with its being a legal relation, but is founded on its being a peculiar legal relation.

2. As to the conditions of its existence, this legal relation is involuntary.

A voluntary legal relation exists when legal norms make entrance into the relation conditional on actions of the obligated party, of which actions the purpose is to bring about the legal relation; for instance, entrance into the relation of tenancy is conditioned on agreeing to a lease. *Per contra*, an involuntary legal relation exists when legal norms do not make entrance

into the relation conditional on any such actions of
the obligated party, as, for instance, a patent is not
conditioned on any action of those who are bound by
it, and the sentence of a criminal is at least not
conditioned on any action whereby he intended to
bring it about.

If the State were a voluntary legal relation, a
supreme authority could exist only for those inhabitants of a territory who had acknowledged it. But the
supreme authority exists for all inhabitants of the
territory, whether they have acknowledged it or not;
the legal relation is therefore involuntary.

3. The substance of this legal relation is, that a
supreme authority exists in a territory.

An authority exists in a territory by virtue of a
legal relation when, according to the legal norms
which found the relation, the will of some men—or
even merely of a man—is regulative for the inhabitants of this territory. A supreme authority exists in
a territory by virtue of a legal relation when according to those norms the will of some men is finally regulative for the inhabitants of the territory,—that is, is
decisive when authorities disagree. What we here
designate as a supreme authority, therefore, is not the
men on whose will the legal norms in force in a territory are based, but rather their highest agents, whose
will they would have finally regulative within the
territory.

What men it is whose will is finally regulative for
the inhabitants of a territory by virtue of a legal relation—for instance, members of a royal family according to a certain order of inheritance, or persons

elected according to a certain election law—depends on the legal norms by which the legal relation is determined.   On these legal norms, too, depends the question within what limits the will of these men is regulative.   But this limited nature of the authority does not stand in the way of its being a supreme authority; the highest agent need not be an agent with unrestricted powers.

Here one might perhaps object that in federal States, in the German empire for instance, the individual States have not supreme authority.   But in reality they have it.   For, even if there are a multitude of subjects in reference to which the highest authority of the individual States of the German empire has to bow to the imperial authority, yet there are also subjects enough about which the highest authority of the individual States gives a final decision.   As long as there are such subjects, a supreme authority exists in the individual States; if some day there should no longer be such, one could no longer speak of individual States.

4.   As a legal relation, by virtue of which a supreme authority exists in a territory, the State is distinguished from all other objects, even from those that most resemble it.

By being a legal relation it is distinguished on the one hand from institutions such as would exist in a conceivable kingdom of God or of reason, on the basis of the moral law, and on the other hand from the dominion of a conqueror in the conquered country, which can never be anything but an arbitrary dominion.

Being an involuntary legal relation, the State is distinguished from a conceivable association of men who should set up a supreme authority among themselves by an agreement, as well as from leagues under international law, in which a supreme authority exists on the basis of an agreement.

The fact that by virtue of a legal relation an authority over a territory is given distinguishes the State from the tribal community of nomads and from the Church; for in the former there is given an authority over people of a certain descent, in the latter over people of a certain faith, but in neither over people of a certain territory. And finally, in the fact that this territorial authority is a supreme authority lies the difference between the State and towns, counties, or provinces; in the latter there is indeed a territorial authority instituted, but one that by the very intent of its institution must bow to a higher authority.

5. What is briefly summed up in the definition of the State may be expanded as follows, if one takes into consideration on the one hand the previous definition of a legal norm and on the other hand the above explanations of the definition of the State:

Some inhabitants of a territory are so powerful that their will is competent to affect the inhabitants of this territory in their procedure, and these men will have it that for all the inhabitants of the territory, for themselves as well as for the rest, the will of men picked out in a certain way shall within certain limits be finally regulative. When such is the condition of things, a State exists.

4.—PROPERTY

Property is a legal relation, by virtue of which some one has, within a certain group of men, the exclusive privilege of ultimately disposing of a thing.
1. Property is a legal relation.

As has already been stated, a legal relation is the relation of an obligated party, one to whom a procedure is prescribed by legal norms, to an entitled party, one for whose sake it is prescribed.

Property is the legal relation of all the members of a group of men who by legal norms are excluded from ultimately disposing of a thing, to him—or to those—for whose sake they are excluded from it. Here the circle of the obligated is much broader than that of the entitled; the former embraces, say, all the inhabitants of a territory or all who belong to a tribe, the latter only those among them in whom certain further conditions (for instance, transfer, prescription, appropriation) are fulfilled.

2. As to the conditions of its existence, this legal relation is involuntary.

As discussion has already shown, a voluntary legal relation exists when legal norms make entrance into the relation conditional on actions of the obligated party, of which actions the purpose is to bring about the legal relation; *per contra*, an involuntary legal relation exists when legal norms do not make entrance into the relation conditional on any such actions of the obligated party.

If property were a voluntary legal relation, then there could be excluded from ultimately disposing of a

thing only those members of a group of men who had
consented to this exclusion.   But all members of the
group—for instance, all the inhabitants of a territory,
all who belong to a tribe—are excluded, whether they
have consented or not.

3. The substance of this legal relation consists in
some one's having, within a certain group of men, the
exclusive privilege of ultimately disposing of a thing.

Some one's having, within a certain group of men,
the exclusive privilege of ultimately disposing of a
thing means that this group is excluded from the
thing in his favor; that is, they must not hinder him
from dealing with the thing according to his will,
nor may they themselves deal with it against his will.
Now, the exclusive disposition of a thing within a certain group of men may by virtue of a legal relation
belong to several, part by part, in this way: that
some—or one—of them have it in this or that particular respect (for instance, as to the usufruct), and one
—or some—in all other respects which are not individually alienated.   Whoever thus has, within a group
of men, the exclusive disposition of a thing in all those
respects which are not individually alienated, to him
belongs, within that group, the exclusive privilege of
ultimately disposing of the thing.

To whom this belongs by virtue of the legal relation—whether, for instance, it belongs among others
to him who by labor has made a thing into some new
thing—depends on the legal norms by which the legal
relation is determined.   On them also depends the
question, within what limits this belongs to him: the
dispository authority of him to whom the exclusive

disposition of a thing within a group of men ultimately belongs is limited, not only by the dispository authority of those to whom the exclusive disposition within the group proximately belongs, but also by the limits within which such dispository authority is at all allowed to anybody in the group. Especially, it depends on these legal norms whether a privilege of exclusive ultimate disposition belongs to individuals as well as to corporations, or only to corporations, and whether it applies to every kind of things or only to one kind or another.

4. As a legal relation by virtue of which some one has, within a certain group of men, the exclusive privilege of ultimately disposing of a thing, property is distinguished from all other objects, even from those which most resemble it.

By being a legal relation it is distinguished from all the relations in which one has the exclusive ultimate disposition of a thing guaranteed to him solely by the reasonableness of the men who surround him, or solely by his own might, as might be the case in a conceivable kingdom of God or of reason, and as is often the case in a conquered country.

Being an involuntary legal relation, it is distinguished from those legal relations by virtue of which the exclusive privilege of ultimately disposing of a thing belongs to some one solely on the ground of a contract, and solely as against the other contracting parties.

That by virtue of this legal relation some one has, within a group of men, the exclusive privilege of ultimately disposing of a thing, distinguishes property from copyright, by virtue of which some one has exclusively, within a group of men, not the disposition of a thing, but somewhat else; and furthermore from rights in the property of others, by virtue of which some one has, within a group of men, the exclusive privilege of disposing of a thing, but not of ultimately disposing of it.

5. What is briefly summed up in the definition of property may be expanded as follows, if one takes into consideration on the one hand the previously given definition of a legal norm, and on the other the above explanations of the definition of property.

Some men are so powerful that their will is able to affect in its procedure a group of men which embraces them, and these men will have it that no member of this group shall, within certain limits, hinder a member picked out in a certain way from dealing with a thing according to his will, nor, within these limits, himself deal with the thing against the will of that member, so far as the will of another member is not already in particular respects regulative with respect to that thing equally with the will of that member. When such is the condition of things, property exists.

[Distinguishing the State from arbitrary dominion as he here does (p. 34), and then saying that Anarchism consists solely in the negation of the State, Eltzbacher implies the unsound conclusion that Anarchism does not involve the negation of arbitrary dominion. This is because he incautiously takes the word of the learned public that the only cardinal points of Anarchism are law, the State, and property, without making sure that those who say this are using the term " State " in the precise sense defined by him. But are not many of his " arbitrary commands " law and State by his definitions? Every robber in his band (p. 31) is as much required to keep the secret as are the peasantry, and under the same penalties. In restraining a subject population I restrict my liberty of emigration or investment, and forbid myself to be an accomplice in certain things.]

CHAPTER III

GODWIN'S TEACHING

1.—GENERAL

1. William Godwin was born in 1756 at Wisbeach, Cambridgeshire. He studied theology at Hoxton, beginning in 1773. In 1778 he became preacher at Ware, Hertfordshire; in 1780, preacher at Stowmarket, Suffolk. In 1782 he gave up this position. From this time on he lived in London as an author. He died there in 1836.

Godwin published numerous works in the departments of philosophy, economics, and history; also stories, tragedies, and juvenile books.

2. Godwin's teaching about law, the State, and property is contained mainly in the two-volume work "An Enquiry Concerning Political Justice and its Influence on General Virtue and Happiness" (1793).

"The printing of this treatise," says Godwin himself, "was commenced long before the composition was finished. The ideas of the author became more perspicuous and digested as his inquiries advanced. This circumstance has led him into some inaccuracies of language and reasoning, particularly in the earlier part of the work. He did not enter upon the subject without being aware that government by its very nature counteracts the improvement of individual intellect; but he understood the proposition more completely as he proceeded, and saw more distinctly into

40

the nature of the remedy."* Godwin's teaching is here presented exclusively in the developed form which it shows in the second part of the work.

3. Godwin does not call his teaching about law, the State, and property " Anarchism." Yet this word causes him no terror. " Anarchy is a horrible calamity, but it is less horrible than despotism. Where anarchy has slain its hundreds, despotism has sacrificed millions upon millions, with this only effect, to perpetuate the ignorance, the vices, and the misery of mankind. Anarchy is a short-lived mischief, while despotism is all but immortal. It is unquestionably a dreadful remedy, for the people to yield to all their furious passions, till the spectacle of their effects gives strength to recovering reason: but, though it be a dreadful remedy, it is a sure one."†

2.—BASIS

According to Godwin, our supreme law is the general welfare.

What is the general welfare? " Its nature is defined by the nature of mind."‡ It is unchangeable; as long as men are men it remains the same.§ "That will most contribute to it which expands the understanding, supplies incitements to virtue, fills us with a generous consciousness of our independence, and carefully removes whatever can impede our exertions."‖

The general welfare is our supreme law. " Duty is that mode of action on the part of the individual,

---

* Godwin pp. IX-X [1. VI-VII].　　† *Ib.* pp. 548-9 [2. 132-3].
‡ *Ib.* p. 90 [1. 120].　　§ *Ib.* p. 150 [1, 164].　　‖ *Ib.* p. 90 [1.120-21].

which constitutes the best possible application of his
capacity to the general benefit."* "Justice is the
sum of all moral duty;"† "if there be such a thing, I
am bound to do for the general weal everything in my
power."‡ "Virtue is a desire to promote the benefit
of intelligent beings in general, the quantity of virtue
being as the quantity of desire;"§ "the last perfection
of this feeling consists in that state of mind which
bids us rejoice as fully in the good that is done by
others, as if it were done by ourselves."‖

"The truly wise man "¶ strives only for the welfare
of the whole. He is "actuated neither by interest nor
ambition, the love of honor nor the love of fame.
[He knows no jealousy. He is not disquieted by the
comparison of what he has attained with what others
have attained, but by the comparison with what
ought to be attained.] He has a duty indeed obliging
him to seek the good of the whole; but that good is
his only object. If that good be effected by another
hand, he feels no disappointment. All men are his
fellow laborers, but he is the rival of no man."**

3.—LAW

I. *Looking to the general good, Godwin rejects
law, not only for particular local and temporary conditions, but altogether.*

"Law is an institution of the most pernicious tendency."†† "The institution once begun, can never be
brought to a close. No action of any man was ever
the same as any other action, had ever the same de-

---

*Godwin p. 101 [1. 134].   †Ib. pp. 150, 80 [1. 120, 112].   ‡Ib. p. 81 [1. 117-18?].
§Ib. p. 254 [1. 253].   ‖Ib. pp. 360-61 [1. 342].   ¶Ib. p. 361. [Not in ed. 2.]
**Ib. p. 361 [1. 342 ; bracketed words omitted in ed. 2].   ††Ib. p. 771 [2. 294].

gree of utility or injury. As new cases occur, the law is perpetually found deficient. It is therefore perpetually necessary to make new laws. The volume in which justice records her prescriptions is for ever increasing, and the world would not contain the books that might be written."* " The consequence of the infinitude of law is its uncertainty. Law was made that a plain man might know what he had to expect, and yet the most skilful practitioners differ about the event of my suit."† " A farther consideration is that it is of the nature of prophecy. Its task is to describe what will be the actions of mankind, and to dictate decisions respecting them."‡

" Law we sometimes call the wisdom of our ancestors. But this is a strange imposition. It was as frequently the dictate of their passion, of timidity, jealousy, a monopolizing spirit, and a lust of power that knew no bounds. Are we not obliged perpetually to revise and remodel this misnamed wisdom of our ancestors? to correct it by a detection of their ignorance, and a censure of their intolerance?"§

" Legislation, as it has been usually understood, is not an affair of human competence. Reason is [our sole legislator, and her decrees are unchangeable and everywhere the same.]"‖ " Men cannot do more than declare and interpret law; nor can there be an authority so paramount, as to have the prerogative of making that to be law, which abstract and immutable justice had not made to be law previously to that interposition."¶

---

* Godwin pp. 766-7 [2. 290-91].   † Ib. p. 768 [2. 291].   ‡ Ib. p. 769 [2. 292].
§ Ib. p. 773 [2. 295].   ‖ Ib. p. 166 [1. 182, except bracketed words].
¶ Ib. p. 381 [2. 3].

To be sure, " it must be admitted that we are imperfect, ignorant, and slaves of appearances."* But " whatever inconveniences may arise from the passions of men, the introduction of fixed laws cannot be the genuine remedy."† " As long as a man is held in the trammels of obedience, and habituated to look to some foreign guidance for the direction of his conduct, his understanding and the vigor of his mind will sleep. Do I desire to raise him to the energy of which he is capable? I must teach him to feel himself, to bow to no authority, to examine the principles he entertains, and render to his mind the reason of his conduct."‡

II. *The general welfare requires that in future it itself should be men's rule of action in place of the law.*

" If every shilling of our property, [every hour of our time,] and every faculty of our mind, have received their destination from the principles of unalterable justice,"§ that is, of the general good,‖ then no other decree can any longer control it. " The true principle which ought to be substituted in the room of law, is that of reason exercising an uncontrolled jurisdiction upon the circumstances of the case."¶

" To this principle no objection can arise on the score of wisdom. It is not to be supposed that there are not men now existing, whose intellectual accomplishments rise to the level of law. But, if men can be found among us whose wisdom is equal to the wisdom of law, it will scarcely be maintained, that the

---

* Godwin p. 774 [2. 296].   † *Ib.* p. 775 [2. 296].   ‡ *Ib.* p. 776 [2. 297].
§ *Ib.* p. 151 [1. 165, except bracketed words].
‖ *Ib.* pp. 121, 81 [1. 145, 118].   ¶ *Ib.* p. 773 [2. 295].

truths they have to communicate will be the worse for having no authority, but that which they derive from the reasons that support them."*

"The juridical decisions that were made immediately after the abolition of law, would differ little from those during its empire. They would be the decisions of prejudice and habit. But habit, having lost the centre about which it revolved, would diminish in the regularity of its operations. Those to whom the arbitration of any question was entrusted would frequently recollect that the whole case was committed to their deliberation, and they could not fail occasionally to examine themselves, respecting the reason of those principles which had hitherto passed uncontroverted. Their understandings would grow enlarged, in proportion as they felt the importance of their trust, and the unbounded freedom of their investigation. Here then would commence an auspicious order of things, of which no understanding man at present in existence can foretell the result, the dethronement of implicit faith, and the inauguration of unclouded justice."†

4.—THE STATE

I. *Since Godwin unconditionally rejects law, he necessarily has to reject the State as unconditionally. Nay, he regards it as a legal institution peculiarly repugnant to the general welfare.*

Some base the State on force, others on divine right, others on contract.‡ But "the hypothesis of force appears to proceed upon the total negation of

---

*Godwin pp. 773-4 [2. 295]. †*Ib.* p. 778 [2. 298-9]. ‡*Ib.* p. 140-1 [1. 156].

abstract and immutable justice, affirming every government to be right, that is possessed of power sufficient to enforce its decrees. It puts a violent termination upon all political science, and is calculated for nothing farther than to persuade men, to sit down quietly under their present disadvantages, whatever they may be, and not exert themselves to discover a remedy for the evils they suffer. The second hypothesis is of an equivocal nature. It either coincides with the first, and affirms all existing power to be alike of divine derivation; or it must remain totally useless, till a criterion can be found, to distinguish those governments which are approved by God, from those which cannot lay claim to that sanction."* The third hypothesis would mean that one "should make over to another the control of his conscience and the judging of his duties."† "But we cannot renounce our moral independence; it is a property that we can neither sell nor give away; and consequently no government can derive its authority from an original contract."‡

"All government corresponds in a certain degree to what the Greeks denominated a tyranny. The difference is, that in despotic countries mind is depressed by a uniform usurpation; while in republics it preserves a greater portion of its activity, and the usurpation more easily conforms itself to the fluctuations of opinion."§ "By its very nature positive institution has a tendency to suspend the elasticity and progress of mind."‖ "We should not forget that gov-

---

*Godwin p. 141 [2. 156].   † Ib. p. 148. [Not in ed. 2.]
‡Ib. p. 149. [Not in ed. 2.]   §Ib. p. 572 [2. 149-50].   ‖ Ib. p. 185 [1. 200].

ernment is, abstractedly taken, an evil, a usurpation
upon the private judgment and individual conscience
of mankind."*

II. *The general welfare demands that a social human life based solely on its precepts should take the
place of the State.*

1. Men are to live together in society even after
the abolition of the State. "A fundamental distinction exists between society and government. Men
associated at first for the sake of mutual assistance."†
It was not till later that restraint appeared in these
associations, in consequence of the errors and per-
verseness of a few. "Society and government are different in themselves, and have different origins. Society is produced by our wants, and government by
our wickedness. Society is in every state a blessing;
government even in its best state but a necessary
evil."‡

But what is to hold men together in "society with-
out government"?§ Not a promise,|| at any rate.
No promise can bind me; for either what I have
promised is good, then I must do it even if there had
been no promise; or it is bad, then not even the
promise can make it my duty.¶ "The fact that I
have committed an error does not oblige me to make
myself guilty of a second also."** "Suppose I had
promised a sum of money for a good and worthy object. In the interval between the promise and its
fulfilment a greater and nobler object presents itself to

* Godwin p. 380 [2. 2].   † *Ib.* p. 79 [1. 111].   ‡ *Ib.* p. 79 [1. 111 ; credited
to Paine's "Common Sense," p. 1].   § *Ib.* p. 788 [2. 305].
|| *Ib.* p. 163 [1. 174-6 ? 180 ?].   ¶ *Ib.* p. 151 [1. 164-5 ; but see *per contra* p. 170].
** *Ib.* p. 156.   [Not in ed. 2.]

me, and imperiously demands my co-operation. To
which shall I give the preference? To the one that
deserves it. My promise can make no difference. I
must be guided by the value of things, not by an external and alien point of view. But the value of
things is not affected by my having taken upon me
an obligation."*

"Common deliberation regarding the general
good "† is to hold men together in societies hereafter.
This is highly in harmony with the general welfare.
"That a nation should exercise undiminished its
function of common deliberation, is a step gained,
and a step that inevitably leads to an improvement of
the character of individuals. That men should agree
in the assertion of truth, is no unpleasing evidence of
their virtue. Lastly, that an individual, however
great may be his imaginary elevation, should be
obliged to yield his personal pretensions to the sense
of the community, at least bears the appearance of a
practical confirmation of the great principle, that all
private considerations must yield to the general
good."‡

2. The societies are to be small, and to have as
little intercourse with each other as possible.

Small territories are everywhere to administer their
affairs independently.§ "No association of men, so
long as they adhered to the principles of reason, could
possibly have any interest in extending their territory."‖ "Whatever evils are included in the abstract idea of government, are all of them extremely

---

*Godwin p. 151. [Not in ed. 2.] † Ib. pp. 161-2 [1. 179]. ‡ Ib. 164-5 [1. 181].
§ Ib. p. 561 [2. 142]. ‖ Ib. 566 [2. 145].

aggravated by the extensiveness of its jurisdiction, and softened under circumstances of an opposite species. Ambition, which may be no less formidable than a pestilence in the former, has no room to unfold itself in the latter. Popular commotion is like the waves of the sea, capable where the surface is large of producing the most tragical effects, but mild and innocuous when confined within the circuit of a humble lake. Sobriety and equity are the obvious characteristics of a limited circle."*—"The desire to gain a more extensive territory, to conquer or to hold in awe our neighboring States, to surpass them in arts or arms, is a desire founded in prejudice and error. Power is not happiness. Security and peace are more to be desired than a name at which nations tremble. Mankind are brethren. We associate in a particular district or under a particular climate, because association is necessary to our internal tranquillity, or to defend us against the wanton attacks of a common enemy. But the rivalship of nations is a creature of the imagination."†

The little independently-administered territories are to have as little to do with each other as possible. "Individuals cannot have too frequent or unlimited intercourse with each other; but societies of men have no interests to explain and adjust, except so far as error and violence may render explanation necessary. This consideration annihilates at once the principal objects of that mysterious and crooked policy which has hitherto occupied the attention of governments. Before this principle officers of the army and the navy,

---

* Godwin p. 562 [2. 142].   † *Ib.* 559 [2. 140].

ambassadors and negotiators, and all the train of arti-
fices that has been invented to hold other nations at
bay, to penetrate their secrets, to traverse their mach-
inations, to form alliances and counter-alliances, sink
into nothing."*

3. But how are the functions that the State performs at present to be performed in the future societies? " Government can have no more than two
legitimate purposes, the suppression of injustice
against individuals within the community " (which
includes the settling of controversies between different
districts†), " and the common defence against external
invasion."‡

" The first of these purposes, which alone can have
an uninterrupted claim upon us, is sufficiently
answered by an association of such an extent as to
afford room for the institution of a jury, to decide
upon the offences of individuals within the community,
and upon the questions and controversies respecting
property which may chance to arise."§   This jury
would decide not according to any system of law, but
according to reason.‖—" It might be easy indeed for
an offender to escape from the limits of so petty a
jurisdiction; and it might seem necessary at first that
the neighboring parishes or jurisdictions should be
governed in a similar manner, or at least should be
willing, whatever was their form of government, to co-

---

* Godwin p. 561 [2. 141. Obviously Eltzbacher has misunderstood this
passage. His German translation shows that he mistook " interests" for
" interest" in the sense of " incentive." Note also that Godwin expressly
restricts the application of this paragraph, even in its right sense, on
pp. 111, 145].
    † Ib. p. 566 [2. 145].   ‡ Ib. p. 564 [2. 144].   § Ib. 564-5 [2. 144].
    ‖ Ib. pp. 773, 778, 779-80 [2. 295, 298-300].

operate with us in the removal or reformation of an offender whose present habits were alike injurious to us and to them. But there will be no need of any express compact, and still less of any common centre of authority, for this purpose. General justice and mutual interest are found more capable of binding men than signatures and seals."*

The second function would present itself to us only from time to time. "However irrational might be the controversy of parish with parish in such a state of society, it would not be the less possible. Such emergencies can only be provided against by the concert of several districts, declaring and, if needful, enforcing the dictates of justice."† Foreign invasions too would make such a concert necessary, and would to this extent resemble those controversies.‡ Therefore it would be "necessary upon certain occasions to have recourse to national assemblies, or in other words assemblies instituted for the joint purpose of adjusting the differences between district and district, and of consulting respecting the best mode of repelling foreign invasion."§—But they "ought to be employed as sparingly as the nature of the case will admit."‖ For, in the first place, the decision is given by the number of votes, and "is determined, at best, by the weakest heads in the assembly, but, as it not less frequently happens, by the most corrupt and dishonorable intentions."¶ In the second place, as a rule the members are guided in their decisions by all

---

* Godwin p. 565 [2. 144]. † Ib. p. 566 [2. 145]. ‡ Ib. p. 566 [2. 145].
§ Ib. pp. 573-4 [2. 150-51]. ‖ Ib. pp. 573-4 [2. 150-51].
¶ Ib. pp. 568-9, 571-2 [2. 146, 149].

sorts of external reasons, and not solely by the results of their free reflection.* In the third place, they are forced to waste their strength on petty matters, while they cannot possibly let themselves be quietly influenced by argument.† Therefore national assemblies should "either never be elected but upon extraordinary emergencies, like the dictator of the ancient Romans, or else sit periodically, one day for example in a year, with a power of continuing their sessions within a certain limit. The former is greatly to be preferred."‡

But what would be the authority of these national assemblies and those juries? Mankind is so corrupted by present institutions that at first the issuing of commands, and some degree of coercion, would be necessary; but later it would be sufficient for juries to recommend a certain mode of adjusting controversies, and for national assemblies to invite their constituencies to co-operate for the common advantage.§ "If juries might at length cease to decide and be contented to invite, if force might gradually be withdrawn and reason trusted alone, shall we not one day find that juries themselves, and every other species of public institution, may be laid aside as unnecessary? Will not the reasonings of one wise man be as effectual as those of twelve? Will not the competence of one individual to instruct his neighbors be a matter of sufficient notoriety, without the formality of an election? Will there be many vices to correct and much obstinacy to conquer? This is one of the most

---

* Godwin pp. 569-70 [2. 148[.   † Ib. pp. 570-71 [2. 148-49].
‡ Ib. p. 574 [2. 151].   § Ib. pp. 576-8 [2, 152-3].

memorable stages of human improvement. With what delight must every well-informed friend of mankind look forward to the auspicious period, the dissolution of political government, of that brute engine, which has been the only perennial cause of the vices of mankind, and which has mischiefs of various sorts incorporated with its substance, and no otherwise to be removed than by its utter annihilation!"*

5.—PROPERTY

I. *In consequence of his unconditional rejection of law, Godwin necessarily has to reject property also without any limitation. Nay, property, or, as he expresses himself, " the present system of property,"†— that is, the distribution of wealth at present established by law,—appears to him to be a legal institution that is peculiarly injurious to the general welfare.* "The wisdom of law-makers and parliaments has been applied to creating the most wretched and senseless distribution of property, which mocks alike at human nature and at the principles of justice."‡

The present system of property distributes commodities in the most unequal and most arbitrary way. "On account of the accident of birth, it piles upon a single man enormous wealth. If one who has been a beggar becomes a well-to-do man, we usually know that he has not precisely his honesty or usefulness to thank for this change. It is often hard enough for the most diligent and industrious member of society to preserve his family from starvation."§ " And if I

---

*Godwin pp. 578-9 [2. 154].   † *Ib.* p. 794 |2. 326].
‡ *Ib.* p. 803. [Not in ed. 2.]   § *Ib.* p. 794. [Not in ed. 2.]

receive the reward of my work, they give me a hundred times more food than I can eat, and a hundred times more clothes than I can wear. Where is the justice in this? If I am the greatest benefactor of the human race, is that a reason for giving me what I do not need, especially when my superfluity might be of the greatest use to thousands? "*
This unequal distribution of commodities is altogether opposed to the general welfare. It hampers intellectual progress. "Accumulated property treads the powers of thought in the dust, extinguishes the sparks of genius, and reduces the great mass of mankind to be immersed in sordid cares, beside depriving the rich of the most salubrious and effectual motives to activity."† And the rich man can buy with his superfluity "nothing but glitter and envy, nothing but the dismal pleasure of restoring to the poor man as alms that to which reason gives him an undeniable right."‡
But the unequal distribution of commodities is also a hindrance to moral perfection. In the rich it produces ambition, vanity, and ostentation; in the poor, oppression, servility, and fraud, and, in consequence of these, envy, malice, and revenge.§ "The rich man stands forward as the principal object of general esteem and deference. In vain are sobriety, integrity, and industry, in vain the sublimest powers of mind and the most ardent benevolence, if their possessor be narrowed in his circumstances. To acquire wealth

---

*Godwin p. 795. [Not in ed. 2; cf. 2, 312].   † *Ib.* p. 806 [2. 335].
‡ *Ib.* p. 795. [Not in ed. 2.]
§ *Ib.* pp. 811, 810 [2. 339, 338—but the words " in the poor " seem to be added out of Eltzbacher's head].

and to display it, is therefore the universal passion."*
" Force would have died away as reason and civilization advanced, but accumulated property has fixed its
empire."† " The fruitful source of crimes consists in
this circumstance, one man's possessing in abundance
that of which another man is destitute."‡

II. *The general welfare demands that a distribution of commodities based solely on its precepts should
take the place of property.* When Godwin uses the
expression " property " for that portion of commodities which is assigned to an individual by these
precepts, he does so only in a transferred sense; only
a portion assigned by law can be designated as
property in the strict sense.

Now, according to the decrees of the general welfare, every man should have the means for a good life.

1. " How is it to be decided whether an object that
may be used for the benefit of man shall be my property or yours? There is only one answer; according
to justice."§ " The laws of different countries dispose
of property in a thousand different ways; but only
one of them can be most consonant with justice."‖

Justice demands in the first place that every man
have the means for life. " Our animal needs, it is
well known, consist in food, clothing, and shelter. If
justice means anything, nothing can be more unjust
than that any man lacks these and at the same time
another has too much of them. But justice does not
stop here. So far as the general stock of commodities
holds out, every one has a claim not only to the

---

* Godwin p. 802 [2. 332].   † *Ib.* p. 809 [2. 338].   ‡ *Ib.* p. 809 [2. 337].
§ *Ib.* p. 789. [Not in ed. 2 ; cf. 2. 306-7.]   ‖ *Ib.* p. 790 [Not in ed. 2.]

means for life, but to the means for a good life. It is
unjust that a man works to the point of destroying his
health or his life, while another riots in superfluity.
It is unjust that a man has not leisure to cultivate his
mind, while another does not move a finger for the
general welfare."*

2. Such a " state of equality "† would advance the
general welfare in the highest degree. In it labor
would become " so light, as rather to assume the appearance of agreeable relaxation, and gentle exercise."‡ " Every man would have a frugal, yet wholesome diet; every man would go forth to that moderate
exercise of his corporal functions that would give
hilarity to the spirits; none would be made torpid
with fatigue, but all would have leisure to cultivate
the kindly and philanthropical affections, and to let
loose his faculties in the search of intellectual
improvement."§

" How rapid would be the advances of intellect, if
all men were admitted into the field of knowledge!
It is to be presumed that the inequality of mind
would in a certain degree be permanent; but it is
reasonable to believe that the geniuses of such an age
would far surpass the greatest exertions of intellect
that are at present known."‖

And the moral progress would be as great as the
intellectual. The vices which are inseparably joined
to the present system of property " would inevitably
expire in a state of society where men lived in the
midst of plenty, and where all shared alike the boun-

---

* Godwin pp. 790-91. [Not in ed. 2.]   † *Ib.* p. 821 [2. 351].
‡ *Ib.* p. 821 [2. 352].   § *Ib.* p. 806[2. 335].   ‖ *Ib.* p. 807 [2. 336].

ties of nature. The narrow principle of selfishness would vanish. No man being obliged to guard his little store, or provide with anxiety and pain for his restless wants, each would lose his individual existence in the thought of the general good. No man would be an enemy to his neighbor, for they would have no subject of contention; and of consequence philanthropy would resume the empire which reason assigns her."*

3. But how could such a distribution of commodities be effected in a particular case?

"As soon as law was abolished, men would begin to inquire after equity. In this situation let us suppose a litigated succession brought before them, to which there were five heirs, and that the sentence of their old legislation had directed the division of this property into five equal shares. They would begin to inquire into the wants and situation of the claimants. The first we will suppose to have a fair character and be prosperous in the world: he is a respectable member of society, but farther wealth would add little either to his usefulness or his enjoyments. The second is a miserable object, perishing with want, and overwhelmed with calamity. The third, though poor, is yet tranquil; but there is a situation to which his virtue leads him to aspire and in which he may be of uncommon service, but which he cannot with propriety accept, without a capital equal to two-fifths of the whole succession. One of the claimants is an unmarried woman past the age of child-bearing. Another is a widow, unprovided, and with a numerous family

* Godwin p. 810 [2. 338].

depending on her succor. The first question that
would suggest itself to unprejudiced persons having
the allotment of this succession referred to their unlimited decision, would be, what justice is there in the
indiscriminate partition which has hitherto
prevailed?"* And their answer could not be
doubtful.

6.—REALIZATION.

*The change which is called for by the general wel-
fare should, according to Godwin, be effected by those
who have recognized the truth persuading others how
necessary the change is for the general welfare, so
that law, the State, and property would spontaneously
disappear and the new condition would take their
place.*

I. The sole requirement is to convince men that
the general welfare demands the change.

1. Every other way is to be rejected. "Our judgment will always suspect those weapons that can be
used with equal prospect of success on both sides.
Therefore we should regard all force with aversion.
When we enter the lists of battle, we quit the sure domain of truth and leave the decision to the caprice of
chance. The phalanx of reason is invulnerable; it
moves forward with calm, sure step, and nothing can
withstand it. But, when we lay aside arguments, and
have recourse to the sword, the case is altered.
Amidst the clamorous din of civil war, who shall tell
whether the event will be prosperous or adverse? We
must therefore distinguish carefully between instruct-

---

* Godwin pp. 779-80 [2. 299-300].

ing the people and exciting them. We must refuse
indignation, rage, and passion, and desire only sober
reflection, clear judgment, and fearless discussion."*
2. The point is to convince men as generally as
possible. Only when this is accomplished can acts of
violence be avoided. " Why did the revolution in
France and America find all sorts and conditions of
men almost unanimous, while the resistance to
Charles the First divided our nation into two equal
parties? Because the latter occurred in the seventeenth century, the former at the end of the eigh-
teenth. Because at the time of the revolutions in
France and America philosophy had already developed some of the great truths of political science, and
under the influence of Sydney and Locke, of Montesquieu and Rousseau, a number of strong and
thoughtful minds had perceived what an evil force is.
If these revolutions had taken place still later, not a
drop of civic blood would have been shed by civic
hands, not in a single case would force have been
used against persons or things."†
3. The means to convince men as generally as possible of the necessity of a change consist in " proof
and persuasion. The best warrant of a happy outcome lies in free, unrestricted discussion. In this
arena truth must always be victor. If, therefore, we
would improve the social institutions of mankind, we
must seek to convince by spoken and written words.
This activity has no limits; this endeavor admits of
no interruption. Every means must be used, not so

---

* Godwin p. 203 [1, 223, only the two sentences beginning at " But "].
† Ib. pp. 203-4. [Not in ed. 2.]

much to draw men's attention and bring them over to
our opinion by persuasion, as rather to remove every
barrier to thought and to open to everybody the tem-
ple of science and the field of study."*

"Therefore the man who has at heart the regenera-
tion of his species should always bear in mind two
principles, to regard hourly progress in the discovery
and dissemination of truth as essential, and calmly to
let years pass before he urges the carrying into effect
of his teaching. With all his prudence, it may be
that the boisterous multitude will hurry ahead of the
calm, quiet progress of reason; then he will not condemn the revolution that takes place some years before
the time set by wisdom. But if he is ruled by strict
prudence he can without doubt frustrate many over-
hasty attempts, and considerably prolong the general
quietness."†

"This does not mean, as one might think, that the
changing of our conditions lies at an immeasurable
distance. It is the nature of human affairs that great
alterations take place suddenly, and great discoveries
are made unexpectedly, as it were accidentally.
When I cultivate a young person's mind, when I exert myself to influence that of an older person, it will
long seem as if I had accomplished little, and the
fruits will show themselves when I least expect them.
The kingdom of truth comes quietly. The seed of
virtue may spring up when it was fancied to be lost."‡
"If the true philanthropist but tirelessly proclaims
the truth and vigilantly opposes all that hinders its

---

* Godwin pp. 202-3.   [Not in ed. 2.]   † *Ib.* p. 204.   [Not in ed. 2.]
‡ *Ib.* p. 223.   [Not in ed. 2 ; cf. 1. 226.]

progress, he may look forward, with heart at rest, to a speedy and favorable outcome."*

II. As soon as the conviction that the general welfare demands a change in our condition has made itself generally felt, law, the State, and property will disappear spontaneously and give way to the new condition. "Reform, under this meaning of the term, can scarcely be considered as of the nature of action. [It is a general enlightenment.] Men feel their situation; and the restraints that shackled them before, vanish like a deception. When such a crisis has arrived, not a sword will need to be drawn, not a finger to be lifted up in purposes of violence. The adversaries will be too few and too feeble, to be able to entertain a serious thought of resistance against the universal sense of mankind."†

In what way may the change of our conditions take place?

1. "The opinion most popular in France at the time that the national convention entered upon its functions, was that the business of the convention extended only to the presenting a draft of a constitution, to be submitted in the sequel to the approbation of the districts, and then only to be considered as law."‡

"The first idea that suggests itself respecting this opinion is, that, if constitutional laws ought to be subjected to the revision of the districts, then all laws ought to undergo the same process. [But if the approbation of the districts to any declarations is not

---

* Godwin p. 225. [Not in ed. 2.]
† *Ib.* pp. 222-3 [1. 222, except bracketed words]. ‡ *Ib.* pp. 657-8 [2. 210].

to be delusive, the discussion of these declarations in the districts must be unlimited. Then] a transaction will be begun to which it is not easy to foresee a termination. Some districts will object to certain articles; and, if these articles be modeled to obtain their approbation, it is possible that the very alteration introduced to please one part of the community may render the code less acceptable to another."*

"This principle of a consent of districts has an immediate tendency, by a salutary gradation perhaps, to lead to the dissolution of all government."† It is indeed "desirable that the most important acts of the national representatives should be subject to the approbation or rejection of the districts whose representatives they are, for exactly the same reason as it is desirable that the acts of the districts themselves should, as speedily as practicability will admit, be in force only so far as relates to the individuals by whom those acts are approved."‡

2. This system would have the effect, first, that the constitution would be very short. The impracticability of obtaining the free approbation of a great number of districts to an extensive code would speedily manifest itself; and the whole constitution might consist of a scheme for the division of the country into parts equal in their population, and the fixing of stated periods for the election of a national assembly, not to say that the latter of these articles may very probably be dispensed with.§

---

*Godwin pp. 658-9 [2. 211-12 ; bracketed words a paraphrase].
† Ib. pp. 659-60 [2. 212].   ‡ Ib. p. 660 [2. 212].
§ Ib. pp. 660-61 [2. 212-13].

A second effect would be, that it would soon be found a proceeding unnecessarily circuitous to send laws to the districts for their revision, unless in cases essential to the general safety, and that in as many instances as possible the districts would be suffered to make laws for themselves. "Thus, that which was at first a great empire with legislative unity would speedily be transformed into a confederacy of lesser republics, with a general congress or Amphictyonic council, answering the purpose of a point of co-operation upon extraordinary occasions."*

A third effect would consist in the gradual cessation of legislation. "A great assembly collected from the different provinces of an extensive territory, and constituted the sole legislator of those by whom the territory is inhabited, immediately conjures up to itself an idea of the vast multitude of laws that are necessary. A large city, impelled by the principles of commercial jealousy, is not slow to digest the volume of its by-laws and exclusive privileges. But the inhabitants of a small parish, living with some degree of that simplicity which best corresponds with nature, would soon be led to suspect that general laws were unnecessary, and would adjudge the causes that came before them, not according to certain axioms previously written, but according to the circumstances and demands of each particular cause."†

A fourth effect would be that the abrogation of property would be favored. "All equalization of rank and station strongly tends toward an equaliza-

---

* Godwin pp. 661-2 [2. 213-14].   † *Ib.* p. 662 [2. 214].

tion of possessions."* So not only the lower orders, but also the higher, would see the injustice of the present distribution of property.† "The rich and great are far from callous to views of general felicity, when such views are brought before them with that evidence and attraction of which they are susceptible."‡ But even so far as they might think only of their own emolument and ease, it would not be difficult to show them that it is in vain to fight against truth, and dangerous to bring upon themselves the hatred of the people, and that it might be to their own interest to make up their minds to concessions at least.§

---

* Godwin p. 888 [cf. 2. 396].   † *Ib.* pp. 888-9 [2. 396].
‡ *Ib.* pp. 882-3 [2. 392].   § *Ib.* pp. 883-84 [2. 393].

CHAPTER IV

PROUDHON'S TEACHING

1.—GENERAL

1. Pierre-Joseph Proudhon was born at Besançon in 1809. At first he followed the occupation of a printer there and in other cities. In 1838 a stipend of the Academy of Besançon enabled him to go to Paris for scientific studies. In 1843 he took a mercantile position at Lyons. In 1847 he gave it up and moved to Paris.

Here, in the years from 1848 to 1850, Proudhon published several periodicals, one after the other. In 1848 he became a member of the National Assembly. In 1849 he founded a People's Bank. Soon after this he was condemned to three years' imprisonment for an offence against the press laws, and served his time without having to interrupt his activity as an author.

In 1852 Proudhon was released from prison. He remained in Paris till, in 1858, he was again condemned to three years' imprisonment for an offence against the press laws. He fled and settled in Brussels. In 1860 he was pardoned, and returned to France. Thenceforth he lived at Passy. He died there in 1865.

Proudhon published many books and other writings, especially in the fields of jurisprudence, political economy, and politics.

2. Of special importance for Proudhon's teaching about law, the State, and property are, among the

writings before 1848, the book "*Qu'est-ce que la propriété ? ou recherches sur le principe du droit et du gouvernement*" (1840) and the two-volume work "*Système des contradictions économiques, ou philosophie de la misère*" (1846); among the writings from 1848 to 1851 the "*Confessions d'un révolutionnaire*" (1849) and the "*Idée générale de la révolution au XIXe siècle*" (1851); and lastly, among the writings after 1851, the three-volume work "*De la justice dans la révolution et dans l'Eglise, nouveaux principes de philosophie pratique*" (1858) and the book "*Du principe fédératif et de la nécessité de reconstituer le parti de la révolution*" (1863).*

Proudhon's teaching regarding law, the State, and property underwent changes in minor points, but remained the same in its essentials; the opinion that it changed also in essentials is caused by Proudhon's arbitrary and varying use of language. Since no history of the evolution of Proudhon's teaching can be given here, I shall present, so far as concerns such minor points, only the teaching of 1848–51, in which years Proudhon developed his views with especial clearness and did especially forcible work for them.

3. Proudhon calls his teaching about law, the State, and property " Anarchism." " ' What form of government shall we prefer?' ' Can you ask?' replies one of my younger readers without doubt; ' you are a Republican.' ' Republican, yes; but this word makes nothing definite. *Res publica* is " the public thing "; now, whoever wants the public thing, under whatever form of government, may call himself a Republican.

---

* Not (as stated by Diehl vol. 2 p. 116, Zenker p. 61) 1852.

Even kings are Republicans.' 'Well, you are a Democrat.' 'No.' 'What? can you be a Monarchist?' 'No.' 'A Constitutionalist?' 'I should hope not.' 'You are an Aristocrat then?' 'Not a bit.' 'You want a mixed government, then?' 'Still less.' 'What are you then?' 'I am an Anarchist.' "*

2.—BASIS

According to Proudhon the supreme law for us is justice.

What is justice? "Justice is respect, spontaneously felt and mutually guaranteed, for human dignity, in whatever person and under whatever circumstances we find it compromised, and to whatever risk its defence may expose us."†

"I ought to respect my neighbor, and make others respect him, as myself; such is the law of my conscience. In consideration of what do I owe him this respect? In consideration of his strength, his talent, his wealth? No, what chance gives is not what makes the human person worthy of respect. In consideration of the respect which he in turn pays to me? No, justice assumes reciprocity of respect, but does not wait for it. It asserts and wills respect for human dignity even in an enemy, which causes the existence of *laws of war;* even in the murderer whom we kill as having fallen from his manhood, which causes the ex-

---

*Proudhon "*Propriété*" p. 295 [212. Bracketed references under Proudhon are to the collected edition of his "*Œuvres complètes,*" Paris, 1866-83. —The passage quoted above is probably the first case in history where anybody called himself an Anarchist, though the word had long been in use as a term of reproach for enemies].

† Pr. "*Justice*" 1. 182-3 [1. 224-5].

istence of *penal laws*.   It is not the gifts of nature or
the advantages of fortune that make me respect my
neighbor; it is not his ox, his ass, or his maid-ser-
vant, as the decalogue says; it is not even the welfare
that he owes to me as I owe mine to him; it is his
manhood."*

" Justice is at once a reality and an idea."†
" Justice is a faculty of the soul, the foremost of all,
that which constitutes a social being.   But it is more
than a faculty; it is an idea, it indicates a relation,
an equation.   As a faculty it may be developed; this
development is what constitutes the education of humanity.   As an equation it presents nothing anti-
nomic; it is absolute and immutable like every law,
and, like every law, very intelligible."‡
Justice is for us the supreme law.   " Justice is the
inviolable yardstick of all human actions."§
" By it the facts of social life, by nature indeterminate
and contradictory, become susceptible of definition
and arrangement."‖

" Justice is the central star which governs societies,
the pole about which the political world revolves, the
principle and rule of all transactions.   Nothing is
done among men that is not in the name of *right ;*
nothing without invoking justice.   Justice is not the
work of the law; on the contrary, the law is never
anything but a declaration and application of what is
just."‖   " Suppose a society where justice is out-
ranked, however little, by another principle, say reli-

---

*Pr. " *Justice* " 1. 184-5 [1. 227].
† *Ib.* 1. 73 [132? but there he says *must be*, not *is*].
‡ *Ib.* 1. 185 [1. 228].   § *Ib.* 1. 195 [1. 235].   ‖ *Ib.* 1. 185 [1. 228[.

gion; or in which certain individuals are regarded
more highly, by however little, than others; I say
that, justice being virtually annulled, it is inevitable
that the society will perish sooner or later.*
" It is the privilege of justice that the faith which
it inspires is unshakable, and that it cannot be dog-
matically denied or rejected. All peoples invoke it;
reasons of State, even while they violate it, profess to
be based on it; religion exists only for it; skepticism
dissembles before it; irony has power only in its
name; crime and hypocrisy do it homage. [If liberty
is not an empty phrase, it acts only in the service of
right; even when it rebels against right, at bottom it
does not curse it.]"† " All the most rational teachings of human wisdom about justice are summed up
in this famous adage: *Do to others what you would
have done to you ; Do not to others what you would
not have done to you.*"‡

3.—LAW

I. *In the name of justice Proudhon rejects, not law
indeed, but almost all individual legal norms, and the
State laws in particular.*

The State makes laws, and " as many laws as the
interests which it meets with; and, since interests are
innumerable, the legislation-machine must work uninterruptedly. Laws and ordinances fall like hail on
the poor populace. After a while the political soil

---

* Pr. " *Justice* " 1. 195 [1. 235].
† *Ib.* 3. 45 [3. 276, but with the bracketed sentence much abridged. For
the phrase " rebel against right," remember that in French *right* and *common law* are one and the same word].
‡ Pr. " *Propriété* " p. 18 [24-5].

will be covered with a layer of paper, and all the
geologists will have to do will be to list it, under the
name of *papyraceous formation*, among the epochs of
the earth's history. The Convention, in three years
one month and four days, issued eleven thousand six
hundred laws and decrees; the Constituent and Legislative Assemblies had produced hardly less; the empire and the later governments have wrought as
industriously. At present the '*Bulletin des Lois*' contains, they say, more than fifty thousand; if our
representatives did their duty this enormous figure
would soon be doubled. Do you believe that the
populace, or the government itself, can keep its sanity
in this labyrinth? "*

"But what am I saying? Laws for him who
thinks for himself, and is responsible only for his own
acts! laws for him who would be free, and feels himself destined to become free! I am ready to make
terms, but I will have no laws; I acknowledge none;
I protest against every order which an ostensibly necessary authority shall please to impose on my free
will. Laws! we know what they are and what they
are worth. Cobwebs for the powerful and the rich,
chains which no steel can break for the little and the
poor, fishers' nets in the hands of the government."†

"You say they shall make *few* laws, make them
simple, make them *good*. But it is impossible.
Must not government adjust all interests, decide all
disputes? Now interests are by the nature of society
innumerable, relationships infinitely variable and
mobile; how is it possible that only a few laws should

---

* Pr. "*Idée*" 147-8 [136-7[.   † *Ib*. 149 [138].

be made? how can they be simple? how can the best law escape soon being detestable? "*

II. *Justice requires that only one legal norm be in force: to wit, the norm that contracts must be lived up to.*

"What do we mean by a *contract?* A contract, says the civil code, art. 1101, is an agreement whereby one or more persons bind themselves to one or more others to do or not to do something."†
"That I may remain free, that I may be subjected to no law but my own, and that I may govern myself, the edifice of society must be rebuilt upon the idea of CONTRACT."‡ "We must start with the idea of contract as the dominant idea of politics."§ This norm, that contracts must be lived up to, is to be based not only on its justice, but at the same time on the fact that among men who live together there prevails a will to enforce the keeping of contracts, if necessary, with violence; ‖ so it is to be not only a commandment of morality, but also a legal norm.

"Several of your fellow-men have agreed to treat each other with good faith and fair play,—that is, to respect those rules of action which the nature of things points out to them as being alone capable of assuring to them, in the fullest measure, prosperity, safety, and peace. Are you willing to join their league? to form a part of their society? Do you promise to respect the honor, the liberty, the goods, of your brothers? Do you promise never to appropriate

---

* Pr. "*Idée*" pp. 149-50 [138].   † Pr. "*Principe*" p. 64 [44].
‡ Pr. "*Idée*" p. 235 [215].   § Pr. "*Principe*" p. 64 [44].
‖ Pr. "*Idée*" p. 343 [312].

to yourself, neither by violence, by fraud, by usury, nor by speculation, another's product or possession? Do you promise never to lie and deceive, neither in court, in trade, nor in any of your dealings? You are free to accept or to refuse.

" If you refuse, you form a part of the society of savages. Having left the fellowship of the human race, you come under suspicion. Nothing protects you. At the least insult anybody you meet may knock you down, without incurring any other charge than that of cruelty to animals.

" If you swear to the league, on the contrary, you form a part of the society of free men. All your brothers enter into an engagement with you, promising you fidelity, friendship, help, service, commerce. In case of infraction on their part or on yours, through negligence, hot blood, or evil intent, you are responsible to one another, for the damage and also for the scandal and insecurity which you have caused; this responsibility may extend, according to the seriousness of the perjury or the repetition of the crime, as far as to excommunication and death."*

4.—THE STATE

I. Since Proudhon approves only the single legal norm that contracts must be lived up to, he can sanction only a single legal relation, that of parties to a contract. Hence he must necessarily reject the State; for it is established by particular legal norms, and, as an involuntary legal relation, it binds even those who have not entered into any contract at all. *Proudhon*

---

*Pr. " *Idée* " pp. 342-3 [311-12].

*does accordingly reject the State absolutely, without
any spatial or temporal limitation; he even regards it
as a legal relation which offends against justice to an
unusual degree.*

" The government of man by man is slavery."*
" Whoever lays his hand on me to govern me is a
usurper and a tyrant; I declare him my enemy."†
" In a given society the authority of man over man is
in inverse ratio to the intellectual development which
this society has attained, and the probable duration of
this authority may be calculated from the more or less
general desire for a true—that is, a scientific—
government."‡
" Royalty is never legitimate. Neither heredity,
election, universal suffrage, the excellence of the
sovereign, nor the consecration of religion and time,
makes royalty legitimate. In whatever form it may
appear, monarchical, oligarchic, democratic,—royalty,
or the government of man by man, is illegal and
absurd."§ Democracy in particular " is nothing but
a constitutional arbitrary power succeeding another
constitutional arbitrary power; it has no scientific
value, and we must see in it only a preparation for
the REPUBLIC, one and indivisible."‖
" Authority was no sooner begun on earth than it
became the object of universal competition. Authority, Government, Power, State,—these words all denote the same thing,—each man sees in it the means
of oppressing and exploiting his fellows. Absolutists,

---

* Pr. *Confessions* " p. 8]29]. † *Ib.* p. 6 [23].
‡ Pr. " *Propriété* " p. 301 [216]. § *Ib.* pp. 298-9 [214].
‖ Pr. " *Solution* " p. 54 [39].

doctrinaires, demagogues, and socialists, turned their eyes incessantly to authority as their sole cynosure."* " All parties without exception, in so far as they seek for power, are varieties of absolutism; and there will be no liberty for citizens, no order for societies, no union among workingmen, till in the political cate- chism the renunciation of authority shall have re- placed faith in authority. *No more parties, no more authority, absolute liberty of man and citizen,*—there, in three words, is my political and social confession of faith."†

II. *Justice demands, in place of the State, a social human life on the basis of the legal norm that con- tracts must be lived up to.* Proudhon calls this social life " anarchy "‡ and later " federation "§ also.

1. After the abrogation of the State men are still to live together in society. As early as 1841 Prou- dhon says that the point is " to discover a system of absolute equality, in which all present institutions, minus property or the sum of the abuses of property, might not only find a place, but be themselves means to equality; individual liberty, the division of powers, the cabinet, the jury, the administrative and judiciary organization."‖

But men are not to be kept together in society by any supreme authority, but only by the legally bind- ing force of contract. " When I bargain for any

---

*Pr. " *Confessions* " p. 7 [24]. † *Ib.* p. 7 [25-6].
‡ Pr. " *Propriété* " p. 301 [216], " *Confessions* " p. 68 [192], " *Solution* " p. 119 [87].
§ Pr. " *Principe* " p. 67 [46].—Proudhon's teaching was not. as asserted by Diehl vol. 2 p. 116, vol. 3 pp. 166-7, and Zenker p. 61, Anarchism till 1852 and Federalism thenceforward ; his Anarchism was Federalism from the start, only he later gave it the add'tional name of Federalism.
‖ Pr. " *Propriété* " pp. XIX-XX [10-11].

object with one or more of my fellow-citizens, it is
clear that then my will alone is my law; it is I myself
who, in fulfilling my obligation, am my government.
If then I could make that contract with all, which I
do make with some; if all could renew it with each
other; if every group of citizens, commune, canton,
department, corporation, company, etc., formed by
such a contract and considered as a moral person,
could then, always on the same terms, treat with each
of the other groups and with all, it would be exactly
as if my will was repeated *ad infinitum.* I should be
sure that the law thus made on all points that concern
the republic, on the various motions of millions of persons, would never be anything but my law; and, if
this new order of things was called government, that
this government would be mine. The *régime of contracts,* substituted for the *régime of laws,* would constitute the true government of man and of the citizen,
the true sovereignty of the people, the REPUBLIC."*

" The Republic is the organization by which, all
opinions and all activities remaining free, the People,
by the very divergence of opinions and of wills, thinks
and acts as a single man. In the Republic every citizen, in doing what he wishes and nothing but what he
wishes, participates directly in legislation and government, just as he participates in the production and
circulation of wealth. There every citizen is king;
for he has plenary power, he reigns and governs.
The Republic is a positive anarchy. It is neither
liberty subjected TO order, as in the constitutional
monarchy, nor liberty imprisoned IN order, as the pro-

* Pr. "*Idée*" pp. 235-6 [215-16].

visional government would have it.   It is liberty delivered from all its hobbles, superstition, prejudice, sophism, speculation, authority; it is mutual liberty, not self-limiting liberty; liberty, not the daughter but the MOTHER of order."*

2. Anarchy may easily seem to us "the acme of disorder and the expression of chaos.   They say that when a Parisian burgher of the seventeenth century once heard that in Venice there was no king, the good man could not get over his astonishment, and thought he should die of laughing.   Such is our prejudice."†   As against this, Proudhon draws a picture of how men's life in society under anarchy might perhaps shape itself in detail, to execute the functions now belonging to the State.

He begins with an example.   " For many centuries the spiritual power has been separated, within traditional limits, from the temporal power.   [But there has never been a complete separation, and therefore, to the great detriment of the church's authority and of believers, centralization has never been sufficient.]   There would be a complete separation if the temporal power not only did not concern itself with the celebration of mysteries, the administration of sacraments, the government of parishes, etc., but did not intervene in the nomination of bishops either.   There would ensue a greater centralization, and consequently a more regular government, if in each parish the people had the right to choose for themselves their vicars and curates, or to have none at all; if in each diocese the priests elected their bishop; if the assembly of

---

*Pr. "Solution " p. 119 [87],   † Pr, " Propriété " pp. 301-2 [216].

bishops, or a primate of the Gauls, had sole charge of the regulation of religious affairs, theological instruction, and worship. By this separation the clergy would cease to be, in the hands of political power, an instrument of tyranny over the people; and by this application of universal suffrage the ecclesiastical government, centralized in itself, receiving its inspirations from the people and not from the government or the pope, would be in constant harmony with the needs of society and with the moral and intellectual condition of the citizens. We must, then, in order to return to truth, organic, political, economic, or social (for here all these are one), first, abolish the constitutional cumulation by taking from the State the nomination of the bishops, and definitively separating the spiritual from the temporal; second, centralize the church in itself by a system of graded elections; third, give to the ecclesiastical power, as we do to all the other powers in the State, the vote of the citizens as a basis. By this system what to-day is GOVERNMENT will no longer be anything but *administration;* all France is centralized, so far as concerns ecclesiastical functions; the country, by the mere fact of its electoral initiative, governs itself in matters of eternal life as well as in those of this world. And one may already see that if it were possible to organize the entire country in temporal matters on the same bases, the most perfect order and the most vigorous centralization would exist without there being anything of what we to-day call constituted authority or government."*

Proudhon gives a second example in judicial

---

*Pr. " *Confessions* " p. 65 [180-3 ; bracketed words a paraphrase.]

authority. "The judicial functions, by their different
specialties, their hierarchy, [their permanent tenure of
office,] their convergence under a single departmental
head, show an unequivocal tendency to separation and
centralization. But they are in no way dependent on
those who are under their jurisdiction; they are all at
the disposal of the executive power, which is appointed
by the people once in four years with authority that
cannot be diminished; they are subordinated not to
the country by election, but to the government, president or prince, by appointment. It follows that those
who are under the jurisdiction of a court are given
over to their 'natural' judges just as are parishioners
to their vicars; that the people belong to the magis-
trate like an inheritance; that the litigant is the
judge's, not the judge the litigant's. Apply universal
suffrage and graded election to the judicial as well
as the ecclesiastical functions; suppress the permanent
tenure of office, which is an alienation of the electoral
right; take away from the State all action, all
influence, on the judicial body; let this body,
separately centralized in itself, no longer depend on
any but the people,—and, in the first place, you will
have deprived power of its mightiest instrument of
tyranny; you will have made justice a principle of
liberty as well as of order. And, unless you suppose
that the people, from whom all powers should spring
by universal suffrage, is in contradiction with itself,—
that what it wants in religion it does not want in justice,—you are assured that the separation of powers
can beget no conflict; you may boldly lay it down as
a principle that *separation* and *equilibrium* are hence-

forth synonymous."*

Then Proudhon goes on to the army, the custom-houses, the public departments of agriculture and commerce, public works, public education, and finance; for each of these administrations he demands independence and centralization on the basis of general suffrage.†

"That a nation may manifest itself in its unity, it must be centralized in its religion, centralized in its justice, centralized in its army, centralized in its agriculture, industry, and commerce, centralized in its finances,—in a word, centralized in all its functions and faculties; the centralization must work from the bottom to the top, from the circumference to the centre; all the functions must be independent and severally self-governing.

" Would you then make this invisible unity perceptible by a special organ, preserve the image of the old government? Group these different administrations by their heads; you have your cabinet, your *executive*, which can then very well do without a Council of State.

" Set up above all this a grand jury, legislature, or national assembly, appointed directly by the whole country, and charged not with appointing the cabinet officers,—they have their investiture from their particular constituents,—but with auditing the accounts, making the laws, settling the budget, deciding controversies between the administrations, all after having heard the reports of the Public Department, or De-

---

* Pr. " *Confessions* " pp. 65-6 [183-4, except bracketed words].
† *Ib.* pp. 66-8 [185-9].

partment of the Interior, to which the whole government will thenceforth be reduced; and you will have a
centralization the stronger the more you multiply its
foci, a responsibility the more real the more clear-cut
is the separation between the powers; you have a
constitution at once political and social."*

5.—PROPERTY

I. Since Proudhon sanctions only the one legal
norm that contracts must be kept, he can approve
only one legal relation, that between contracting parties. Hence he must necessarily reject property as
well as the State, since it is established by particular
legal norms, and, as an involuntary legal relation,
binds even such as have in no way entered into a contract. *And he does reject property† absolutely, without any spatial or temporal limitation; nay, it even
appears to him to be a legal relation which is particularly repugnant to justice.*

" According to its definition, property is the right
of using and abusing; that is to say, it is the absolute, irresponsible domain of man over his person and
his goods. If property ceased to be the right to
abuse, it would cease to be property. Has not the
proprietor the right to give his goods to whomever he

---

* Pr. " *Confessions* " p. 68 [191-2].
† Pfau pp. 227-31, Adler p. 372, Zenker pp. 26, 41, fail to see this, being
influenced by the improper sense in which Proudhon uses the word " property " for a contractually guaranteed share of goods. [Eltzbacher's statement, on the other hand, is not so much drawn from Proudhon himself as
deduced from a comparison of Eltzbacher's definition of property with the
statement that Proudhon admits no law but the law of contract. I do not
think this last statement is correct; I think Proudhon would have his voluntary contractual associations protect their members in certain definable
respects—among others, in the possession of goods—against those who
stood outside the contract as well as against those within. Then this
would be, by Eltzbacher's definitions, both law and property.]

will, to let his neighbor burn without crying fire, to
oppose the public good, to squander his patrimony,
to exploit the laborer and hold him to ransom, to
produce bad goods and sell them badly? Can he be
judicially constrained to use his property well? can he,
be disturbed in the abuse of it? What am I saying?
Is not property, precisely because it is full of abuse,
the most sacred thing in the world for the legislator?
Can one conceive of a property whose use the police
power should determine, whose abuse it should re-
press? Is it not clear, in fine, that if one undertook
to introduce justice into property, one would destroy
property, just as the law, by introducing propriety
into concubinage, destroyed concubinage?"*

"Men steal: first, by violence on the highway;
second, alone or in a band; third, by burglary;
fourth, by embezzlement; fifth, by fraudulent bankruptcy; sixth, by forgery; seventh, by counterfeiting.
Eighth, by pocket-picking; ninth, by swindling;
tenth, by breach of trust; eleventh, by gambling and
lotteries.—Twelfth, by usury. Thirteenth, by rent-
taking.—Fourteenth, by commerce, when the profits
are more than fair wages for the trader's work.—Fif-
teenth, by selling one's own product at a profit, and
by accepting a sinecure or a fat salary."† "In theft
such as the laws forbid, force and fraud are employed
alone and openly; in authorized theft they are dis-
guised under a produced utility, which they use as a
device for plundering their victim. The direct use of
violence and force was early and unanimously re-

---

* Pr, " Contradictions " 2. 303-4 [2. 237-8].
† Pr. " Propriété " pp. 285-90 [205-9].

jected; no nation has yet reached the point of delivering itself from theft when united with talent, labor, and possession."* In this sense property is "theft,"† "the exploitation of the weak by the strong,"‡ "contrary to right,"§ "the suicide of society."‖

II. *Justice demands, in place of property, a distribution of goods based on the legal norm that contracts must be lived up to.*

Proudhon calls that portion of goods which is assigned to the individual by contract, "property." In 1840 he had demanded that individual possession be substituted for property; with this one change evil would disappear from the earth.¶ But in 1841 he is already explaining that by property he means only its abuses;** nay, he even then describes as necessary the creation of an immediately applicable social system in which the rights of barter and sale, of direct and collateral inheritance, of primogeniture and bequest, should find their place.†† In 1846 he says, "Some day transformed property will be an idea positive, complete, social, and true; a property which will abolish the old property and will become equally effective and beneficent for all."‡‡ In 1848 he is declaring that "property, as to its principle or substance, which is human personality, must never perish; it must remain in man's heart as a perpetual stimulus to labor, as the antagonist whose absence would cause labor to fall into idleness and death."§§ And in 1850 he announces: "What I sought for

---

* Pr. "*Propriété*" p. 293 [211].   † *Ib.* pp. 1-2 [13].   ‡ *Ib.* p. 283 [204].
§ *Ib.* p. 311 [223].   ‖ *Ib.* p. 311 [223].   ¶ *Ib.* p. 311 [223].
** *Ib.* pp. XVIII-XIX [10; consult the passage].   †† *Ib.* pp. XIX-XX [11].
‡‡ Pr. "*Contradictions*" 2. 234-5 [2. 184].   §§ Pr. "*Droit*" p. 50 [230].

as far back as 1840, in defining property, what I am
wanting now, is not a destruction; I have said it till
I am tired.   That would have been to fall with Rousseau, Plato, Louis Blanc himself, and all the adversaries of property, into *Communism*, against which I
protest with all my might; what I ask for property is
a BALANCE,"*—that is, "justice."†

In all these pronouncements property means
nothing else than that portion of goods which falls
to the individual on the basis of contracts, on which
society is to be built up.‡   The property which
Proudhon sanctions cannot be a special legal relation,
but only a possible part of the substance of the one
legal relation which he approves, the relation of contract.   It can afford no protection against a group of
men whose extent is determined by legal norms, but
only against a group of men who have mutually
secured a certain portion of goods to each other by
contract.   Proudhon, therefore, is here using the
word "property" in an inexact sense; in the strict
sense it can denote only a portion of goods set apart
in an involuntary legal relation by particular legal
norms.

Accordingly, when in the name of justice Proudhon
demands a certain distribution of property, this means
nothing more than that the contracts on which society
is to be built should make a certain sort of provision
with respect to the distribution of goods.   And the
way in which they should determine it is this: that
every man is to have the product of his labor.

---

* Pr. "*Justice*" 1. 302-3 [1. 324-5].   † *Ib.* 303 [1. 325].
‡ Pr. "*Idée*" p. 235 [215] ; "*Principe*" p. 64 [44].

" Let us conceive of wealth as a mass whose elements are held together permanently by a chemical force, and into which new elements incessantly enter and combine in different proportions, but according to a definite law: value is the proportion (the measure) in which each of these elements forms a part of the whole. "* " I suppose, therefore, a force which combines the elements of wealth in definite proportions and makes of them a homogeneous whole."† " This force is LABOR. It is labor, labor alone, that produces all the elements of wealth and combines them, to the last molecule, according to a variable but definite law of proportionality."‡ " Every product is a representative sign of labor."§

" Every product can consequently be exchanged for another."‖ " If then the tailor, in return for furnishing the value of one day of his work, consumes ten times the weaver's day, it is as if the weaver gave ten days of his life for one day of the tailor's. This is precisely what occurs when a peasant pays a lawyer twelve francs for a document that it costs one hour to draw up; and this inequality, this iniquity in exchange, is the mightiest cause of poverty. Every error in commutative justice is an immolation of the laborer, a transfusion of a man's blood into another man's body."¶

" What I demand with respect to property is a BALANCE. It is not for nothing that the genius of nations has equipped Justice with this instrument of

---

* Pr. " *Contradictions* " 1. 51 [1. 74].   † *Ib*. 1. 53 [1. 75].
‡ *Ib*. 1. 55. [1. 76-7].   § *Ib*. 1. 68 [1. 87].   ‖ *Ib*. 1. 68 [1. 87].
¶ *Ib*. 1. 83 [1. 98-9].

precision. Justice applied to economy is in fact
nothing but a perpetual balance; or, to express myself still more precisely, justice as regards the distribution of goods is nothing but the obligation which
rests upon every citizen and every State, in their business relations, to conform to that law of equilibrium
which manifests itself everywhere in economy, and
whose violation, accidental or voluntary, is the fundamental principle of poverty."*

2. That every man should enjoy the product of his
labor is possible only through reciprocity, according
to Proudhon; therefore he calls his doctrine " the
theory of *mutuality* or of the *mutuum*."† " RECI-
PROCITY is expressed in the precept, ' Do to others
what you would have done to you,' a precept which
political economy has translated into its celebrated
formula, ' Products exchange for products.' Now the
evil which is devouring us results from the fact that
the law of reciprocity is unrecognized, violated. The
remedy consists altogether in the promulgation of this
law. The organization of our mutual and reciprocal
relations is the whole of social science."‡

And so Proudhon, in the solemn declaration which
he prefixed to the constitution of the People's Bank
when he first published it, gives the following assur-
ance: " I protest that in criticising property, or
rather the whole body of institutions of which property is the pivot, I never meant either to attack the
individual rights recognized by previous laws, or to

---

* Pr. " *Justice* " 1. 302-3 [1. 325].
† Pr. " *Contradictions* " 2. 528 [2. 414].
‡ Pr. " *Organisation* " p. 5 [93].

dispute the legitimacy of acquired possessions, or to instigate an arbitrary distribution of goods, or to put an obstacle in the way of the free and regular acquisition of properties by bargain and sale; or even to prohibit or suppress by sovereign decree land-rent and interest on capital. I think that all these manifestations of human activity should remain free and optional for all; I would admit no other modifications, restrictions, or suppressions of them than naturally and necessarily result from the universalization of the principle of reciprocity and of the law of synthesis which I propound. This is my last will and testament. I allow only him to suspect its sincerity, who could tell a lie in the moment of death."*

6.—REALIZATION

The change which justice calls for is to come about in this way, that those men who have recognized the truth are to convince others how necessary the change is for the sake of justice, and that hereby, spontaneously, law is to transform itself, the State and property to drop away, and the new condition to appear. The new condition will appear " as soon as the idea is popularized "; † that it may appear, we must " popularize the idea."‡

I. Nothing is requisite but to convince men that justice commands the change.

1. Proudhon rejects all other methods. His doctrine is " in accord with the constitution and the laws."§ " Accomplish the Revolution, they say, and

---

* Pr. "*Banque*" pp. 3-4 [260].
† Pr. "*Justice*" 1. 515 [2. 133].   ‡ *Ib.* 1. 515 [2. 133].
‡ Pr. *Confessions* " p. 71 [201].

after this everything will be cleared up. As if the
Revolution itself could be accomplished without a
leading idea!"* "To secure justice to one's self by
bloodshed is an extremity to which the Californians,
gathered since yesterday to seek for gold, may be reduced; but may the luck of France preserve us from
it!"†

"Despite the violence which we witness, I do not
believe that hereafter liberty will need to use force to
claim its rights and avenge its wrongs. Reason will
serve us better; and patience, like the Revolution, is
invincible."‡

2. But how shall we convince men, "how popularize the idea, if the *bourgeoisie* remains hostile; if the
populace, brutalized by servitude, full of prejudices
and bad instincts, remains plunged in indifference; if
the professors, the academicians, the press, are calum-
niating you; if the courts are truculent; if the powers
that be muffle your voice? Don't worry. Just as
the lack of ideas makes one lose the most promising
games, war against ideas can only push forward the
Revolution. Do you not see already that the *régime*
of authority, of inequality, of predestination, of
eternal salvation, and of reasons of State, is daily becoming still more intolerable for the well-to-do classes,
whose conscience and reason it tortures, than for the
mass, whose stomach cries out against it? "§

---

* Pr. "*Justice*" 1, 515 [2, 133. Eltzbacher finds the sense "all will be enlightened" where I translate "everything will be cleared up." Eltzbacher's view of the sense—that to those who say "Enlightenment must
come by the Revolution" Proudhon replies, "No, the Revolution must
come by enlightenment"—correctly gives the thought brought out in the
context].
† Pr. "*Justice*" 1. 466 [2. 90]. ‡ *Ib.* 1. 470-71 [2. 94]. § *Ib.* 1. 515 [2. 133-4].

3. The most effective means for convincing men, according to Proudhon, is to present to the people, within the State and without violating its law, " an example of centralization spontaneous, independent, and social," thus applying even now the principles of the future constitution of society.* " Rouse that collective action without which the condition of the people will forever be unhappy and its efforts powerless. Teach it to produce wealth and order with its own hands, without the help of the authorities."†

Proudhon sought to give such an example by the founding of the People's Bank.‡

The People's Bank was to " insure work and prosperity to all producers by organizing them as beginning and end of production with regard to one another,—that is, as capitalists and as consumers."§

" The People's Bank was to be the property of all the citizens who accepted its services, who for this purpose furnished money to it if they thought that it could not yet for some time do without a metallic basis, and who, in every case, promised it their preference in discounting paper, and received its notes as cash. Accordingly the People's Bank, working for the profit of its customers themselves, had no occasion to take interest for its loans nor to charge a discount on commercial paper; it had only to take a very slight allowance to cover salaries and expenses. So credit was GRATUITOUS!—The principle being realized, the consequences unfolded themselves *ad infinitum*."‖

" So the People's Bank, giving an example of pop-

---

* Pr. " *Confessions* " p. 69 [196].   † *Ib.* p. 72 [203].   ‡ *Ib.* p. 69 [196].
§ *Ib.* p. 69 [196].   ‖ *Ib.* pp. 69-70 [197].

ular initiative alike in government and in public economy, which thenceforth were to be identified in a single synthesis, was becoming for the *prolétariat* at once the principle and the instrument of their emancipation; it was creating political and industrial liberty. And, as every philosophy and every religion is the metaphysical or symbolic expression of social economy, the People's Bank, changing the material basis of society, was ushering in the revolution of philosophy and religion; it was thus, at least, that its founders had conceived of it."*

All this can best be made clear by reproducing some provisions from the constitution of the People's Bank.

Art. 1. By these presents a commercial company is founded under the name of *Société de la Banque du Peuple,* consisting of Citizen Proudhon, here present, and the persons who shall give their assent to this constitution by becoming stockholders.

Art. 3. . . . . For the present the company will exist as a partnership in which Citizen Proudhon shall be general partner, and the other parties concerned shall be limited partners who shall in no case be responsible for more than the value of their shares.

Art. 5. . . . . The firm name shall be P. J. Proudhon & Co.

Art. 6. Besides the members of the company proper, every citizen is invited to form a part of the People's Bank as a cooperator. For this it suffices to assent to the bank's constitution and to accept its paper.

Art. 7. The People's Bank Company being capable of indefinite extension, its virtual duration is endless. However, to conform to the requirements of the law, it fixes its duration at ninety-nine years, which shall commence on the day of its definitive organization.

Art. 9. . . . . The People's Bank, having as its *basis* the essential gratuitousness of credit and exchange, as its *object* the circulation, not the production, of values, and as its *means* the

---

* Pr. " *Confessions* " p. 70 [197-8].

mutual consent of producers and consumers, can and should work without capital.

This end will be reached when the entire mass of producers and consumers shall have assented to the constitution of the company.

Till then the People's Bank Company, having to conform to established custom and the requirements of law, and especially in order more effectively to invite citizens to join it, will provide itself with capital.

Art. 10. The capital of the People's Bank shall be five million francs, divided into shares of five francs each.

. . . . The company shall be definitively organized, and its business shall begin, when ten thousand shares are taken.

Art. 12. Stock shall be issued only at par. It shall bear no interest.

Art. 15. The principal businesses of the People's Bank are, 1, to increase its cash on hand by issuing notes; 2, discounting endorsed commercial paper; 3, discounting accepted orders *(commandes)* and bills *(factures)*; 4, loans on personal property; 5, loans on personal security; 6, advances on annuities and collateral security; 7, payments and collections; 8, advances to productive and industrial enterprises *(la commande)*.

To these departments the People's Bank will add: 9, the functions of a savings bank and endowment insurance; 10, insurance; 11, safe deposit vaults; 12, the service of the budget.*

Art. 18. In distinction from ordinary bank notes, payable in *specie* to some one's *order,* the paper of the People's Bank is an order for goods, vested with a social character, rendered perpetual, and is payable at sight by every stockholder and co-operator in the *products* or *services* of his industry or profession.

Art. 21. Every co-operator agrees to trade by preference, for all goods which the company can offer him, with the co-operators of the bank, and to reserve his orders exclusively for his fellow stockholders and fellow co-operators.

In return, every producer or tradesman co-operating with the bank agrees to furnish his goods to the other co-operators at a reduced price.

Art. 62. The People's Bank has its headquarters in Paris.

---

*[French dictionaries leave us somewhat in the lurch as to commercial usages which differ from the English. Eltzbacher translates 8, "invest-ment as silent partner"; 12, "balancing accounts."]

Its aim is, in the course of time, to establish a branch in every *arrondissement* and a correspondent in every commune.

Art. 63. As soon as circumstances permit, the present company shall be converted into a corporation, since this form allows us to realize, according to the wish of the founders, the threefold principle, first, of election; second, of the separation and the independence of the branches of work; third, of the personal responsibility of every employee.*

II. If once men are convinced that justice commands the change, then will " despotism fall of itself by its very uselessness."† The State and property disappear, law is transformed, and the new condition of things begins.

" The Revolution does not act after the fashion of the old governmental, aristocratic, or dynastic principle. It is Right, the balance of forces, equality. It has no conquests to pursue, no nations to reduce to servitude, no frontiers to defend, no fortresses to build, no armies to feed, no laurels to pluck, no preponderance to maintain. The might of its economic institutions, the gratuitousness of its credit, the brilliancy of its thought, are its sufficient means for converting the universe."‡ " The Revolution has for allies all who suffer oppression and exploitation; let it appear, and the universe stretches its arms to it."§

" I want the peaceable revolution. I want you to make the very institutions which I charge you to abolish, and the principles of law which you will have to complete, serve toward the realization of my wishes, so that the new society shall appear as the spontaneous, natural, and necessary development of the old, and that the Revolution, while abrogating the old

---

*Pr. "*Banque*" pp. 5-20 [261-77]. † Pr. " *Confessions* " p. 72 [202-3].
‡Pr. "*Justice* " 1. 509 [2. 128-9]. §*Ib.* 1. 510 [2. 129].

order of things, shall nevertheless be the progress of that order."* " When the people, once enlightened regarding its true interests, declares its will not to reform the government but to revolutionize society,"† then " the dissolution of government in the economic organism "‡ will follow in a way about which one can at present only make guesses.§

---

*Pr. "*Idée*" pp. 196-7 [181].   † *Ib.* p. 197 [181].

‡ *Ib.* p. 277 [253].   § *Ib.* pp. 195, 197 [180-81].

CHAPTER V

STIRNER'S TEACHING

1. Johann Kaspar Schmidt was born in 1806, at Bayreuth in Bavaria. He studied philosophy and theology at Berlin from 1826 to 1828, at Erlangen from 1828 to 1829. In 1829 he interrupted his studies, made a prolonged tour through Germany, and then lived alternately at Koenigsberg and Kulm till 1832. From 1832 to 1834 he studied at Berlin again; in 1835 he passed his tests there as *Gymnasiallehrer*. He received no government appointment, however, and in 1839 became teacher in a young ladies' seminary in Berlin. He gave up this place in 1844, but continued to live in Berlin, and died there in 1856.

In part under the pseudonym Max Stirner, in part anonymously, Schmidt published a small number of works, mostly of a philosophical nature.

2. Stirner's teaching about law, the State, and property is contained chiefly in his book "*Der Einzige und sein Eigentum*" (1845).

—But here arises the question, Can we speak of such a thing as a "teaching" of Stirner's?

Stirner recognizes no *ought*. "Men are such as they should be—can be. What should they be? Surely not more than they can be! And what can they be? Not more, again, than they—can, *i. e.*

than they have the ability, the strength, to be."*
"A man is 'called' to nothing, and has no 'proper
business,' no 'function,' as little as a plant or beast
has a 'vocation.' He has not a vocation; but he has
powers, which express themselves where they are, because their being consists only in their expression, and
which can remain idle as little as life, which would no
longer be life if it 'stood still' but for a second.
Now one might cry to man, 'Use your power.' But
this imperative would be given the meaning that it
was man's proper business to use his power. It is not
so. Rather, every one really does use his power,
without first regarding this as his vocation; every one
uses in every moment as much power as he
possesses."†

Nay, Stirner acknowledges no such thing as truth.
"Truths are phrases, ways of speaking, words
(*logos*); brought into connection, or arranged by
ranks and files, they form logic, science, philosophy."‡
"Nor is there a truth,—not right, not liberty, humanity, etc.,—which could subsist before me, and to which
I would submit."§ "If there is a single truth to
which man must consecrate his life and his powers because he is man, then he is subjected to a rule, dominion, law, etc.; he is a man in service."‖ "As long as
you believe in truth, you do not believe in yourself;
you are a—servant, a—religious man. You alone

---

*Stirner p. 439. [The page-numbers of Stirner's first edition, here cited,
agree almost exactly with those of the English translation under the title
"The Ego and His Own." Any passage quoted here will in general be
found in the English translation either on the page whose number is given
or on the preceding page ; for the early pages, subtract two or three from
the number.]
†*Ib.* pp. 435-6.   ‡*Ib.* p. 465.   §*Ib.* p. 464.   ‖*Ib.* p. 466.

are truth; or rather, you are more than truth, which is nothing at all before you."*

If one chose to draw the extreme ·inference from this, Stirner's book would be only a self-avowal, an expression of thoughts without any claim to general validity; in it Stirner would not be informing us what he thinks to be true, or what in his opinion we ought to do, but only giving us an opportunity to observe the play of his ideas. Stirner did not draw this inference,† and one should not let the style of the book, which speaks mostly of Stirner's " I," lead him to think that Stirner did draw it. He calls that man " blinded, who wants to be only ' Man '."‡ He takes the floor against " the erroneous consciousness of not being able to entitle myself to as much as I want."§ He mocks at our grandmothers' belief in ghosts.‖ He declares that " penalty must make room for satisfaction,"¶ that man " should defend himself against man."** And he asserts that " over the door of our time stands not Apollo's ' Know thyself,' but a ' Turn yourself to account!' "†† So Stirner intends not only to give us information about his inward condition at the time he composed his book, but to tell us what he thinks to be true and what we ought to do; his book is not a mere self-avowal, but a scientific teaching.

3. Stirner does not call his teaching about law, the State, and property " Anarchism." He prefers to use the epithet " anarchic " to designate political liberalism, which he combats.‡‡

---

*Stirner p. 473.
† No more do his adherents, e. g. Mackay, "Stirner " pp. 164-5.
‡Stirner p. 322.   §Ib. p. 343.   ‖Ib. p. 45.   ¶Ib. p. 318.
**Ib. p. 318.   ††Ib. p. 420.   ‡‡Ib. pp. 189-90.

2.—BASIS

*According to Stirner the supreme law for each one
of us is his own welfare.*
What does one's own welfare mean?   " Let us seek
out the enjoyment of life! "*   " Henceforth the question is not how one can acquire life, but how he can
expend it, enjoy it; not how one is to produce in himself the true ego, but how he is to dissolve himself, to
live himself out."†   " If the enjoyment of life is to
triumph over the longing or hope for life, it must
overcome it in its double significance which Schiller
brings out in ' The Ideal and Life '; it must crush
spiritual and temporal poverty, abolish the ideal and
—the want of daily bread.   He who must lay out his
life in prolonging life cannot enjoy it, and he who is
still seeking his life does not have it, and can as little
enjoy it; both are poor."‡
Our own welfare is our supreme law.   Stirner
recognizes no duty.§   " Whether what I think and do
is Christian, what do I care?   Whether it is human,
humane, liberal, or unhuman, inhumane, illiberal,
what do I ask about that?   If only it aims at what I
would have, if only I satisfy myself in it, then fit it
with predicates as you like; it is all one to me."‖
" So then my relation to the world is this: I no longer
do anything for it ' for God's sake ', I do nothing ' for
man's sake ', but what I do I do ' for my sake '."¶
" Where the world comes in my way—and it comes in
my way everywhere—I devour it to appease the hun-

---

*Stirner p. 427.   † *Ib.* p. 428.   ‡ *Ib.* p. 429.
§ *Ib.* p. 258.   ‖ *Ib.* p. 478.   ¶ *Ib.* p. 426.

ger of my egoism. You are to me nothing but—my food, just as I also am fed upon and used up by you. We have only one relation to each other, that of utility, of usableness, of use."* " I too love men, not merely individuals, but every one. But I love them with the consciousness of egoism; I love them because love makes me happy, I love because love is natural to me, because it pleases me. I know no ' commandment of love '."†

3.—LAW

I. *Looking to each one's own welfare, Stirner rejects law, and that without any limitation to particular spatial or temporal conditions.*

Law‡ exists not by the individual's recognizing it as favorable to his interests, but by his holding it sacred. " Who can ask about ' right' if he is not occupying the religious standpoint just like other people? Is not ' right' a religious concept, *i. e.* something sacred?"§ " When the Revolution stamped

---

* Stirner p. 395.　　† *Ib.* p. 387.

‡ [To understand some of the following citations it is necessary to remember that in German " law " (in the sense of common law, or including this) and " right " are one and the same word.—While it is probably not fair to say that these assaults of Stirner are directed only against some laws, it does seem fair to say that they deny to the laws only some sorts of validity. We have very little material for compiling the constructive side of Stirner's teaching, for he avoided specifying what things the Egoists or their unions were to do in his future social order; he said explicitly that the only way to know what a slave will do when he breaks his fetters is to wait and see. But, while he may nowhere have stated a law which is to obtain in the good time coming, neither has he said anything which authorizes us to declare that none of his unions will ever make laws on such a basis as (for instance) the rules of the Stock Exchange. On page 114 below is quoted a passage where he distinctly and approvingly contemplates the possibility that a union of his followers may fix a minimum wage, and may threaten violence to any person who consents to work below the scale. This would be law, and might easily be the germ of a State. On pages 108 and 109 are quoted passages which strongly suggest that the Egoistic union would undertake to defend its member against all interference with his possession of certain goods; this would be both law and property.]

§ Stirner p. 247.

liberty as a 'right' it took refuge in the religious sphere, in the region of the sacred, the ideal."* I am to revere the sultanic law in a sultanate, the popular law in republics, the canon law in Catholic communities, etc. I am to subordinate myself to these laws, I am to count them sacred."† "The law is sacred, and he who outrages it is a criminal."‡ "There are no criminals except against something sacred"; § crime falls when the sacred disappears.‖ Punishment has a meaning only in relation to something sacred.¶ "What does the priest who admonishes the criminal do? He sets forth to him the great wrong of having by his act desecrated that which was hallowed by the State, its property (in which, you will see, the lives of those who belong to the State must be included)."**

But law is no more sacred than it is favorable to the individual's welfare. "Right—is a delusion, bestowed by a ghost."†† Men have "not recovered the mastery over the thought of 'right,' which they themselves created; their creature is running away with them."‡‡ "Let the individual man claim ever so many rights; what do I care for his right and his claim?"§§ I do not respect them.—"What you have the might to be you have the right to be. I deduce all right and all entitlement from myself; I am entitled to everything that I have might over. I am entitled to overthrow Zeus, Jehovah, God, etc., if I can; if I cannot, then these gods will always remain in the right and in the might as against me."‖‖

---

* Stirner p. 248.   † Ib. p. 246.   ‡ Ib. p. 314.   § Ib. p. 268.

‖ Ib. p. 317.   ¶ Ib. pp. 317, 316.   ** Ib. pp. 265-6.   †† Ib. p. 276.

‡‡ Ib. p. 270.   §§ Ib. pp. 326-7.   ‖‖ Ib. pp. 248-9.

" Right crumbles into its nothingness when it is swallowed up by force,"* " but with the concept the word too loses its meaning."† " The people will perhaps be against the blasphemer; hence a law against blasphemy. Shall I therefore not blaspheme? Is this law to be more to me than an order? "‡ " He who has might ' stands above the law '."§ " The earth belongs to him who knows how to take it, or who does not let it be taken from him, does not let himself be deprived of it. If he appropriates it, then not merely the earth, but also the right to it, belongs to him. This is egoistic right; *i. e.*, it suits me, therefore it is right."‖

II. *Self-welfare commands that in future it itself should be men's rule of action in place of the law.*

Each of us is " unique,"¶ " a world's history for himself,"** and, when he " knows himself as unique,"†† he is a " self-owner."‡‡ " God and mankind have made nothing their object, nothing but themselves. Let me then likewise make myself my object, who am, as well as God, the nothing of all else, who am my all, who am the Unique."§§ " Away then with every business that is not altogether my business! You think at least the ' good cause ' must be my business? What good, what bad? Why, I myself am my business, and I am neither good nor bad. Neither has meaning for me. What is divine is God's business, what is human ' Man's.' My business is neither what is divine nor what is human, it is

---

* Stirner p. 275. † *Ib.* p. 275. ‡ *Ib.* pp. 259, 256. § *Ib.* p. 220. ‖ *Ib.* p. 251. [The German idiom for " it suits me " is " it is right to me "]. ¶ *Ib.* p. 8. ** *Ib.* p. 490. †† *Ib.* p. 491. ‡‡ *Ib.* p. 491. §§ *Ib.* p. 7.

not what is true, good, right, free, etc., but only what is mine; and it is no general business, but is—unique, as I am unique. Nothing is more to me than myself!"*

"What a difference between freedom and self-ownership! I am free from what I am rid of; I am owner of what I have in my power."† "My freedom becomes complete only when it is my—might; but by this I cease to be a mere freeman and become a self-owner."‡ "Each must say to himself, I am all to myself and I do all for my sake. If it ever became clear to you that God, the commandments, etc., do you only harm, that they encroach on you and ruin you, you would certainly cast them from you just as the Christians once condemned Apollo or Minerva or heathen morality."§ "How one acts only from himself, and asks no questions about anything further, the Christians have made concrete in the idea of 'God.' He acts 'as pleases him'."‖

"Might is a fine thing and useful for many things; for 'one gets farther with a handful of might than with a bagful of right.' You long for freedom? You fools! If you took might, freedom would come of itself. See, he who has might 'stands above the law.' How does this prospect taste to you, you 'law-abiding' people? But you have no taste!"¶

4.—THE STATE

I. *Together with law Stirner necessarily has to reject also, just as unconditionally, the legal institution*

---

*Stirner p. 8.   † *Ib.* p. 207.   ‡ *Ib.* p. 219.
§ *Ib.* p. 214.   ‖ *Ib.* p. 212.   ¶ *Ib.* p. 220.

which is called State. Without law the State is not possible. "'Respect for the statutes!' By this cement the whole fabric of the State is held together."*

The State as well as the law, then, exists, not by the individual's recognizing it as favorable to his welfare, but rather by his counting it sacred, by "our being entangled in the error that it is an I, as which it applies to itself the name of a 'moral, mystical, or political person.' I, who really am I, must pull off this lion's skin of the I from the parading thistle-eater."† The same holds good of the State as of the family. "If each one who belongs to the family is to recognize and maintain that family in its permanent existence, then to each the tie of blood must be sacred, and his feeling for it must be that of family piety, of respect for the ties of blood, whereby every blood-relative becomes hallowed to him. So, also, to every member of the State-community this community must be sacred, and the concept which is supreme to the State must be supreme to him too."‡ The State is "not only entitled, but compelled, to demand" this.§

But the State is not sacred. "The State's behavior is violence, and it calls its violence 'law', but that of the individual 'crime'."‖ If I do not do what it wishes, "then the State turns against me with all the force of its lion-paws and eagle-talons; for it is the king of beasts, it is lion and eagle."¶ "Even if you do overpower your opponent as a power, it does not follow that you are to him a hallowed authority, un-

<hr>

*Stirner p. 314.   † *Ib.* p. 295.   ‡ *Ib.* pp. 231-2.
§ *Ib.* p. 231.   ‖ *Ib.* p. 259.   ¶ *Ib.* p. 337.

less he is a degenerate. He does not owe you respect, and reverence, even if he will be wary of your might."*

Nor is the State favorable to the individual's welfare. "I am the mortal enemy of the State."†

"The general welfare as such is not my welfare, but only the extremity of self-denial. The general welfare may exult aloud while I must lie like a hushed dog; the State may be in splendor while I starve."‡

"Every State is a despotism, whether the despot be one or many, or whether, as people usually conceive to be the case in a republic, all are masters, i. e. each tyrannizes over the others."§   "Doubtless the State leaves the individuals as free play as possible, only they must not turn the play to earnest, must not forget it. The State has never any object but to limit the individual, to tame him, to subordinate him, to subject him to something general; it lasts only so long as the individual is not all in all, and is only the clear-cut limitation of me, my limitedness, my slavery."||

"A State never aims to bring about the free activity of individuals, but only that activity which is bound to the State's purpose."¶   "The State seeks to hinder every free activity by its censorship, its oversight, its police, and counts this hindering as its duty, because it is in truth a duty of self-preservation."**

"I am not allowed to do all the work I can, but only so much as the State permits; I must not turn my thoughts to account, nor my work, nor, in general,

---

*Stirner p. 258.   † Ib. p. 339.   ‡ Ib. p. 280.   § Ib. p. 257.
|| Ib. p. 298.   ¶ Ib. p. 298.   ** Ib. p. 299.

anything that is mine."* " Pauperism is the value-lessness of Me, the phenomenon of my being unable to turn myself to account. Therefore State and pauperism are one and the same. The State does not let me attain my value, and exists only by my valuelessness; its goal is always to get some benefit out of me, *i. e.* to exploit me, to use me up, even if this using consisted only in my providing a *proles* (*prolétariat*); it wants me to be ' its creature '."†

" The State cannot brook man's standing in a direct relation to man; it must come between as a— mediator, it must—intervene. It tears man from man, to put itself as ' spirit ' in the middle. The laborers who demand a higher wage are treated as criminals so soon as they want to get it by compulsion. What are they to do? Without compulsion they don't get it, and in compulsion the State sees a self-help, a price fixed by the ego, a real, free turning to account of one's property, which it cannot permit."‡

II. *Every man's own welfare demands that a social human life solely on the basis of its precepts should take the place of the State.* Stirner calls this sort of social life " the union of egoists."§

1. Even after the State is abolished men are to live together in society. "Self-owners will fight for the unity which is their own will, for union."‖ But what is to keep men together in the union?

Not a promise, at any rate. " If I were bound to-day and hereafter to my will of yesterday," my will

---

*Stirner p. 298.   †*Ib.* p. 336.   ‡*Ib.* pp. 337-8.
§*Ib.* p. 235 ; Stirner " *Vierteljahrsschrift* " p. 192.   ‖ Stirner p. 304.

would "be benumbed. My creature, *viz.*, a particular expression of will, would have become my domin-
ator. Because I was a fool yesterday I must remain
such all my life."* "The union is my own creation,
my creature, not sacred, not a spiritual power above
my spirit, as little as any association of whatever sort..
As I am not willing to be a slave to my maxims, but
lay them bare to my constant criticism without any
warrant, and admit no bail whatever for their continu-
ance, so still less do I pledge myself to the union for
my future and swear away my soul to it as men are
said to do with the devil, and as is really the case with
the State and all intellectual authority; but I am and
remain more to myself than State, Church, God, and
the like, and, consequently, also infinitely more than
the union."†

Rather, men are to be held together in the union
by the advantage which each individual has from the
union at every moment. If I can "use" my fellow-
men, "then I am likely to come to an understanding
and unite myself with them, in order to strengthen my
power by the agreement, and to do more by joint
force than individual force could accomplish. In this
joinder I see nothing at all else than a multiplication
of my strength, and only so long as it is my multi-
plied strength do I retain it."‡

Hence the union is something quite different from
"that society which Communism means to found."§
"You bring into the union your whole power, your
ability, and assert yourself; in society you with your
labor-strength are spent. In the former you live ego-

---

*Stirner p. 258.   †*Ib.* p. 411.   ‡*Ib.* p. 416.   §*Ib.* p. 411.

istically, in the latter humanly, *i. e.* religiously, as a
'member in the body of this Lord'. You owe to
society what you have, and are in duty bound to it,
are—possessed by 'social duties'; you utilize the
union, and, undutiful and unfaithful, give it up when
you are no longer able to get any use out of it. If
society is more than you, then it is of more consequence to you than yourself; the union is only your
tool, or the sword with which you sharpen and enlarge your natural strength; the union exists for you
and by you, society contrariwise claims you for itself
and exists even without you ; in short, society is
sacred, the union is your own ; society uses you up,
you use up the union."*

2. But what form may such a social life take in
detail? In reply to his critic, Moses Hess, Stirner
gives some examples of unions that already exist.

" Perhaps at this moment children are running together under his window for a comradeship of play ;
let him look at them, and he will espy merry egoistic
unions. Perhaps Hess has a friend or a sweetheart;
then he may know how heart joins itself to heart, how
two of them unite egoistically in order to have the
enjoyment of each other, and how neither ' gets the
worst of the bargain.' Perhaps he meets a few pleas-
ant acquaintances on the street and is invited to
accompany them into a wine-shop ; does he go with
them in order to do an act of kindness to them, or
does he ' unite ' with them because he promises himself enjoyment from it? Do they have to give him
their best thanks for his ' self-sacrifice ', or do they

---

* Stirner pp. 417-18.

know that for an hour they formed an 'egoistic union' together?"*   Stirner even thinks of a "German Union."†

5.—PROPERTY

I. *Together with law Stirner necessarily has to reject also, and just as unconditionally, the legal institution of property.* This " lives by grace of the law. It has its guarantee only in the law; it is not a fact, but a fiction, a thought.   This is law-property, legal property, warranted property.   It is mine not by me, but by—law."‡

" Property in this sense, as well as the law and the State, is based not on the individual's recognizing it as favorable to his welfare, but on his counting it sacred.   " Property in the civil sense means sacred property, in such a way that I must respect your property.   ' Have respect for property!'   Therefore the political liberals would like every one to have his bit of property, and have in part brought about an incredible parcellation by their efforts in this direction. Every one must have his bone, on which he may find something to bite."§

But property is not sacred.   " I do not step timidly back from your property, be you one or many, but look upon it always as my property, in which I have no need to 'respect' anything.   Now do the like with what you call my property!"‖

Nor is property favorable to the individual's welfare.   " Property, as the civic liberals understand it,

---

*Stirner " *Vierteljahrsschrift* " pp. 193-4.   † Stirner p. 305.
‡ *Ib.* p. 332.   § *Ib.* pp. 327-8.   ‖ *Ib.* pp. 328, 326.

is untenable, because the civic proprietor is really
nothing but a propertyless man, a man everywhere excluded. Instead of the world's belonging to him, as
it might, there belongs to him not even the paltry
point on which he turns around."*

II. *Every one's own welfare commands that a distribution of commodities based solely on its precepts
should take the place of property.* When Stirner designates as " property " the share of commodities assigned to the individual by these precepts, it is in the
improper sense in which he constantly uses the word
property: in the proper sense only a share of commodities assigned by law can be called property.†

Now, according to the decrees of his own welfare,
every man should have all that he is powerful enough
to obtain.

" What they are not competent to tear from me the
power over, that remains my property: all right, then
let power decide about property, and I will expect
everything from my power! Alien power, power that
I leave to another, makes me a slave; then let own
power make me an owner."‡ " To what property am
I entitled? To any to which I—empower myself. I
give myself the right of property in taking property to
myself, or giving myself the proprietor's power, plenary power, empowerment."§ " What I am competent
to have is my ' competence.' "‖ " The sick, children,
the aged, are still competent for a great deal; *e. g.* to
receive their living instead of taking it. If they are

---

* Stirner pp. 328-9.
† Zenker fails to recognize this when he asserts (p. 80) that Stirner de-
mands property based on the right of occupation.
‡ Stirner p. 340.   § *Ib.* p. 339.   ‖ *Ib.* p. 351.

competent to control you to the extent of having you
desire their continued existence, then they have a
power over you."* "What competence the child possesses in its smile, its play, its crying,—in short, in its
mere existence! Are you capable of resisting its demand? or do you not hold out to it, as a mother, your
breast,—as a father, so much of your belongings as it
needs? It puts you under constraint, and therefore
possesses what you call yours."†

"Property, therefore, should not and cannot be
done away with; rather, it must be torn from ghostly
hands and become my property; then will the erroneous consciousness that I cannot entitle myself to as
much as I want vanish.—' But what cannot a man
want? ' Well, he who wants much, and knows how
to get it, has in all times taken it to him, as Napoleon
did the continent, and the French Algeria. Therefore
the only point is just that the respectful ' lower
classes ' should at length learn to take to themselves
what they want. If they reach their hands too far for
you, why, defend yourselves."‡ "What ' man ' wants
does not by any means furnish a scale for me and my
needs; for I may have a use for more, or for less.
Rather, I must have as much as I am competent to
appropriate to myself."§

2. "In this matter, as well as in others, unions will
multiply the individual's means and make secure his
assailed property."‖ "When it is our will no longer
to leave the land to the land-owners, but to appropriate it to ourselves, we unite ourselves for this purpose;
we form a union, a *société*, which makes itself owner;

---

*Stirner p. 351.   †*Ib.* pp. 351-2.   ‡*Ib.* pp. 343-4.   §*Ib.* p. 349.   ‖*Ib.* p. 342.

if we are successful, they cease to be land-owners. And, as we chase them out from land and soil, so we can also from many another property, to make it our own, the property of the—conquerors. The conquerors form a society, which one may conceive of as so great that by degrees it embraces all mankind; but so-called mankind is also, as such, only a thought (ghost); its reality is the individuals. And these individuals as a collective mass will deal not less arbitrarily with land and soil than does an isolated individual."*

" What all want to have a share in will be withdrawn from that individual who wants to have it for himself alone; it is made a common possession. As a common possession every one has a share in it, and this share is his property. Just so, even in our old relations, a house which belongs to five heirs is their common possession; but the fifth part of the proceeds is each one's property. The property which for the present is still withheld from us can be better made use of when it is in the hands of us all. Let us therefore associate ourselves for the purpose of this robbery."†

6.—REALIZATION

According to Stirner the change which every one's own welfare requires is to come about in this way,— that men in sufficient number first undergo an inward change and recognize their own welfare as their highest law, and that these men then bring to pass by force the outward change also: to wit, the abrogation of

---

*Stirner pp. 329-30. [See footnote on page 97.]   † *Ib.* p. 330.

*law, State, and property, and the introduction of the
new condition.*
  I. The first and most important thing is the inward
change of men.
  " Revolution and insurrection must not be regarded
as synonymous. The former consists in an overturn-
ing of conditions, of the existing condition. or state,
the State or society, and so is a political or social act;
the latter has indeed a transformation of conditions as
its inevitable consequence, but starts not from this but
from men's discontent with themselves, is not a lifting
of shields but a lifting of individuals, a coming up,
without regard to the arrangements that spring from
it. The Revolution aimed at new arrangements: the
Insurrection leads to no longer having ourselves arranged but arranging ourselves, and sets no brilliant
hope on ' institutions.' It is not a fight against the
existing order, since, if it prospers, the existing order
collapses of itself; it is only a working my way out of
the existing order. If I leave the existing order, it is
dead and passes into decay. Now, since my purpose
is not the upsetting of an existing order but the lifting of myself above it, my aim and act are not political or social, but, as directed upon myself and my
ownness alone, egoistic."*
  Why was the founder of Christianity " not a revolutionist, not a demagogue as the Jews would have
liked to see him; why was he not a Liberal? Because he expected no salvation from a change of *conditions*, and this whole business was indifferent to
him. He was not a revolutionist, like Cæsar for in-

---

*Stirner pp. 421-2.

stance, but an insurgent; not an overturner of the
State, but one who straightened *himself* up. He
waged no Liberal or political war against the existing
authorities, but wanted to go his own way regardless
of these authorities and undisturbed by them."*
"Everything sacred is a bond, a fetter. Everything sacred will be, must be, perverted by perverters
of law; therefore our present time has such perverters
by the quantity in all spheres. They are preparing
for the break of the law, for lawlessness."† "Regard
yourself as more powerful than they allege you to be,
and you have more power; regard yourself as more,
and you are more."‡ "The poor become free and
proprietors only when they—'rise'."§ Only from
egoism can the lower classes get help, and this help
they must give to themselves and—will give to themselves. If they do not let themselves be constrained
into fear, they are a power."‖
II. Furthermore, in order to bring about the
"transformation of conditions "¶ and put the new
condition in the place of law, State, and property,
violent insurrection against the condition that has
hitherto existed is requisite.
1. "The State can be overcome only by a violent
arbitrariness."** "The individual's violence [*Gewalt*]
is called crime [*Verbrechen*], and only by crime does
he break [*brechen*] the State's authority [*Gewalt*] when
he opines that the State is not above him, but he
above the State."†† "Here too the result is that the
thinkers' combat against the government is wrong,

*Stirner p. 423. † Ib. p. 284. ‡ Ib. p. 483. § Ib. p. 344.
‖ Ib. p, 343. ¶ Ib. p. 422. ** Ib. p. 199. †† Ib. p. 259.

viz. in impotence, so far as it cannot bring into the field anything but thoughts against a personal power (the egoistic power stops the mouths of the thinkers). The theoretical combat cannot complete the victory, and the sacred power of thought succumbs to the might of egoism. It is only the egoistic combat, the combat of egoists on both sides, that clears up everything."*

"The property question cannot be solved so gently as the Socialists, even the Communists, dream. It is solved only by the war of all against all."† "Let me then retract the might which I have conceded to others out of ignorance regarding the strength of my own might! Let me say to myself, 'Whatever my might reaches to is my property,' and then claim as property all that I feel myself strong enough to attain; and let me make my real property extend as far as I entitle (*i. e.* empower) myself to take."‡ "In order to extirpate the unpossessing rabble, egoism does not say, ' Wait and see what the Board of Equity will—donate to you in the name of the collectivity ', but ' Put your hand to it and take what you need! ' "§

In this combat Stirner agrees to all methods. "I will not draw back with a shudder from any act because there dwells in it a spirit of godlessness, immorality, wrongfulness, as little as St. Boniface was disposed to abstain from chopping down the heathens'

---

* Stirner pp. 198-9.
† *Ib.* p. 344. [But Stirner does not mean that all are to fight against all; they are merely to declare themselves no longer bound by the obligations of peace, and then those who are able to agree with each other can at once make terms to suit themselves.]
‡ *Ib.* p. 340.   § *Ib.* p. 341.

sacred oak on account of religious scruples."*   "The power over life and death, which Church and State reserved to themselves, this too I call—mine."†   "The life of the individual man I rate only at what it is worth.   His goods, the material and the spiritual alike, are mine, and I dispose of them as proprietor to the extent of my—might."‡

2. Stirner depicts for us a single event in this violent transformation of conditions.   He assumes that certain men come to realize that they occupy a disproportionately unfavorable position in the State as compared with others who receive the preference.

"Those who are in the unfavorable position take courage to ask the question, ' By what, then, is your property secure, you favored ones? ' and give themselves the answer, ' By our refraining from interference!   By our protection, therefore!   And what do you give us for it?   Kicks and contempt you give the " common people "; police oversight, and a catechism with the chief sentence " Respect what is not yours, what belongs to others! respect others, and especially superiors! "   But we reply, " If you want our respect, buy it for a price that shall be acceptable to us." We will leave you your property, if you pay duly for this leaving.   With what, indeed, does the general in time of peace pay for the many thousands of his yearly income? or Another for the sheer hundred-thousands and millions?   With what do you pay us for chewing potatoes and looking quietly on while you swallow oysters?   Only buy the oysters from us as dear as we have to buy the potatoes from you, and

---

*Stirner p. 479.   † *Ib.* p. 424.   ‡ *Ib.* pp. 326-7.

you may go on eating them. Or do you suppose the
oysters do not belong to us as much as to you? You
will make an outcry about violence if we take hold
and help eat them, and you are right. Without
violence we do not get them, as you no less have them
by doing violence to us.

"'But take the oysters and done with it, and let us
come to what is in a closer way our property (for this
other is only possession)—to labor. We toil twelve
hours in the sweat of our foreheads, and you offer us a
few groschen for it. Then take the like for your
labor too. We will come to terms all right if only we
have first agreed on the point that neither any longer
needs to—donate anything to the other. For centuries we have offered you alms in our kindly—stupidity,
have given the mite of the poor and rendered to the
masters what is—not the masters'; now just open your
bags, for henceforth there is a tremendous rise in the
price of our ware. We will take nothing away from
you, nothing at all, only you shall pay better for what
you want to have. What have you then? "I have
an estate of a thousand acres." And I am your plow-
man, and will hereafter do your plowing only for a
thaler a day wages. "Then I'll get another." You
will not find one, for we plowmen are no longer doing
anything different, and if one presents himself who
takes less, let him beware of us.' "†

---

* Stirner pp. 359-60.

CHAPTER VI

BAKUNIN'S TEACHING

1.—GENERAL

1. Mikhail Alexandrovitch Bakunin was born in 1814 at Pryamukhino, district of Torshok, government of Tver. In 1834 he entered the Artillery School at St. Petersburg; in 1835 he became an officer, but resigned his commission in the same year. He then lived alternately in Pryamukhino and in Moscow.

In 1840 Bakunin left Russia. In the following years revolutionary plans took him now to this part of Europe, now to that; in Paris he associated much with Proudhon. In 1849 he was condemned to death in Saxony, but was pardoned; in 1850 he was handed over to Austria and was condemned to death there also; in 1851 he was handed over to Russia and was there kept a prisoner first at St. Petersburg, then at Schluesselburg; in 1857 he was sent to Siberia.

From Siberia Bakunin escaped to London in 1865, by way of Japan and California. He took up his revolutionary activities again at once, and thereafter lived by turns in the most various parts of Europe. In 1868 he became a member of the *Association internationale des travailleurs*, and soon afterward he founded the *Alliance internationale de la démocratie socialiste*. In 1869 he came into intimate relations with the fanatic Nechayeff, but broke away from him in the next year. In 1872 he was expelled from the *Association internationale des travailleurs* on the ground that his aims were different from those of the Association. He died at Berne in 1876. Bakunin wrote a number of works of a philosophical and political nature.

2. Bakunin's teaching about law, the State, and property finds its expression especially in the " *Proposition motivée au comité central de la Ligue de la paix et de la liberté* "* offered by him in 1868; in the principles† of the *Alliance internationale de la démocratie socialiste*, drawn up by him in 1868; and in his work " *Dieu et l'Etat* "‡ (1871).

Writings which cannot with certainty be assigned to Bakunin are here disregarded. Among such we may name especially the two works " The Principles of the Revolution "§ and ''Catechism of the Revolution," || in which Nechayeff's views are set forth. They are indeed ascribed to Bakunin by some,¶ but their matter is in contradiction to his other utterances as well as to his deeds; he even used vehement language on several occasions against Nechayeff's

---

* Printed in " *Œuvres de Michel Bakounine* " (1895) pp. 1-205, under the title " *Fédéralisme, socialisme, et antithéologisme.*"

† Printed in " *L'Alliance de la démocratie socialiste et l'Association internationale des travailleurs* " (1873) pp. 118-35.

‡ Only fragments have been printed : one under the title '' *L'Empire knoutogermanique et la Révolution sociale* " (1871), a second under the title " *Dieu et l'État* " (1882), a third under the same title in " *Œuvres de Michel Bakounine* " (1895) pp. 261-326.

§ Printed in Dragomanoff, '' *Michaïl Bakunins sozial-politischer Briefwechsel mit Alexander Iw. Herzen und Ogarjow,*" German translation by Minzès (1895) pp. 358-64.

|| A part is printed in French translation, in " *L'Alliance de la démocratie socialiste et l'Association internationale des travailleurs* " (1873) pp. 90-95, the rest in Dragomanoff pp. 371-83.

¶ " *L'Alliance de la démocratie socialiste et l'Association internationale des travailleurs* " p. 89 ; Dragomanoff p. IX.

" Machiavellianism and Jesuitism."* Even on the
assumption that they are by Bakunin, they would at
any rate express only a very insignificant chapter in
his development.

3. Bakunin designates his teaching about law, the
State, and property as " Anarchism." " In a word,
we reject all legislation, all authority, all privileged,
chartered, official, and legal influence,—even if it were
created by universal suffrage,—in the conviction that
such things can but redound always to the advantage
of a ruling minority of exploiters and to the disadvantage of the vast enslaved majority. In this sense
we are in truth Anarchists."†

2.—BASIS

*Bakunin regards the evolutionary law of the pro-
gress of mankind from a less perfect existence to the
most perfect possible existence as the law which has
supreme validity for man.*

" Science has no other task than the careful intellectual reproduction, in the most systematic form possible, of the natural laws of corporeal, mental, and
moral life, alike in the physical and in the social
world, which two worlds constitute in fact only a
single natural world."‡

Now " science—that is, true, unselfish science "§—
teaches us the following: " Every evolution signifies
the negation of its starting-point. Since according to
the materialists the basis or starting-point is material,
the negation must necessarily be ideal."‖ That is,

* Ba. "*Briefe*" pp. 223, 233, 266, 272.
† Ba. "*Dieu*" p. 34.   ‡ *Ib.* p. 33.   § *Ib.* p. 3.   ‖ *Ib.* p. 52.

" everything that lives makes the effort to perfect itself
as fully as possible."*

Thus, " according to the conception of materialists,
man's historical evolution also moves in a constantly
ascending line."† " It is an altogether natural movement from the simple to the compound, from down to
up, from the lower to the higher."‡ " History consists in the progressive negation of man's original
bestiality by the evolution of his humanity."§

" Man is originally a wild beast, a cousin of the
gorilla. But he has already come out of the deep
night of bestial impulses to make his way to the light
of the mind. This explains all his former missteps in
the most natural way, and comforts us somewhat with
regard to his present aberrations. He has turned his
back on bestial slavery, and is now moving toward
freedom through the realm of slavery to God, which
lies between his bestial and his human existence.
Behind us, therefore, lies our bestial existence, before
us our human; the light of humanity, which alone
can light us and warm us, deliver us and exalt us,
make us free, happy, and brothers, stands never at the
beginning of history, but always only at its end."∥

This " historical negation of the past takes place
now slowly, sluggishly, sleepily, but now again pas-
sionately and violently."¶ It always takes place with
the inevitable certainty of natural law: " we believe in
the final triumph of humanity on earth."** " We
yearn for the coming of this triumph, and seek to hasten it with united effort "; ** " we must never look

---

* Ba. " *Proposition* " p. 104.   † Ba. " *Dieu* " p. 52.   ‡ *Ib.* p. 7.
§ *Ib.* p. 16.   ∥ *Ib.* p. 16.   ¶ *Ib.* p. 16.   ** Ba. " *Proposition*" p. 155.

back, always forward alone; before us is our sun, before us our bliss."*

3.—LAW

I. *In the progress of mankind from its bestial existence to a human existence, one of the next steps, according to Bakunin, will be the disappearance—not indeed of law, but—of enacted law.*

Enacted law belongs to a low stage of evolution. "A political legislation, whether it is based on a ruler's will or on the votes of representatives chosen by universal suffrage, can never correspond to the laws of nature, and is always baleful, hostile to the liberty of the masses, if only because it forces upon them a system of external and consequently despotic laws."† No legislation has ever "had another aim than that of confirming, and exalting into a system, the exploitation of the laboring populace by the ruling classes."‡ Thus every legislation "has for its consequence at once the enslavement of society and the depravation of the legislators."§

But mankind will soon leave behind it the stage of evolution to which law belongs. Enacted law is indissolubly connected with the State: "the State is a historically necessary evil,"‖ "a transitory form of society";¶ "with the State, law in the jurists' sense, the so-called legal regulation of popular life from above downward by legislation, must necessarily fall."** Everybody feels already that this moment is approach-

---

* Ba. "*Dieu*" p. 16.   † *Ib.* pp. 27-8.   ‡ Ba. "*Programme*" p. 382.
§ Ba. "*Dieu*" p. 30.   ‖ Ba. "*Dieu*" *Œuvres* p. 287.   ¶ *Ib.* p. 285.
** Ba. "*Programme*" p. 382.

ing,* the transformation is at hand,† it is to be
expected within the nineteenth century.‡

II. *In the next stage of evolution, which mankind
must speedily reach, there will be no enacted law to be
sure, but there will be law even there.* What Bakunin
predicts with regard to this next stage of evolution
enables us to perceive that according to his expecta-
tion norms will then prevail which " are based on a
general will,"§ and which even secure obedience by
forcible compulsion if necessary,‖ so that they are
legal norms.

Among such legal norms of our next stage of evolution Bakunin mentions that by virtue of which there
exists a " right to independence."¶ For me as an individual this means " that I as a man am entitled to
obey no other man, and to act only in accordance
with my own judgment."** But, furthermore,
" every nation, every province, and every commune
has the unlimited right to complete independence,
provided that its internal constitution does not
threaten the independence and liberty of the adjoining
territories."††

Likewise Bakunin regards it as a legal norm of the
next stage of evolution that contracts must be lived up
to. To be sure, the obligation of contracts has its
limits. " Human justice cannot recognize anything as
creating an obligation in perpetuity. All rights and
duties are founded on liberty. The right of freely
uniting and separating is the first and most important

* Ba. " *Articles* " p. 113.   † Ba. " *Statuts* " p. 125.   ‡ *Ib.* p. 125.
§ Ba. " *Dieu* " *Œuvres* p. 281.   ‖ Ba. " *Statuts* " pp. 129-31.
¶ Ba. " *Proposition* " pp. 17-18.   ** Ba. " *Dieu* " *Œuvres* p. 281.
†† Ba. " *Proposition* " pp. 17-18,

of all political rights."*

Another legal norm mentioned by Bakunin as belonging to the next stage of evolution is that by virtue of which "the land, the instruments of labor, and all other capital, as the collective property of the whole of society, will exclusively serve for the use of the agricultural and industrial associations."†

4.—THE STATE

I. *In the progress of mankind from its bestial existence to a human existence the State will shortly, according to Bakunin, disappear.* "The State is a historically temporary arrangement, a transitory form of society."‡

1. The State belongs to a low stage of evolution.

" Man takes the first step from his bestial existence to a human existence by religion; but so long as he remains religious he will never reach his goal; for every religion condemns him to absurdity, guides him into a wrong course, and makes him seek the divine in place of the human."§ " All religions, with their gods, demigods, and prophets, their Messiahs and saints, are products of the credulous fancy of men who had not yet come to the full development and entire possession of their intellectual powers." ‖ This holds good also, and particularly, of Christianity: it is " the complete inversion of common-sense and reason."¶

The State is a product of religion. " In all lands it is born of a marriage of violence, robbery, spoli-

---

* Ba. " *Proposition* " p. 18.   † Ba. " *Statuts* " p. 133.
‡ Ba. " *Dieu* " *Œuvres* p. 285.
§ Ba. " *Proposition* " p. 134.   ‖ Ba. " *Dieu*" p. 19.   ¶ *Ib.* p. 87.

ation,—in short, of war and conquest,—with the gods whom the religious enthusiasm of the nations had gradually created."* "He who speaks of revelation speaks thereby of revealers enlightened by God, of Messiahs, prophets, priests, and lawgivers; and, if once these are recognized on earth as representatives of the Deity, as sacred teachers of mankind chosen by God himself, then of course they have unlimited authority. All men owe them blind obedience; for no human reason, no human justice, is valid against the divine reason and justice. As slaves of God, men must be also slaves of the Church, and of the State so far as the Church hallows the State."†

"No State is without religion, and none can be without religion. Take the freest States in the world, —for instance, the United States of America or the Swiss Confederacy,—and see what an important part divine providence plays in all public utterances there."‡ "It is not without good reason that governments hold the belief in God to be an essential condition of their power."§ "There is a class of people who, even if they do not believe, must necessarily act as if they believed. This class embraces all mankind's tormentors, oppressors, and exploiters. Priests, monarchs, statesmen, soldiers, financiers, office-holders of all sorts; policemen, *gendarmes*, jailers, and executioners; capitalists, usurers, heads of business, and house-owners; lawyers, economists, politicians of all shades,—all of them, down to the smallest grocer, will always repeat in chorus the words of Voltaire, that, if there were no God, it would be necessary to invent

---

* Ba. "*Dieu*" *Œuvres* p. 287.   † Ba. "*Dieu*" p. 20.   ‡ *Ib.* p. 97.   § *Ib.* p. 9.

him; 'for must not the populace have its religion?' It is the very safety-valve.'"*

2. The characteristics of the State correspond to the low stage of evolution to which it belongs.

The State enslaves the governed. "The State is force; nay, it is the silly parading of force. It does not propose to win love or to make converts; if it puts its finger into anything, it does so only in an unfriendly way; for its essence consists not in persuasion, but in command and compulsion. However much pains it may take, it cannot conceal the fact that it is the legal maimer of our will, the constant negation of our liberty. Even when it commands the good, it makes this valueless by commanding it; for every command slaps liberty in the face; as soon as the good is commanded, it is transformed into the evil in the eyes of true (that is, human, by no means divine) morality, of the dignity of man, of liberty; for man's liberty, morality, and dignity consist precisely in doing the good not because he is commanded to but because he recognizes it, wills it, and loves it."†

At the same time the State depraves those who govern. "It is characteristic of privilege, and of every privileged position, that they poison the minds and hearts of men. He who is politically or economically privileged has his mind and heart depraved. This is a law of social life, which admits of no exceptions and is applicable to entire nations as well as to classes, corporations, and individuals. It is the law of equality, the foremost of the conditions of liberty and humanity."‡

---

* *Ib.* p. 11.   † Ba. " *Dieu* " *Œuvres* p. 288.   ‡ Ba. " *Dieu* " pp. 29-30.

" Powerful States can maintain themselves only by crime, little States are virtuous only from weakness."* " We abhor monarchy with all our hearts; but at the same time we are convinced that a great republic too, with army, bureaucracy, and political centralization, will make a business of conquest without and oppression within, and will be incapable of guaranteeing happiness and liberty to its subjects even if it calls them citizens."† " Even in the purest democracies, such as the United States and Switzerland, a privileged minority faces the vast enslaved majority."‡

3. But the stage of mankind's evolution to which the State belongs will soon be left behind.

" From the beginning of historic society to this day, there has always been oppression of the nations by the State. Is it to be inferred that this oppression is inseparably connected with the existence of human society?"§ Certainly not! " The great, true goal of history, the only one for which there is justification, is our humanization and deliverance, the genuine liberty and prosperity of all socially-living men."‖ " In the triumph of humanity is at the same time the goal and the essential meaning of history, and this triumph can be brought about only by liberty."¶ " As in the past the State was a historically necessary evil, it must just as necessarily, sooner or later, disappear altogether."** Everybody feels already that this moment is approaching,†† the transformation is at hand,‡‡ it is to be expected within the nineteenth

---

* Ba. " *Proposition* " p. 154.   † *Ib.* p. 10.
‡ Ba. " *Dieu* " *Œuvres* pp. 287-8.   § Ba. " *Dieu* " p. 14.   ‖ *Ib.* p. 65.
¶ *Ib.* p. 53.   ** Ba. " *Dieu* " *Œuvres* p. 287.   †† Ba. " *Articles* " p. 113.
‡‡ Ba. " *Statuts* " p. 125.

century.*

II. *In the next stage of evolution, which mankind must speedily reach, the place of the State will be taken by a social human life on the basis of the legal norm that contracts must be lived up to.*

1. Even after the State is done away, men will live together socially. The goal of human evolution, "complete humanity,"† can be attained only in a society. "Man becomes man, and his humanity becomes conscious and real, only in society and by the joint activity of society. He frees himself from the yoke of external nature only by joint—that is, societary—labor: it alone is capable of making the surface of the earth fit for the evolution of mankind; but without such external liberation neither intellectual nor moral liberation is possible. Furthermore, man gets free from the yoke of his own nature only by education and instruction: they alone make it possible for him to subordinate the impulses and motions of his body to the guidance of his more and more developed mind; but education and instruction are of an exclusively societary nature. Outside of society man would have remained forever a wild beast, or, what comes to about the same thing, a saint. Finally, in his isolation man cannot have the consciousness of liberty. What liberty means for man is that he is recognized as free, and treated as free, by those who surround him; liberty is not a matter of isolation, therefore, but of mutuality—not of separateness, bnt of combination; for every man it is only the mirroring of his humanity (that is, of his human rights) in the

---

*Ba. "*Statuts*" p. 125.　　† Ba. "*Dieu*" p. 11.

consciousness of his brothers."*

But men will be held together in society no longer by a supreme authority, but by the legally binding force of contract. Complete humanity can be attained only in a free society. "My liberty, or, what means the same, my human dignity, consists in my being entitled, as man, to obey no other man and to act only on my own judgment."† "I myself am a free man only so far as I recognize the humanity and liberty of all the men who surround me. In respecting their humanity I respect my own. A cannibal, who treats his prisoner as a wild beast and eats him, is himself not a man, but a beast. A slaveholder is not a man, but a master."‡ "The more free men surround me, and the deeper and broader their freedom is, so much deeper, broader, and more powerful is my freedom too. On the other hand, every enslavement of men is at the same time a limitation of my freedom, or, what is the same thing, a negation of my human existence by its bestial existence."§ But a free society cannot be held together by authority,‖ but only by contract.¶

2. How will the future society shape itself in detail?

"Unity is the goal toward which mankind ceaselessly moves."** Therefore men will unite with the utmost amplitude. But "the place of the old organization, built from above downward upon force and authority, will be taken by a new one which has no

---

* Ba. "*Dieu*" *Œuvres* pp. 277-8.   † *Ib.* p. 281.   ‡ *Ib.* p. 279.
§ *Ib.* p. 281.   ‖ *Ib.* p. 283.   ¶ Ba. "*Proposition*" pp. 16-18.
** *Ib.* p. 20.

other basis than the natural needs, inclinations, and endeavors of men."* Thus we come to a " free union of individuals into communes, of communes into provinces, of provinces into nations, and finally of nations into the United States of Europe and later of the whole world."†

" Every nation,—be it great or small, strong or weak,—every province, and every commune has the unlimited right to complete independence, provided that its internal constitution does not threaten the independence and liberty of the adjoining territories."‡

" All of what are known as the historic rights of nations are totally done away; all questions regarding natural, political, strategic, and economic boundaries are henceforth to be classed as ancient history and resolutely disallowed."§

" By the fact that a territory has once belonged to a State, even by a voluntary adhesion, it is in no wise bound to remain always united with this State. Human justice, the only justice that means anything to us, cannot recognize anything as creating an obligation in perpetuity. All rights and duties are founded on liberty. The right of freely uniting and separating is the first and most important of all political rights. Without this right the League would be merely a concealed centralization still."‖

5.—PROPERTY

I. *In the progress of mankind from its bestial ex-*

---

* Ba. " *Proposition* " p. 16.   † *Ib.* pp. 16-17.   ‡ *Ib.* pp. 17-18.
§ *Ib.* p. 17.   ‖ *Ib.* p. 18.

istence to a human existence, according to Bakunin, we must shortly come to the disappearance—not indeed of property, but—of property's present form, unlimited private property.

1. Private property, so far as it fastens upon all things without distinction, belongs to the same low stage of evolution as the State.

" Private property is at once the consequence and the basis of the State."* " Every government is necessarily based on exploitation on the one hand, and on the other hand has exploitation for its goal and bestows upon exploitation protection and legality."†
In every State there exist "two kinds of relationship, —to wit, government and exploitation. If really governing means sacrificing one's self for the good of the governed, then indeed the second relationship is in direct contradiction to the first. But let us only understand our point rightly! From the ideal standpoint, be it theological or metaphysical, the good of the masses can of course not mean their temporal welfare: what are a few decades of earthly life in comparison to eternity? Hence one must govern the masses with regard not to this coarse earthly happiness, but to their eternal good. Outward sufferings and privations may even be welcomed from the educator's standpoint, since an excess of sensual enjoyment kills the immortal soul. But now the contradiction disappears. Exploiting and governing mean the same; the one completes the other, and serves as its means and its end."‡

2. Private property, when it exists in all things

---

*Ba. " Statuts " p. 128,   † Ba. " Dieu " Œuvres p. 324.   ‡ Ib. pp. 323-4.

without distinction, has such characteristics as correspond to the low stage of evolution to which it belongs.

" On the privileged representatives of head-work (who at present are called to be the representatives of society, not because they have more sense, but only because they were born in the privileged class) such property bestows all the blessings and also all the debasement of our civilization: wealth, luxury, profuse expenditure, comfort, the pleasures of family life, the exclusive enjoyment of political liberty, and hence the possibility of exploiting millions of laborers and governing them at discretion in one's own interest. What is there left for the representatives of handwork, these numberless millions of proletarians or of small farmers? Hopeless misery, not even the joys of the family (for the family soon becomes a burden to the poor man), ignorance, barbarism, an almost bestial existence, and this for consolation with it all, that they are serving as pedestal for the culture, liberty, and depravity of a minority."*

The freer and more highly developed trade and industry are in any place, " the more complete is the demoralization of the privileged few on the one hand, and the greater are the misery, the complaints, and the just indignation of the laboring masses on the other. England, Belgium, France, Germany, are certainly the countries of Europe in which trade and industry enjoy greatest freedom and have made most progress. In these very countries the most cruel pauperism prevails, the gulf between capitalists and

---

* Ba. " *Proposition* " pp. 32-3.

landlords on the one hand and the laboring class on the other is greater than in any other country.   In Russia, in the Scandinavian countries, in Italy, in Spain, where trade and industry are still embryonic, people but seldom die of hunger except on extraordinary occasions. In England starvation is an every-day thing. And not only individuals starve, but thousands, tens of thousands, hundreds of thousands."[*]

3. But mankind will soon have passed the low stage of evolution to which private property belongs. As there has at all times been oppression of the nations by the State, so has there also always been "exploitation of the masses of slaves, serfs, wage-workers, by a ruling minority."[†] But this exploitation is no more " inseparably united with the existence of human society "[‡] than is that oppression. " By the force of things themselves "[§] unlimited private property will be done away. Everybody feels already that this moment is approaching,[||] the transformation is already at hand,[¶] it is to be expected within the nineteenth century.[**]

II. *In the next stage of evolution, which mankind must speedily reach, property will be so constituted that there will indeed be private property in the objects of consumption, but in land, instruments of labor, and all other capital, there will be only social property.* The future society will be collectivist.

In this way every laborer has the product of his labor guaranteed to him.

---

* Ba. "*Proposition*" pp. 26-7,   † Ba. "*Dieu*" p. 14.   ‡ *Ib.* p. 14.
§ Ba. "*Programme*" p. 382. || Ba. "*Articles*" p. 113,
¶ Ba, "*Statuts*" p. 125.   ** *Ib.* p. 125.

1. "Justice must serve as basis for the new world: without it, no liberty, no living together, no prosperity, no peace."* "Justice, not that of jurists, nor yet that of theologians, nor yet that of metaphysicians, but simple human justice, commands "† that " in future every man's enjoyment corresponds to the quantity of goods produced by him."‡ The thing is, then, to find a means "which makes it impossible for any one, whoever he may be, to exploit the labor of another, and permits each to share in the enjoyment of society's stock of goods (which is solely a product of labor) only so far as he has, by his labor, directly contributed to the production of this stock of goods."§

This means consists in the principle " that the land, the instruments of labor, and all other capital, as the collective property of the whole of society, shall exclusively serve for the use of the laborers,—that is, of their agricultural and industrial associations."‖ " I am not a Communist, but a Collectivist."¶

2. The collectivism of the future society " by no means demands the setting up of any supreme authority. In the name of liberty, on which alone an economic or a political organization can be founded, we shall always protest against everything that looks even remotely similar to Communism or State Socialism."** " I would have the organization of society, and of the collective or social property, from below upward by the voice of free union, not from above downward by means of any authority."††

* Ba. "Proposition " pp. 54-5.   † Ib. p. 59.   ‡ Ba. " Statuts " p. 133.
§ Ba. " Proposition " p. 55.   ‖ Ba. " Statuts " p. 133.
¶ Ba. " Discours " p. 27.   ** Ba. " Proposition " p. 56.
†† Ba. " Discours " p. 28.

6.—REALIZATION

*The change that is promptly to be expected in the
course of mankind's progress from its bestial existence
to a human existence,—the disappearance of the State,
the transformation of law and property, and the appearance of the new condition,—will come to pass, according to Bakunin, by a social revolution; that is, by
a violent subversion of the old order, which will be
automatically brought about by the power of things,
but which those who foresee the course of evolution
have the task of hastening and facilitating.*

I. " To escape its wretched lot the populace has
three ways, two imaginary and one real.   The two
first are the rum-shop and the church, the third is the
social revolution."*   " A cure is possible only
through the social revolution,"†—that is, through
" the destruction of all institutions of inequality, and
the establishment of economic and social equality."‡
The revolution will not be made by anybody.   " Revolutions are never made, neither by individuals nor
yet by secret societies.   They come about automatically, in a measure; the power of things, the current
of events and facts, produces them.   They are long
preparing in the depth of the obscure consciousness of
the masses—then they break out suddenly, not seldom
on apparently slight occasion."§   The revolution is
already at hand to-day; ‖ everybody feels its approach; ¶ we are to expect it within the nineteenth
century.**

---

* Ba. " *Dieu* " p. 10.   † *Ib.* p. 18.   ‡ *Ib.* p. 45.
§ Ba. " *Statuts* " p. 132.   ‖ *Ib.* p. 125.   ¶ Ba. " *Articles* " p. 113.
** Ba. " *Statuts* " p. 125.

1. " By the revolution we understand the unchaining of everything that is to-day called 'evil passions,' and the destruction of everything that in the same language is called ' public order '."*

The revolution will rage not against men, but against relations and things.† " Bloody revolutions are often necessary, thanks to human stupidity; yet they are always an evil, a monstrous evil and a great disaster, not only with regard to the victims, but also for the sake of the purity and perfection of the purpose in whose name they take place."‡ " One must not wonder if in the first moment of their uprising the people kill many oppressors and exploiters—this misfortune, which is of no more importance anyhow than the damage done by a thunderstorm, can perhaps not be avoided. But this natural fact will be neither moral nor even useful. Political massacres have never killed parties; particularly have they always shown themselves impotent against the privileged classes; for authority is vested far less in men than in the position which the privileged acquire by any institutions, particularly by the State and private property. If one would make a thorough revolution, therefore, one must attack things and relationships, destroy property and the State: then there is no need of destroying men and exposing one's self to the inevitable reaction which the slaughtering of men always has provoked and always will provoke in every society. But, in order to have the right to deal humanely with men without danger to the revolution, one must be inexorable toward things and relationships, destroy every-

---

* Ba. " *Statuts* " p. 129.   † *Ib.* p. 126.   ‡ Ba. " *Volkssache* " p. 309.

thing, and first and foremost property and its inevitable consequence the State. This is the whole secret of the revolution."*

" The revolution, as the power of things to-day necessarily presents it before us, will not be national, but international,—that is, universal. In view of the threatened league of all privileged interests and all reactionary powers in Europe, in view of the terrible instrumentalities that a shrewd organization puts at their disposal, in view of the deep chasm that to-day yawns between the *bourgeoisie* and the laborers everywhere, no revolution can count on success if it does not speedily extend itself beyond the individual nation to all other nations. But the revolution can never cross the frontiers and become general unless it has in it the foundations for this generality; that is, unless it is pronouncedly socialistic, and, by equality and justice, destroys the State and establishes liberty. For nothing can better inspire and uplift the sole true power of the century, the laborers, than the complete liberation of labor and the shattering of all institutions for the protection of hereditary property and of capital."† " A political and national revolution cannot win, therefore, unless the political revolution becomes social, and the national revolution, by the very fact of its fundamentally socialistic and State-destroying character, becomes a universal revolution."‡

2. " The revolution, as we understand it, must on its very first day completely and fundamentally destroy the State and all State institutions. This destruction will have the following natural and neces-

* Ba. " *Statuts* " pp. 127-8.   † *Ib.* p. 125.   ‡ *Ib.* p. 131.

sary effects. (a) The bankruptcy of the State.
(b) The cessation of State collection of private debts,
whose payment is thenceforth left to the debtor's
pleasure. (c) The cessation of the payment of taxes,
and of the levying of direct or indirect imposts. (d)
The dissolution of the army, the courts, the corps of
office-holders, the police, and the clergy. (e) The
stoppage of the official administration of justice, the
abolition of all that is called juristic law and of its
exercise. Hence, the valuelessness, and the consign-
ment to an *auto-da-fe*, of all titles to property, testa-
mentary dispositions, bills of sale, deeds of gift, judgments of courts—in short, of the whole mass of papers
relating to private law. Everywhere, and in regard
to everything, the revolutionary fact in place of the
law created and guaranteed by the State. (f) The
confiscation of all productive capital and instruments
of labor in favor of the associations of laborers, which
will use them for collective production. (g) The confiscation of all Church and State property, as well as
of the bullion in private hands, for the benefit of the
commune formed by the league of the associations of
laborers. In return for the confiscated goods, those
who are affected by the confiscation receive from the
commune their absolute necessities; they are free to
acquire more afterward by their labor."*

The destruction will be followed by the reshaping.

---

* Ba. " *Statuts* " pp. 129-30. [Bakunin is writing in a world where the
Church is everywhere part of the State machine. Would his words about
Church property apply equally, according to him, in the United States,
where the Church property is in general made up of the free gifts of individual believers? Perhaps; for he would have no love for the Church even
here, and he is obviously hostile to anything in the nature of mortmain. If
so, how about college property?]

Hence, (h) "The organization of the commune by the permanent association of the barricades and by its organ, the council of the revolutionary commune, to which every barricade, every street, every quarter, sends one or two responsible and revocable representatives with binding instructions. The council of the commune can appoint executive committees out of its membership for the various branches of the revolutionary administration. (i) The declaration of the capital, insurgent and organized as a commune, that, after the righteous destruction of the State of authority and guardianship, it renounces the right (or rather the usurpation) of governing the provinces and setting a standard for them. (k) The summons to all provinces, communities, and associations, to follow the example given by the capital, first to organize themselves in revolutionary form, then to send to a specified meeting-place responsible and revocable representatives with binding instructions, and so to constitute the league of the insurgent associations, communities, and provinces, and to organize a revolutionary power capable of defeating the reaction. The sending, not of official commissioners of the revolution with some sort of badges, but of agitators for the revolution, to all the provinces and communities—especially to the peasants, who cannot be revolutionized by scientific principles nor yet by the edicts of any dictatorship, but only by the revolutionary fact itself: that is, by the inevitable effects of the complete cessation of official State activity in all the communities. The abolition of the national State, not only in other senses, but in this,—that all foreign countries, provinces, communities, associations, nay, all individuals who have risen in the name of the same principles, without regard to the present State boundaries, are accepted as part of the new political system and nationality; and that, on the other hand, it shall exclude from membership those provinces, communities, associations, or personages, of the same country, who take the side of the reaction. Thus must the universal revolution, by the very fact of its binding the insurgent countries together for joint defence, march on unchecked over the abolished boundaries and the ruins of the formerly existing States to its triumph."[*]

II. "To serve, to organize, and to hasten"[†] "the revolution, which must everywhere be the work of the people"[‡]—this alone is the task of those who foresee the course of evolution. We have to perform " midwife's services "[§] for the new time, " to help on the birth of the revolution."[||]

To this end we must, " first, spread among the masses thoughts that correspond to the instincts of the masses."[¶] " What keeps the salvation-bringing thought from going through the laboring masses with a rush? Their ignorance; and particularly the political and religious prejudices which, thanks to the exertions of the ruling classes, to this day obscure the laborer's natural thought and healthy feelings."[**] " Hence the aim must consist in making him completely conscious of what he wants, evoking in him the thought that corresponds to his impulses. If once

---

[*] Ba. " *Statuts* " pp. 130-31. [†] *Ib.* p. 125. [‡] *Ib.* p. 131.
[§] Ba. " *Volkssache* " p. 309. [||] Ba. " *Statuts* " p. 132. [¶] *Ib.* p. 132.
[**] Ba. " *Articles* " p. 103.

the thoughts of the laboring masses have mounted to
the level of their impulses, then will their will be soon
determined and their power irresistible."*
Furthermore, we must " form, not indeed the army
of the revolution,—the army can never be anything
but the people,—but yet a sort of staff for the revolutionary army. These must be devoted, energetic,
talented men, who, above all, love the people without
ambition and vanity, and who have the faculty of
mediating between the revolutionary thought and the
instincts of the people. No very great number of such
men is requisite. A hundred revolutionists firmly and
seriously bound together are enough for the international organization of all Europe. Two or three hundred revolutionists are enough for the organization of
the largest country."†
Here, especially, is the field for the activity of
secret societies.‡ " In order to serve, organize, and
hasten the general revolution "§ Bakunin founded the
Alliance internationale de la démocratie socialiste. It
was to pursue a double purpose: " (a) The spreading
of correct views about politics, economics, and philosophical questions of every kind, among the masses in
all countries; an active propaganda by newspapers,
pamphlets, and books, as well as by the founding of
public associations. (b) The winning of all wise,
energetic, silent, well-disposed men who are sincerely
devoted to the idea; the covering of Europe, and
America too so far as possible, with a network of
self-sacrificing revolutionists, strong by unity."‖

---

* Ba. "*Articles*" p. 103.   † Ba. "*Statuts*" p. 132.   ‡ *Ib.* p. 132.
§ *Ib.* p. 125.   ‖ *Ib.* pp. 125-6.

CHAPTER VII

KROPOTKIN'S TEACHING

1. Prince Peter Alexeyevitch Kropotkin was born at Moscow in 1842. From 1862 to 1867 he was an officer of the Cossacks of the Amur; during this time he traveled over a great part of Siberia and Manchuria. From 1867 to 1871 he studied mathematics at St. Petersburg; at this time he was also secretary of the Geographical Society; under its commission he explored the glaciers of Finland and Sweden in 1871.

In 1872 Kropotkin visited Belgium and Switzerland, where he joined the *Association internationale des travailleurs*. In the same year he returned to St. Petersburg and became a prominent member of the Tchaikoffski secret society. This was found out in 1874. He was arrested and kept in prison until in 1876 he succeeded in escaping to England.

From England Kropotkin went to Switzerland in 1877, but was expelled from that country in 1881. Thenceforth he resided alternately in England and France. In France, in 1883, he was condemned to five years' imprisonment for membership in a prohibited association; he was kept in prison till 1886, and then pardoned. Since then he has lived in England.

Kropotkin has published geographical works and accounts of travel, and also writings in the spheres of economics, politics, and the philosophy of law.

2. For Kropotkin's teaching about law, the State, and property, the most important sources are his many short works, newspaper articles, and lectures. The articles that he published from 1879 to 1882 in " *Le Révolté*," of Geneva, appeared in 1885 as a book under the title " *Paroles d'un révolté.*" The only large work in which he develops his teaching is " *La conquête du pain* " (1892).

3. Kropotkin calls his teaching " Anarchism." " When in the bosom of the International there was formed a party which no more acknowledged an authority inside that association than any other authority, this party called itself at first federalist, then anti-authoritarian or hostile to the State. At that time it avoided describing itself as Anarchistic. The word *an-archie* (it was so written at that time) seemed to identify the party too much with the adherents of Proudhon, whose reform ideas the International was opposing. But for this very reason its opponents delighted in using this designation in order to produce confusion; besides, the name made the assertion possible that from the very name of the Anarchists it was evident that they aimed merely at disorder and chaos, without thinking any farther. The Anarchistic party was not slow to adopt the designation that was given to it. At first it still insisted on the hyphen between *an* and *archie*, with the explanation that in this form the word *an-archie*, being of Greek origin, denoted absence of dominion and not ' disorder '; but it soon decided to spare the proof-reader his useless trouble and the reader his lesson in Greek, and used the name as it

stood." * And in fact " the word *anarchie*, which negates the whole of this so-called order and reminds us of the fairest moments in the lives of the nations, is well chosen for a party that looks forward to conquering a better future." †

2.—BASIS

According to Kropotkin, the law which has supreme validity for man is the evolutionary law of the progress of mankind from a less happy existence to an existence as happy as possible; from this law he derives the commandment of justice and the commandment of energy.

1. The supreme law for man is the evolutionary law of the progress of mankind from a less happy existence to an existence as happy as possible.

There is " only one scientific method, the method of the natural sciences,"‡ and we apply this method also " in the sciences that relate to man,"§ particularly in the " science of society."‖ Now, a mighty revolution is at present taking place¶ in the entire realm of science; it is the result of the " philosophy of evolution."** " The idea hitherto prevalent, that everything in nature stands fast, is fallen, destroyed, annihilated. Everything in nature changes; nothing remains: neither the rock which appears to us to be immovable and the continent which we call *terra firma*, nor the inhabitants, their customs, habits, and thoughts. All that we see about us is a transitory phenomenon, and must change, because motionless-

* Kr. " *Paroles* " p. 99.   † *Ib.* p. 104.   ‡ Kr. " *Temps nouveaux* " p. 39
§ *Ib.* p. 39.   ‖ *Ib.* pp. 8, 39.   ¶ *Ib.* p. 5.
** Kr. " Anarchist Communism" p. 4.

ness would be death."* In the case of organisms this
evolution is progress, in consequence of " their admir-
able adaptivity to their conditions of life. They develop such faculties as render more complete both the
adaptations of the aggregates to their surroundings
and those of each of the constituent parts of the aggregate to the needs of free co-operation."† "This
is the ' struggle for existence,' which, therefore, must
not be conceived merely in its restricted sense of a
struggle between individuals for the means of
subsistence."‡

" Evolution never advances so slowly and evenly as
has been asserted. Evolution and revolution alter-
nate, and the revolutions—that is, the times of accel-
erated evolution—belong to the unity of nature just
as much as do the times in which evolution takes
place more slowly."§ " Order is the free equilibrium
of all forces that operate upon the same point; if any
of these forces are interfered with in their operation
by a human will, they operate none the less, but their
effects accumulate till some day they break the arti-
ficial dam and provoke a revolution."||

Kropotkin applies these general propositions to the
social life of men.¶ " A society is an aggregation of
organisms trying to combine the wants of the individual with those of co-operation for the welfare of
the species "; ** it is " a whole which serves toward
the purpose of attaining the largest possible amount
of happiness at the least possible expense of human

---

* Kr. " Studies " p. 9.   † Kr. " Anarchist Communism " pp. 8-9.
‡ Ib. p. 9.   § Kr. " Temps nouveaux " p. 13. || Ib. p. 12.
¶ Ib. p. 7.   ** Kr. " Anarchist Communism " p. 4.

force."* Now human societies evolve,† and one may try to determine the direction of this evolution.‡ Societies advance from lower to higher forms of organization; § but the goal of this evolution—that is, the point towards which it directs itself—consists in " establishing the best conditions for realizing the greatest happiness of humanity."‖ What we call progress is the right path to this goal;¶ humanity may for the time err from this path, but will always be brought back to it at last.**

But not even here does evolution take place without revolutions. What is true of a man's views, of the climate of a country, of the characteristics of a species, is true also of societies: " they evolve slowly, but there are also times of the quickest transformation."†† For circumstances of many kinds may oppose themselves to the effort of human associations to attain to the greatest possible measure of happiness.‡‡ " New thoughts germinate everywhere, try to get to the light, try to get themselves applied in life; but they are kept back by the inertia of those who have an interest in keeping up the old conditions, they are stifled under long-established prejudices and traditions."§§ " Political, economic, and social institutions fall in ruins, and the building which has become uninhabitable hinders the development of what is sprouting in its crevices and around it."‖‖ Then there is need of " great events which rudely break the thread of history and

* Kr. "Studies " p. 24.   † Kr. " Anarchist Communism " p. 7.
‡ Ib. p. 4.   § Ib. p. 7.   ‖ Ib. p. 4.
¶ Kr. " L'Anarchie dans l'évolution socialiste " p. 28.
** Kr. "Paroles " p. 17.   †† Kr. " Temps nouveaux " p. 59.
‡‡ Kr. " Anarchist Communism " p. 4.   §§ Kr. " Paroles " pp. 275-6.
‖‖ Ib. pp. 277-8.

hurl mankind out of its ruts into new roads "; * " the
Revolution becomes a peremptory necessity."†—
" Man has recognized his place in nature; he has
recognized that his institutions are his work and can
be refashioned by him alone."‡ "What has not the
engineer's art dared, and what do not literature, painting, music, the drama dare to-day?"§ Thus must we
also, where any institutions hinder the progress of society, " dare the fight, to make a rich and overflowing
life possible to all."‖

2. From the evolutionary law of the progress of
mankind from a less happy existence to the happiest
existence possible Kropotkin derives the commandment
of justice and the commandment of energy.

In the struggle for existence human societies evolve
toward a condition in which there are given the best
conditions for the attainment of the greatest happiness
of mankind.¶ When we describe anything as
" good," we mean by this that it favors the attainment
of the goal; that is, it is beneficial to the society in
which we live; and we call that " evil " which in our
opinion hinders the attainment of the goal, that is, is
harmful to the society we live in.**

Now, men's views as to what favors and what hinders the establishment of the best conditions for the
attainment of mankind's greatest happiness, and hence
as to what is beneficial or harmful to society, may
certainly change.†† But one fundamental requisite
for the attainment of the goal will always have to be
recognized as such, whatever the diversity of opinions.

* Kr. "Paroles" p. 17. † Ib. p. 275. ‡ Kr. "Studies" p. 9. § Ib. p. 10.
‖ Kr. "Morale" p. 74. ¶ Kr. "Anarchist Communism" p. 4.
** Kr. "Morale" pp. 24, 31. †† Ib. p. 30.

It "may be summed up in the sentence ' Do to others as you would have it done to you in the like case '."* But this sentence " is nothing else than the principle of equality "; † and equality, in turn, " means the same as equity,"‡ " solidarity,"§ "justice."‖ But there is indisputably yet another fundamental requisite for the attainment of the goal. This is " something greater, finer, and mightier than mere equality "; ¶ it may be expressed in the sentence " Be strong; overflow with the passion of thought and action: so shall your understanding, your love, your energy, pour itself into others."**

3.—LAW

I. *In mankind's progress from a less happy existence to an existence as happy as possible, one of the next steps, according to Kropotkin, will be the disappearance—not indeed of law, but—of enacted law.*

1. Enacted law has become a hindrance to mankind's progress toward an existence as happy as possible.

" For thousands of years those who govern have been repeating again and again, ' Respect the law!' "; †† " in the States of to-day a new law is re-

---

* Kr. " *Morale* " pp. 30-31.　　† *Ib.* p. 41.　　‡ *Ib.* p. 42.
§ *Ib.* p. 38 ; Kr. " *Conquête* " p. 296.　　‖ Kr. " *Paroles* " pp. 342, 129.
¶ Kr. " *Morale* " p. 57.　　** *Ib.* pp. 61-2.
* Kr. " *Paroles* " p. 215.　[In Eltzbacher's general discussions, and his summaries of the different writers' views on law, the word translated " law " is everywhere *Recht*, French *droit*, Latin *jus*, law as a body of rights and duties.　But in the quotations from Kropotkin under the heading " Law " the word is everywhere (with the single exception of the phrase " customary law ") *Gesetz*, French *loi*, Latin *lex*, a law as an enacted formula to describe men's actions ; and the same is the word translated " law " in Eltzbacher's summaries under the heading " Basis " in the different chapters.]

garded as the cure for all evils."* But "the law has no claim to men's respect."† "It is an adroit mixture of such customs as are beneficial to society, and would be observed even without a law, with others which are to the advantage only of a ruling minority, but are harmful to the masses and can be upheld only by terror."‡ "The law, which first made its appearance as a collection of customs which serve for the maintenance of society, is now merely an instrument to keep up the exploitation and domination of the industrious masses by wealthy idlers. It has now no longer any civilizing mission; its only mission is to protect exploitation."§ "It puts rigid immobility in the place of progressive development,"‖ "it seeks to confirm permanently the customs that are advantageous to the ruling minority."¶

"If one looks over the millions of laws which mankind obeys, one can distinguish three great classes: protection of property, protection of government, protection of persons. But in examining these three classes one comes in every case to the necessary conclusion that the law is valueless and harmful. What the protection of property is worth, the Socialists know only too well. The laws about property do not exist to secure to individuals or to society the product of their labor. On the contrary, they exist to rob the producer of a part of his product, and to protect a few in the enjoyment of what they have stolen from the producer or from the whole of society."** And as regards the laws for the protection of government, "we

---

* Kr. "*Paroles*" p. 214.   † *Ib.* p. 227.   ‡ *Ib.* p. 227.   § *Ib.* p. 235.
‖ *Ib.* p. 219.   ¶ *Ib.* p. 226.   ** *Ib.* p. 236.

know well that all governments, without exception, have it for their mission to uphold by force the privileges of the propertied classes—the nobility, the clergy, and the *bourgeoisie.* A man has only to examine all these laws, only to observe their every-day working, and he will be convinced that not one is worth keeping."* Equally " superfluous and harmful, finally, are the laws for the protection of persons, for the punishment and prevention of ' crimes '. The fear of punishment never yet restrained a murderer. He who would kill his neighbor, for revenge or for necessity, does not beat his brains about the consequences; and every murderer hitherto has had the firm conviction that he would escape prosecution. If murder were declared not punishable, the number of murders would not increase even by one; rather it would decrease to the extent that murders are at present committed by habitual criminals who have been corrupted in prison."†

2. The stage of evolution to which enacted law belongs will soon be left behind by man.

"The law is a comparatively young formation. Mankind lived for ages without any written law. At that time the relations of men to each other were regulated by mere habits, by customs and usages, which age made venerable, and which every one learned from his childhood in the same way as he learned hunting, cattle-raising, or agriculture."‡ " But when society came to be more and more split into two hostile classes, of which the one wanted to rule and the other to escape from rule, the victor of the moment

---

* Kr. " *Paroles* " p. 239.　† *Ib.* pp. 240-42.　‡ *Ib.* p. 221.

sought to give permanence to the accomplished fact and to hallow it by all that was venerable to the defeated. Consecrated by the priest and protected by the strong hand of the warrior, law appeared."* But its days are already numbered. " Everywhere we find insurgents who will no longer obey the law till they know where it comes from, what it is good for, by what right it demands obedience, and for what reason it is held in honor. They bring under their criticism everything that has until now been respected as the foundation of society, but first and foremost the fetish, law."† The moment of its disappearance, for the hastening of which we must fight,‡ is close at hand,§ perhaps even at the end of the nineteenth century.‖

II. *In the next stage of evolution, which, as has been shown, mankind must soon reach, there will indeed be no enacted law, but there will be law even there.* "The laws will be totally abrogated;"¶ " unwritten customs,"** " ' customary law,' as jurists say,"†† will " suffice to maintain a good understanding."‡‡ These norms of the next stage of evolution will be based on a general will; §§ and conformity to them will be adequately assured " by the necessity, which every one feels, of finding co-operation, support, and sympathy "‖‖ and by the fear of expulsion from the fellowship,¶¶ but also, if necessary, by the inter-

---

* Kr. "*Paroles*" p. 226.   † *Ib.* pp. 218-19.   ‡ Kr. "*Morale*" p. 74.
§ Kr. "*Paroles*" pp. 264-5.
‖ *Ib.* p. 235 ; Kr. "*L'Anarchie dans l'évolution socialiste*" pp. 28-9.
¶ Kr. "*Paroles*" pp. 227, 235.   ** Kr. "Anarchist Communism " p. 29.
†† Kr. "*Paroles*" p. 221.   ‡‡ *Ib.* p. 221.
§§ Kr. "*Conquête*" pp. 229, 109.   ‖‖ Kr. "Anarchist Communism " p. 24.
¶¶ Kr. "*Conquête*" p. 202.

vention of the individual citizen* or of the masses; †
they will therefore be legal norms.

Of legal norms of the next stage of evolution Kropotkin mentions in the first place this,—that contracts
must be lived up to.‡

Furthermore, according to Kropotkin there will obtain in the next stage of evolution a legal norm by
virtue of which not only the means of production, but
all things, are common property.§

An additional legal norm in the next stage of evolution will, according to Kropotkin, be that by virtue
of which " every one who co-operates in production to
a certain extent has, for one thing, the right to live;
for another, the right to live comfortably."‖

4.—THE STATE

I. *According to Kropotkin, in mankind's progress
from a less happy existence to an existence as happy
as possible the State will shortly disappear.*

1. The State has become a hindrance to mankind's
evolution toward a happiness as great as possible.

" What does this monstrous engine serve for, that
we call 'State'? For preventing the exploitation of
the laborer by the capitalist, of the peasant by the
landlord? or for assuring us of work? for providing us
food when the mother has nothing but water left for
her child? No, a thousand times no."¶ But instead
of this the State " meddles in all our affairs, pinions us

---

* Kr. "Studies " p. 30.
† Kr. " *Paroles* " pp. 110, 134-5, " *Conquête* " p. 109.
‡ Kr. " *Conquête* " pp. 169, 128-9, 203-5.
§ Kr. " *Paroles* " pp. 136-7. ‖ Kr. " *Conquête* " p. 229.
* Kr. " *Paroles* " p. 14.

from cradle to grave. It prescribes all our actions, it
piles up mountains of laws and ordinances that be-
wilder the shrewdest lawyer. It creates an army of
office-holders who sit like spiders in their webs and
have never seen the world except through the dingy
panes of their office-window. The immense and ever-
increasing sums that the State collects from the
people are never sufficient: it lives at the expense of
future generations, and steers with all its might
toward bankruptcy. 'State' is tantamount to 'war';
one State seeks to weaken and ruin another in order to
force upon the latter its law, its policy, its commercial
treaties, and to enrich itself at its expense; war is to-
day the usual condition in Europe, there is a thirty
years' supply of causes of war on hand. And civil
war rages at the same time with foreign war; the
State, which was originally to be a protection for all
and especially for the weak, has to-day become a
weapon of the rich against the exploited; of the
propertied against the propertyless."*

In these respects there is no distinction to be made
between the different forms of the State. "Toward
the end of the last century the French people over-
threw the monarchy, and the last absolute king expi-
ated on the scaffold his own crimes and those of his
predecessors."† "Later all the countries of the Continent went through the same evolution: they over-
threw their absolute monarchies and flung themselves
into the arms of parliamentarism."‡ "Now it is
being perceived that parliamentarism, which was entered upon with such great hopes, has everywhere be-

---

* Kr. "*Paroles*" pp. 11-14.   † *Ib.* p. 172.   ‡ *Ib.* p. 173.

come a tool for intrigue and personal enrichment, for efforts hostile to the people and to evolution."*
" Precisely like any despot, the body of representatives of the people—be it called Parliament, Convention, or anything else; be it appointed by the prefects of a Bonaparte or elected with all conceivable freedom by an insurgent city—will always try to enlarge its competence, to strengthen its power by all sorts of meddling, and to displace the activity of the individual and the group by the law."† " It was only a forty years' movement, which occasionally even set fire to grain-fields, that could bring the English Parliament to secure to the tenant the value of the improvements made by him. But if it is a question of protecting the capitalist's interest, threatened by a disturbance or even by agitation,—ah, then every representative of the people is on hand, then it acts with more recklessness and cowardice than any despot. The six-hundred-headed beast without a name has outdone Louis IX and Ivan IV."‡ " Parliamentarism is nauseating to any one who has seen it near at hand."§
" The dominion of men, which calls itself 'government,' is incompatible with a morality founded on solidarity."‖ This is best shown by " the so-called civil rights, whose value and importance the *bourgeois* press is daily praising to us in every key."¶ " Are they made for those who alone need them? Certainly not. Universal suffrage may under some circumstances afford to the *bourgeoisie* a certain protection against encroachments by the central authority, it

---

* Kr. " *Paroles* " p. 175.   † *Ib.* pp. 181-2.   ‡ *Ib.* pp. 183-4.
§ *Ib.* p. 190.   ‖ *Ib.* p. 19.   ¶ *Ib.* p. 33.

may establish a balance between two authorities without its being necessary for the rivals to draw the
knife on each other as formerly; but it is valueless
when the object is to overthrow authority or even to
set bounds to it. For the rulers it is an excellent
means of deciding their disputes; but of what use is
it to the ruled? Just so with the freedom of the
press. To the mind of the *bourgeoisie*, what is the
best thing that has been alleged in its favor? Its
impotence. ' Look at England, Switzerland, the
United States,' they say. ' There the press is free and
yet the dominion of capital is more assured than in
any other country.' Just so they think about the
right of association. ' Why should we not grant full
right of association? ' says the *bourgeoisie*. ' It will
not impair our privileges. What we have to fear is
secret societies; public unions are the best means to
cripple them.' ' The inviolability of the home?
Yes, this we must proclaim aloud, this we must
inscribe in the statute-books,' say the sly *bourgeois*,
' the police certainly must not be looking into our pots
and kettles. If things go wrong some day, we will
snap our fingers at a man's right to his own house,
rummage everything, and, if necessary, arrest people
in their beds.' ' The secrecy of letters? Yes, just
proclaim its inviolability aloud everywhere, our little
privacies certainly must not come to the light. If
we scent a plot against our privileges, we shall not
stand much on ceremony. And if anybody objects,
we shall say what an English minister lately said
among the applause of Parliament: "Yes, gentlemen,
it is with a heavy heart and with the deepest reluc-

tance that we are having letters opened, but the country (that is, the aristocracy and *bourgeoisie*) is in danger!"' That is what political rights are. Freedom of the press and freedom of association, the inviolability of the home, and all the rest, are respected only so long as the people make no use of them against the privileged classes. But on the day when the people begin to use them for the undermining of privileges all these ' rights ' are thrown overboard."*

2. The stage of evolution to which the State belongs will soon be left behind by man. The State is doomed.†

It is " of a relatively modern origin."‡ " The State is a historic formation which, in the life of all nations, has at a certain time gradually taken the place of free associations. Church, law, military power, and wealth acquired by plunder, have for centuries made common cause, have in slow labor piled stone on stone, encroachment on encroachment, and thus created the monstrous institution which has finally fixed itself in every corner of social life—nay, in the brains and hearts of men—and which we call the State."§

It has now begun to decompose. " The peoples— especially those of the Latin races—are bent on destroying its authority, which merely hampers their free development; they want the independence of provinces, communes, and groups of laborers; they

---

* Kr. " *Paroles* " pp. 35-9.
† Kr. " *L'Anarchie dans l'évolution socialiste* " p. 30.
‡ Kr. " Anarchist Communism " p. 7.
§ Kr. " *Temps nouveaux* " pp. 49-50.

want not to submit to any dominion, but to league themselves together freely."* "The dissolution of the States is advancing at frightful speed. They have become decrepit graybeards, with wrinkled skins and tottering feet, gnawed by internal diseases and without understanding for the new thoughts; they are squandering the little strength that they still had left, living at the expense of their numbered years, and hastening their end by falling foul of each other like old women."† The moment of the State's disappearance is therefore close at hand.‡ Kropotkin says now that it will come in a few years,§ now that it will come at the end of the nineteenth century.||

II. *In the next stage of evolution, which, as has been shown, mankind must soon reach, the place of the State will be taken by a social human life on the basis of the legal norm that contracts must be lived up to.* Anarchism is the "inevitable"¶ "next phase,"** "higher form,"†† of society.

1. Even after the State is done away men will live together socially; but they will no longer be held together in society by a governmental authority, but by the legally binding force of contract. "Free expansion of individuals into groups and of groups into associations, free organization from the simple to the complex as need and inclination are felt,"‡‡ will be the future form of society.

We can at present perceive a growing Anarchistic

---

* Kr. "*Paroles*" p. 10.   † *Ib.* pp. 9-10.
‡ *Ib.* pp. 264-5.   § *Ib.* p. 139.
|| *Ib.* p. 235 ; Kr. "*L'Anarchie dans l'évolution socialiste*" pp. 28-9,
¶ Kr. "*L'Anarchie dans l'évolution socialiste*" p. 30.
** Kr. "Anarchist Communism" p. 4.   †† *Ib.* p. 7.
‡‡ Kr. "*L'Anarchic dans l'évolution socialiste*" p. 26.

movement; that is, "a movement towards limiting
more and more the sphere of action of government.
After having tried all kinds of government, humanity
is trying now to free itself from the bonds of any government whatever, and to respond to its needs of organization by the free understanding between individuals prosecuting the same common aims."* "Free
associations are beginning to take to themselves the
entire field of human activity."† "The large organizations resulting merely and simply from free agreement have grown recently. The railway net of
Europe—a confederation of so many scores of separate
societies—is an instance; the Dutch *Beurden*, or
associations of ship and boat owners, are extending
now their organizations over the rivers of Germany,
and even to the shipping trade of the Baltic; the
numberless amalgamated manufacturers' associations,
and the *syndicats* of France, are so many instances in
point. But there also is no lack of free organizations
for nobler pursuits: the Lifeboat Association, the
Hospitals Association, and hundreds of like organizations. One of the most remarkable societies which
has‡ recently arisen is the Red Cross Society. To
slaughter men on the battle-fields, that remains the
duty of the State; but these very States recognize
their inability to take care of their own wounded;
they abandon the task, to a great extent, to private
initiative."§ "These endeavors will attain to free
play, will find a new and vast field for their applica-

---

*Kr. "Anarchist Communism" p. 23.
† Kr. "*Paroles*" pp. 117-18.   ‡ [*Sic*, edition of 1891].
§ Kr. "Anarchist Communism" pp. 25-7.

tion, and will form the foundation of the future society."*

"The agreement between the hundreds of companies to which the European railroads belong has been entered into directly, without the meddling of any central authority that prescribed laws to the several companies. It has been kept up by conventions at which delegates met to consult together and then to lay before their principals plans, not laws. This is a new procedure, utterly different from any government whether monarchical or republican, absolute or constitutional. It is an innovation which at first makes its way into European manners only by hesitating steps, but to which the future belongs."†

2. "To rack our brains to-day about the details of the form which public life shall take in the future society, would be silly. Yet we must come to an agreement now about the main outlines."‡ "We must not forget that perhaps in a year or two we shall be called on to decide all questions of the organization of society."§

Communes will continue to exist; but "these communes are not agglomerations of men in a territory, and know neither walls nor boundaries; the commune is a clustering of like-minded persons, not a closed integer. The various groups in one commune will feel themselves drawn to similar groups in other communes; they will unite themselves with these as firmly as with their fellow-citizens; and thus there will come about communities of interest whose members are

---

* Kr. "Paroles" p. 118.   † Kr. "Conquête" p. 174.
‡ Kr. "Studies" p. 25.   § Ib. p. 26.

scattered over a thousand cities and villages."*
Men will join themselves together by "contracts "†
to form such communes. They will "take upon
themselves duties to society,"‡ which on its part en-
gages to do certain things for them.§ It will not be
necessary to compel the fulfilment of these contracts,‖
there will be no need of penalties and judges.¶ Fulfilment will be sufficiently assured by "the necessity,
which every one feels, of finding co-operation, support,
and sympathy among his neighbors;"** he who does
not live up to his obligations can of course be expelled
from fellowship.††

In the commune every one will "do what is necessary himself, without waiting for a government's
orders."‡‡ "The commune will not first destroy the
State and then set it up again."§§ "People will see
that they are freest and happiest when they have no
plenipotentiary agents and depend as little on the
wisdom of representatives as on that of Providence."‖‖
Nor will there be prisons or other penal institutions;¶¶ "for the few anti-social acts that may still
take place the best remedy will consist in loving
treatment, moral influence, and liberty."***

The communes on their part will join themselves
together by contracts††† quite in the same way as do
the members of the individual communes. "The

* Kr. "Paroles" p. 117.   † Kr. "Conquête" pp. 169, 203.
‡ Ib. pp. 145, 136, 128-9.   § Ib. pp. 203-5.
‖ Kr. "Anarchist Communism" pp. 29-30, "Conquête" p. 188
¶ Kr. "Prisons" p. 49.
** Kr. "Anarchist Communism" p. 24. [Kropotkin prefixes "his own
social habits and."]
†† Kr. "Conquête" p. 202.   ‡‡ Kr. "Paroles" p. 139.
§§ Ib. p. 111.   ‖‖ Ib. p. 175.   ¶¶ Kr. "Prisons" p. 49.
*** Ib. pp. 58-9.   ††† Kr. "Conquête" pp. 44-5.

commune will recognize nothing above it except the interests of the league that it has of its own accord made with other communes."* " Owing to the multiplicity of our needs, a single league will soon not be enough; the commune will feel the necessity of entering into other connections also, joining this or that other league. For the purpose of obtaining food it is already a member of one group; now it must join a second in order to obtain other objects that it needs,— metal, for instance,—and then a third and fourth too, that will supply it with cloth and works of art. If one takes up an economic atlas of any country, one sees that there are no economic boundaries: the areas of production and exchange for the different objects are blended, interlaced, superimposed. Thus the combinations of the communes also, if they followed their natural development, would soon intertwine in the same way and form an infinitely denser network and a far more consummate ' unity ' than the States, whose individual parts, after all, only lie side by side like the rods around the lictor's axe."†

3. The future society will be able easily to accomplish the tasks that the State accomplishes at present.

" Suppose there is need of a street. Well, then let the inhabitants of the neighboring communes come to an understanding about it, and they will do their business better than the Minister of Public Works would do it. Or a railroad is needed. Here too the communes that are concerned will produce something very different from the work of the promoters who only build bad pieces of track and make millions by it.

---

*Kr. " *Paroles* " p. 108.   † *Ib.* pp. 115-16.

Or schools are required. People can fit them up for themselves at least as well as the gentlemen at Paris. Or the enemy invades the country. Then we defend ourselves instead of relying on generals who would merely betray us. Or the farmer must have tools and machines. Then he comes to an understanding with the city workingmen, these supply him with them at cost in return for his products, and the middleman, who now robs both the farmer and the workingman, is superfluous."* " Or there comes up a little dispute, or a stronger man tries to push down a weaker. In the first case the people will know enough to create a court of arbitration, and in the second every citizen will regard it as his duty to interfere himself and not wait for the police; there will be as little need of constables as of judges and turnkeys."†

5.—PROPERTY

I. *According to Kropotkin, the progress of mankind from a less happy existence to an existence as happy as possible will shortly bring us to the disappearance not indeed of property, but of its present form, private property.*

1. Private property has become a hindrance to the evolution of mankind toward a happiness as great as possible.

What are the effects of private property to-day? "The crisis, which was formerly acute, has become chronic; the crisis in the cotton trade, the crisis in the production of metals, the crisis in watchmaking, all the crises, rage concurrently now and do not come

---

* Kr. " *Paroles* " p. 166. † Kr. " Studies " p. 30.

to an end. The unemployed in Europe to-day are
estimated at several million; those who beg their way
from city to city, or gather in mobs to demand ' work
or bread ' with threats, are estimated at tens of thousands. Great branches of industry are destroyed;
great cities, like Sheffield, forsaken. Everything is at
a standstill, want and misery prevail everywhere: the
children are pale, the wife has grown five years older
in one winter, disease and death are rife among the
workingmen—and people talk of over-production! "*
One might reply that in peasant ownership of land, at
least, private property has good effects.†   " But the
golden age is over for the small farmer. To-day he
hardly knows how to make both ends meet. He gets
into debt, becomes a victim of the cattle-dealer, the
real-estate jobber, the usurer; notes and mortgages
ruin whole villages, even more than the frightful taxes
imposed by State and commune. Small proprietor-
ship is in a desperate condition; and even if the small
farmer is still owner in name, he is in fact nothing
more than a tenant paying rent to money-dealers and
usurers."‡

But private property has still more sweeping indirect effects.   " So long as we have a caste of idlers
who have us feed them under the pretext that they
must lead us, so long these idlers will always be a
focus of pestilence to general morality. He who lives
his life in dull laziness, who is always bent merely on
getting new pleasures, who by the very basis of his
existence can know no solidarity, and who by his
course of life cultivates the vilest self-seeking,—he will

---

* Kr. " *Paroles* " pp. 5-6.   † *Ib.* pp. 322-3.   ‡ *Ib.* p. 326.

always pursue the coarsest sensual pleasures and debase everything around him. With his bag full of dollars and his bestial impulses he will go and dishonor women and children, degrade art, the drama, the press, sell his country and its defenders, and, because he is too cowardly to murder with his own hands, will have his proxies murder the choicest of his nation when, some day, he is afraid for his darling money-bag."* " Year by year thousands of children grow up in the physical and moral filth of our great cities, among a population corrupted by the struggle for daily bread, and at the same time they daily see the immorality, idleness, prodigality, and ostentation of which these same cities are full."† " Thus society is incessantly bringing forth beings who are incapable of an honorable and industrious life, and who are full of anti-social feelings. It does homage to them when success crowns their crimes, and sends them to the penitentiary when they are unlucky."‡°

Private property offends against justice. " The labor of all has produced the entire accumulated mass of wealth, that of the present generation as well as that of all that went before. The house in which we happen to be together has value only by its being in Paris, this glorious city in which the labor of twenty generations is piled layer upon layer. If it were removed to the snow-fields of Siberia, it would be worth substantially nothing. This machine, invented and patented by you, has in it the labor of five or six generations; it has a value only as a part of the vast whole that we call nineteenth-century industry. Take

---

*Kr. " *Paroles* " p. 24.   † Kr. " *Prisons* " p. 47.   ‡ *Ib.* p. 49.

your lace-making machine to the Papuans in New Guinea, and it is valueless."* "Science and industry; theory and practice; the invention and the putting the invention in operation, which leads to new inventions again; head work and hand work,—all is connected. Every discovery, every progress, every increase in our wealth, has its origin in the total bodily and mental activity of the past and present. Then by what right can any one appropriate to himself the smallest fraction of this vast total and say 'this belongs to me and not to you'?"†—But this unjust appropriation of what belongs to all has nevertheless taken place. "Among the changes of time a few have taken possession of all that is made possible to man by the production of goods and the increase of his productive power. To-day the land, though it owes its value to the needs of a ceaselessly increasing population, belongs to a minority which can hinder the people from cultivating it, and which does so—or at least does not permit the people to cultivate it in a manner accordant with modern needs. The mines, which represent the toil of centuries, and whose value is based solely on the needs of industry and the necessities of population, belong likewise to a few, and these few limit the mining of coal, or entirely forbid it when they find a better investment for their money. The machines, too, are the property of a handful of men; and, even if a machine has indubitably been brought to its present perfection by three generations of workers, it nevertheless belongs to a few givers of work.

---

* Kr. " *L'Anarchie dans l'évolution socialiste* " p. 10.
† Kr. " *Conquête* " pp. 8-9.

The roads, which would be scrap-iron but for Europe's dense population, industry, trade, and travel, are in the possession of a few shareholders who perhaps do not even know the location of the lines from which they draw princely incomes."[*]

2. Mankind will soon have passed the stage of evolution to which private property belongs. Private property is doomed.[†]

Private property is a historic formation: it "has developed parasitically amidst the free institutions of our earliest ancestors,"[‡] and this in the closest connection with the State. "The political constitution of a society is always the expression, and at the same time the consecration, of its economic constitution."[§]

"The origin of the State, and its reason for existence, lie in the fact that it interferes in favor of the propertied and to the disadvantage of the propertyless."[∥]

"The omnipotence of the State constitutes the foundation of the strength of the *bourgeoisie*."[¶]

But private property is already on the way to dissolution. "The economic chaos can last no longer. The people are tired of the crises which the greed of the ruling classes provokes. They want to work and live, not first drudge a few years for scanty wages and then become for many years victims of want and objects of charity. The workingman sees the incapacity of the ruling classes: he sees how unable they are either to understand his efforts or to manage the pro-

---

[*] Kr. " *Conquête* " pp. 9-10.
[†] Kr. " *L'Anarchie dans l'évolution socialiste* " p. 30.
[‡] Kr. " Anarchist Communism " p. 11.
[§] Kr. " *Paroles* " p. 169.   [∥] Kr. " *Temps nouveaux* " p. 45.
[¶] Kr. " Studies " p. 17.

duction and exchange of goods."* Hence "one of
the leading features of our century is the growth of
Socialism and the rapid spreading of Socialist views
among the working classes."† The moment when
private property is to disappear is near, therefore: be
it in a few years,‡ be it at the end of the nineteenth
century,§ in any case it will come soon.‖

II. *In mankind's next stage of evolution, which, as
has been shown, must soon be attained, property will
take such form that only property of society shall
exist.* The "next phase of evolution,"¶ "higher form
of social organization,"** will "inevitably"†† be not
only Anarchism, but "Anarchistic Communism."‡‡
"The tendencies towards economical and political
freedom are two different manifestations of the very
same need of equality which constitutes the very
essence of all struggles mentioned by history";§§
"these two powerful currents of thought characterize
our century."‖‖

In this way a comfortable life will be guaranteed to
every person who co-operates in production to a
certain extent.

1. Mankind's next stage of evolution will no longer
know any but the property of society.

"In our century the Communist tendency is continually reasserting itself. The penny bridge disappears
before the public bridge; and the turnpike road be-

---

* Kr. "*Paroles*" pp. 7-8.   † Kr. "Anarchist Communism" p. 4.
‡ Kr. "*Paroles*" p. 139, "*L'Anarchie—sa philosophie, son idéal*" p. 25.
§ Kr. "*Paroles*" p. 235, "*L'Anarchie dans l'évolution socialiste*"
pp. 28-9.   ‖ Kr. "*Paroles*" pp. 264-5.
¶ Kr. "Anarchist Communism" p. 4.   ** *Ib.* p. 7.
†† Kr. "*L'Anarchie dans l'évolution socialiste*" p. 30.
‡‡ Kr. "*Paroles*" p. 88, "*L'Anarchie dans l'évolution socialiste*" p. 30.
§§ Kr. "Anarchist Communism" p. 8.   ‖‖ *Ib.* p. 8.

fore the free road. The same spirit pervades thousands of other institutions. Museums, free libraries, and free public schools; parks and pleasure grounds; paved and lighted streets, free for everybody's use; water supplied to private dwellings, with a growing tendency towards disregarding the exact amount of it used by the individual; tramways and railways which have already begun to introduce the season ticket or the uniform tax, and will surely go much further on this line when they are no longer private property: all these are tokens showing in what direction further progress is to be expected."[*]

So will the future society be Communistic. "The first act of the nineteenth-century commune will consist in laying hands on the entire capital accumulated in its bosom."[†] This applies "to the materials for consumption as well as to those for production."[‡] "People have tried to make a distinction between the capital that serves for the production of goods and that which satisfies the wants of life, and have said that machines, factories, raw materials, the means of transportation, and the land are destined to become the property of the community; while dwellings, finished products, clothing, and provisions will remain private property. This distinction is erroneous and impracticable. The house that shelters us, the coal and gas that we burn, the nutriment that our body burns up, the clothing that covers us, and the book from which we draw instruction, are all essential to our existence and are just as necessary for successful

---

[*] Kr. "Anarchist Communism" p. 21.
[†] Kr. "*Paroles*" p. 110.   [‡] *Ib.* p. 137.

production and for the further development of mankind as are machines, factories, raw materials, and other factors of production.   With private property in the former goods, there would still remain inequality, oppression, and exploitation; a half-way abolition of private property would have its effectiveness crippled in advance."*

There is no fear that the Communistic communes will isolate themselves.†   " If to-day a great city transforms itself into a Communistic commune, and introduces community of the materials for both work and enjoyment, then in a very few days, if it is not shut in by hostile armies, trains of wagons will appear in its markets, and raw materials will arrive from distant ports; and the city's industrial products, when once the wants of the population are satisfied, will go to the ends of the earth seeking purchasers; throngs of strangers will stream in from near and far, and will afterward tell at home of the marvelous life of the free city where everybody works, where there are neither poor nor oppressed, where every one enjoys the fruit of his toil, and no one interferes with another's doing so."‡

2. The Communism of the future society will " not be the Communism of the convent or the barrack, such as was formerly preached, but a free Communism which puts the joint products at the disposal of all while leaving to every one the liberty of using them at home."§   To get an entirely clear idea of every detail of it, indeed, is not as yet possible; " nevertheless we

---

* Kr. " *Paroles* " p. 136.   † *Ib.* p. 114,   ‡ *Ib.* pp. 113-14.
§ Kr. " *L'Anarchie dans l'évolution socialiste* " p. 12.

must come to an agreement about the fundamental features at least."*

What form will production take?

That must first be produced which is requisite " for the satisfaction of man's most urgent wants."† For this it suffices " that all adults, with the exception of those women who are occupied with the education of children, engage to do five hours a day, from the age of twenty or twenty-two to the age or forty-five or fifty, of any one (at their option) of the labors that are regarded as necessary."‡ " For instance, a society would enter into the following contract with each of its members: 'We will guarantee to you the enjoyment of our houses, stores of goods, streets, conveyances, schools, museums, etc., on condition that from your twentieth year to your forty-fifth or fiftieth you apply five hours every day to one of the labors necessary to life. Every moment you will have your choice of the groups you will join, or you may found a new one provided that it proposes to do necessary service. For the rest of your time you may associate yourself with whom you like for the purpose of scientific or artistic recreation at your pleasure. We ask of you, therefore, nothing but twelve or fifteen hundred hours' work annually in one of the groups which produce food, clothing, and shelter, or which care for health, transportation, etc.; and in return we insure to you all that these groups produce or have produced'."§

There will be time enough, therefore, to produce what is requisite for the satisfaction of less urgent

---

* Kr. " Studies " p. 25.   † Kr. " Conquête " p. 239.
‡ Ib. pp. 128-9.   § Ib. pp. 203-4.

wants. " When one has done in the field or the
factory the work that he is under obligation to do
for society, he can devote the other half of his day, his
week, or his year, to the satisfaction of artistic or
scientific wants."* " The lover of music who wishes a
piano will enter the association of instrument-makers;
he will devote part of his half-days, and will soon
possess the longed-for piano. Or the enthusiast in
astronomy will join the astronomers' association with
its philosophers, observers, calculators, and opticians,
its scholars and amateurs; and he will obtain the
telescope he wishes, if only he dedicates some work to
the common cause—for there is a deal of rough work
necessary for an observatory, masons' work, car-
penters' work, founders' work, machinists' work—the
final polish, to be sure, can be given to the instrument of precision by none but the artist. In a word,
the five to seven hours that every one has left, after he
has first devoted some hours to the production of the
necessary, are quite sufficient to render possible for
him every kind of luxury."†

" The separation of agriculture from manufactures
will pass away. The factory workmen will be at the
same time field workmen."‡ " As an eminently peri-
odic industry, which at certain times (and even more
in the making of improvements than in harvest) needs
a large additional force, agriculture will form the link .
between village and city."§ And " the separation of
mental from bodily labor will come to an end "‖ too.
" Poets and scientists will no longer find poor devils

---

* Kr. " *Conquête* " p. 136.   † *Ib*. pp. 150-51.   ‡ *Ib*. p. 96.
§ Kr. " *Paroles* " pp. 330-1.   ‖ Kr. " *Conquête* " pp. 195-6.

who will sell their energies to them for a plate of soup; they will have to get together and print their writings themselves. Then the authors, and their admirers of both sexes, will soon acquire the art of handling the type-case and composing-stick; they will learn the pleasure of producing jointly, with their own hands, a work that they value."* "Every labor will be agreeable."† "If there is still work which is really disagreeable in itself, it is only because our scientific men have never cared to consider the means of rendering it less so: they have always known that there were plenty of starving men who would do it for a few pence a day."‡ "Factories, smelters, mines, can be as sanitary and as splendid as the best laboratories of our universities; and the more perfectly they are fitted up the more they will produce."§ And the product of such labor will be "infinitely better, and considerably greater, than the mass of goods hitherto produced under the goad of slavery, serfdom, and wage-slavery."||

How will distribution take place?

Every one who contributes his part to production will also have his share in the product. But it must not be assumed that this share in the product will correspond to that share in the production. "Each according to his powers; to each according to his wants."¶ "Need will be put above service; it will be recognized that every one who co-operates in production to a certain extent has in the first place the

---

* Kr. " *Conquête* " p. 137.   † *Ib.* p. 153.
‡ Kr. " Anarchist Communism " p. 31.
§ Kr. " *Conquête* " p. 156'₁, || *Ib.* p. 193.
¶ Kr. " *L'Anarchie dans 'évolution socialiste* " p. 12.

right to live, and in the second place the right to live comfortably."* "Every one, no matter how strong or weak, how competent or incompetent he may be, will have the right to live,"† and "to have a comfortable life; he will furthermore have the right to decide for himself what belongs to a comfortable life."‡ Society's stock of goods will quite permit this. "If one considers on the one hand the rapidity with which the productive power of civilized nations is increasing, and on the other hand the limits that are directly or indirectly set to its production by present conditions, one comes to the conclusion that even a moderately sensible economic constitution would permit the civilized nations to heap up in a few years so many useful things that we should have to cry out 'Enough! enough coal! enough bread! enough clothes! Let us rest, take recreation, put our strength to a better use, spend our time in a better way!'"§

However, what if the stock should in fact not suffice for all wants? "The solution is—free taking of everything that exists in superfluity, and rations of that in which there is a possibility of dearth: rations according to needs, with preference to children, the aged, and the weak in general. That is what is done even now in the country. What commune thinks of limiting the use of the meadows so long as there are enough of them? what commune, so long as there are chestnuts and brushwood enough, hinders those who belong to it from taking as much as they please?

---

* Kr. " Conquête " p. 229.　† Ib. p. 26.
‡ Ib. p. 28,　§ Ib. p. 20.

And what does the peasant introduce when there is a prospect that firewood will give out?   Rationing."*

6.—REALIZATION

The change that is promptly to be expected in the course of mankind's progress from a less happy existence to an existence as happy as possible,—the disappearance of the State, the transformation of law and property, and the appearance of the new condition,—will be accomplished, according to Kropotkin, by a social revolution; that is, by a violent subversion of the old order, which will come to pass of itself, but for which it is the function of those who foresee the course of evolution to prepare men's minds.

I. We know that we shall not reach the future condition " without intense perturbations."†   " That justice may be victorious, and the new thoughts become reality, there is need of a frightful storm to sweep away all this rottenness, to vivify torpid souls with its breath, and to restore self-sacrifice, self-denial, and heroism to our senile, decrepit, crumbling society."‡   There is need of "social revolution: that is, the people's taking possession of society's total stock of goods, and the abolition of all authorities."§ " The social revolution is at the door," ‖ " it stands before us at the end of this century,"¶ " it will be here in a few years."**   It is " the task which history sets for us,"†† but " whether we will or not, it will be

---

* Kr. " *L'Anarchie dans l'évolution socialiste* " p. 13.   † *Ib.* p. 28.
‡ Kr. " *Paroles* " p. 280.   § *Ib.* p. 261.   ‖ Kr. "*Conquête* " p. 22.
¶ Kr. " *L'Auarchie dans l'évolution socialiste* " p. 28.   [The nineteenth century, of course, is meant.]
** Kr. " *Paroles* " p. 139.   †† Kr. " *Siècle* " p. 32.

accomplished independently of our will."*

1. " The social revolution will be no uprising of a few days: we shall have to go through a period of three, four, or five years of revolution, till the transformation of the social and economic situation is completed."† " During this time what we have sown today will be coming up and bearing fruit; and he who now is yet indifferent will become a convinced adherent of the new doctrine."‡ Nor will the social revolution be limited to a narrow area. " We must not assume, to be sure, that it will break out in all Europe at once."§ " Germany is nearer the revolution than people think "; ‖ " but whether it start from France, Germany, Spain, or Russia, it will anyhow be a European revolution in the end. It will spread as rapidly as that of our predecessors the heroes of 1848, and set Europe afire."¶

2. The first act of the social revolution will be a work of destruction.** "The impulse to destruction, which is so natural and justifiable because it is at the same time an impulse to renovation, will find its full satisfaction. How much old trash there is to clear away! Does not everything have to be transformed, the houses, the cities, the businesses of manufacturing and farming,—in short, all the arrangements of society? "†† " Everything that it is necessary to abolish should be destroyed without delay: the penitentiaries and prisons, the forts that threaten cities,

---

* Kr. " *L'Anarchie dans l'évolution socialiste* " p. 29.
† Kr. " *Paroles* " p. 90, " Studies " p. 23. ‡ Kr. " *Paroles* " pp. 90-91.
§ Kr. " *Conquête* " p. 85.
‖ Kr. " *L'Anarchie. Sa philosophie—son idéal* " p. 26.
¶ Kr. " *L'Anarchie dans l'évolution socialiste* " pp. 28-9.
** Kr. " *Paroles* " p. 263. †† *Ib.* p. 342.

the slums whose disease-laden air people have breathed so long."*

Yet the social revolution will not be a reign of terror. "Naturally the fight will demand victims. One can understand how it was that the people of Paris, before they hurried to the frontiers, killed the aristocrats in the prisons, who had planned with the enemy for the annihilation of the revolution. He who would blame the people for this should be asked, 'Have you suffered with them and like them? if not, blush and be still.'"† But yet the people will never, like the kings and czars, exalt terror into a system. "They have sympathy for the victims; they are too good-hearted not to feel a speedy repugnance at cruelty. The public prosecutor, the corpse-cart, the guillotine, speedily become repulsive. After a little while it is recognized that such a reign of terror is merely preparing the way for a dictatorship, and the guillotine is abolished."‡

The government will be overthrown first. "There is no need of fearing its strength. Governments only seem terrible; the first collision with the insurgent people ays them prostrate; many have collapsed in a few hours before now."§ "The people rise, and the State machine is already at a standstill; the officials are in confusion and know not what to do; the army has lost confidence in its leaders."‖

But it cannot stop with this. "On the day when the people has swept away the governments, it will also, without waiting for any directions from above,

---

* Kr. "*Paroles*" p. 342.   † Kr. "*Prisons*" p. 57.
‡ Kr. "Studies" p. 16.   § Kr. "*Paroles*" p. 166.   ‖ *Ib.* p. 246.

abolish private property by forcible expropriation."*
" The peasants will drive out the great landlords and
declare their estates common property; they will an-
nul the mortgages and proclaim general release from
debt"; † and in the cities " the people will seize on
the entire wealth accumulated there, turn out the fac-
tory-owners, and undertake the management themselves."‡ " The expropriation will be general;
nothing but an expropriation of the broadest kind can
initiate the re-shaping of society—expropriation on a
small scale would appear like ordinary plunder."§ It
will extend not only to the materials of production,
but also to those of consumption: " the first thing
that the people do after the overthrow of the governments will be to provide itself with sanitary dwellings
and with sufficient food and clothing." ‖—Yet expropriation will " have its limits."¶ " Suppose by pinch-
ing, a poor devil has got himself a house that will
hold him and his family. Will he be thrown on the
street? Certainly not! If the house is just big
enough for him and his family, he shall keep it, and
he shall also continue to work the garden under his
window. Our young-men will even lend him a hand
in case of need. But, if he has rented a room to
somebody else, the people will say to this one, ' You
know, friend, don't you, that you no longer owe the
old fellow anything? Keep your room gratis; you
need no longer fear the officer of the court, we have
the new society!'"** " Expropriation will extend just

---

* Kr. " Paroles " pp. 134-5.   † Ib. p. 167.   ‡ Ib. p. 135.
§ Ib. p. 337.   ‖ Kr. " Conquête " pp. 63.
¶ Ib. p. 56.   ** Ib. p. 109.

to that which makes it possible for any one to exploit another's labor."[*]

3. "The work of destruction will be followed by a work of re-shaping."[†]

Most people conceive of revolution as with "a 'revolutionary government' "[‡]—this in two ways. Some understand by this an elective government. " It is proposed to summon the people to elections, to elect a government as quickly as possible, and entrust to it the work which each of us ought to be doing of his own accord."[§] " But any government which an insurgent people attains by elections must necessarily be a leaden weight on its feet, especially in so immense an economic, political, and moral reorganization as the social revolution."[||] This is perceived by others; "therefore they give up the thought of a 'legal' government, at least for the time of insurrection against all laws, and preach the 'revolutionary dictatorship.' 'The party which has overthrown the government,' say they, ' will forcibly put itself in the government's place. It will seize the authority and adopt a revolutionary procedure. For every one who does not recognize it—the guillotine; for every one who refuses obedience to it—the guillotine likewise.' So talk the little Robespierres. But we Anarchists know that this thought is nothing but an unwholesome fruit of government fetishism, and that any dictatorship, even the best disposed, is the death of the revolution."[¶]

" We will do what is needful ourselves, without

* Kr. " Conquête " p. 56.   † Kr. " Paroles " p. 263.
‡ Ib. p. 246.   § Ib. pp. 248-9. || Ib. p. 253.   ¶ Ib. pp. 253-5.

waiting for the orders of a government."* "If the
dissolution of the State is once started, if once the op-
pression-machine begins to give out, free associations
will be formed quite automatically. Just remember
the voluntary combinations of the armed *bourgeoisie*
during the great Revolution. Remember the societies
which were voluntarily formed in Spain, and which
defended the independence of the country, when the
State was shaken to its foundations by Napoleon's
armies. As soon as the State no longer compels any
co-operation, natural wants bring about a voluntary
co-operation quite automatically. If the State be but
overthrown, free society will rise up at once on its
ruins."†

"The reorganization of production will not be possible in a few days,"‡ especially as the revolution will
presumably not break out in all Europe at a time.§
The people will consequently have to take temporary
measures to assure themselves, first of all, of food,
clothing, and shelter. First the populace of the insurgent cities will take possession of the dealers' stocks
of food, and of the grain warehouses and the slaugh-
ter-houses. Volunteers make an inventory of the provisions found, and distribute printed tabular state-
ments by the million. Henceforth free taking of all
that is present in abundance; rations of what has
to be measured out, with preference to the sick and
the weak; a supply for deficiencies by importation
from the country (which will come in plenty if we
produce things that the farmer needs and put them at

* Kr. "*Paroles*" p. 139.   † *Ib.* pp. 116-17.
‡ Kr. "*Conquéte*" p. 75.   § *Ib.* p. 85.

his disposal) and also by the inhabitants of the city
entering upon the cultivation of the royal parks and
meadows in the vicinity.* The people will take possession of the dwelling-houses in like manner. Again
volunteers make lists of the available dwellings and
distribute them. People come together by streets,
quarters, districts, and agree about the allotment of
the dwellings. But the evils that will at first still have
to be borne are soon to be done away: the artisans
of the building trades need only work a few hours a
day, and soon the over-spacious dwellings that were
on hand will be sensibly altered, and model houses,
entirely new, will be built.† The same procedure will
be followed with regard to clothing. The people take
possession of the great clothiers' establishments, and
volunteers list the stocks. People take freely what is
on hand in abundance, in rations what is limited in
quantity. What is lacking is supplied in the shortest
of time by the factories with their perfected machines.‡

II. "To prepare men's minds "§ for the approaching revolution is the task of those who foresee the
course of evolution. This is especially " the task
of the secret societies and revolutionary organizations."‖ It is the task of " the Anarchist party."¶
The Anarchists " are to-day as yet a minority, but
their number is daily growing, will grow more and
more, and will on the eve of the revolution become a
majority."** " What a dismal sight France presented a few years before the great Revolution, and

* Kr. " *Conquête* " pp. 76-96.   † *Ib.* pp. 104-7.   ‡ *Ib.* pp. 114-16.
§ Kr. " *Paroles* " p. 260.   ‖ *Ib.* p. 260.
¶ *Ib.* pp. 99, 254; Kr. " *Temps nouveaux* " p. 54.
** Kr. " *Paroles* " p. 90.

how weak was the minority of those who thought of the abolition of royalty and feudalism; but what a change three or four years later! the minority had begun the revolution and had carried the masses with it."*—But how are men's minds to be prepared for the revolution?

1. First and foremost, the aim of the revolution is to be made generally known. " It is to be proclaimed by word and deed till it is thoroughly popularized, so that on the day of the rising it is in everybody's mouth. This task is greater and more serious than is generally assumed; for, if some few do have the aim clearly before their eyes, it is quite otherwise with the masses, constantly worked upon as they are by the *bourgeois* press."†

But this does not suffice. "The spirit of insurrection must be aroused; the sense of independence and the wild boldness without which no revolution comes about must awake."‡ " Between the peaceable discussion of evils and tumult, insurrection, lies a chasm —the same chasm that in the greater part of mankind separates reflection from act, thought from will."§

2. The way to obtain these two results is " action —constant, incessant action by minorities. Courage, devotion, self-sacrifice are as contagious as cowardice, servility, and apprehension."‖

" What forms is the propaganda to take? Every form that is prescribed by the situation, by opportunity, and propensity. It may be now serious, now jocular; but it must always be bold. It must never leave

---

* Kr. " *Paroles* " pp. 92-5.   † *Ib.* p. 312.   ‡ *Ib.* p. 285.
§ *Ib.* p. 283.   ‖ *Ib.* p. 284.

a means unused, never leave a fact of public life un-
observed, to keep minds alert, to give aliment and expression to discontent, to stir hate against exploiters,
to make the government ridiculous, and to demonstrate its impotence. But above all, to arouse boldness and the spirit of insurrection, it must continually
preach by example."*

"Men of courage, willing not only to speak but to
act; pure characters who prefer prison, exile, and
death to a life that contradicts their principles; bold
natures who know that in order to win one must dare,
—these are the advance-guard who open the fight long
before the masses are ripe to lift the banner of insurrection openly and to seek their rights arms in hand.
In the midst of the complaining, talking, discussing,
comes a mutinous deed by one or more persons, which
incarnates the longings of all."†

"Perhaps at first the masses remain indifferent and
believe the wise ones who regard the act as 'crazy',
but soon they are privately applauding the crazy and
imitating them. While the first of them are filling
the penitentiaries, others are already continuing their
work. The declarations of war against present-day
society, the mutinous deeds, the acts of revenge, multiply. General attention is aroused; the new thought
makes its way into men's heads and wins their hearts.
A single deed makes more propaganda in a few days
than a thousand pamphlets. The government defends
itself, it rages pitilessly; but by this it only causes
further deeds to be committed by one or more persons,
and drives the insurgents to heroism. One deed

---

* Kr. "*Paroles*" p. 284.   † *Ib.* p. 285.

brings forth another; opponents join the mutiny; the government splits into factions; harshness intensifies the conflict; concessions come too late; the revolution breaks out."*

3. To make still clearer the means by which the aim of the revolution is to be made generally known and the spirit of insurrection is to be aroused, Kropotkin tells some of the history of what preceded the Revolution of 1789.

He tells how at that time thousands of lampoons acquainted the people with the vices of the court, and how a multitude of satirical songs flagellated crowned heads and stirred hatred against the nobility and clergy. He sets before us how in placards the king, the queen, the farmers-general, were threatened, reviled, and jeered at; how enemies of the people were hanged or burned or quartered in effigy. He describes to us the way in which the insurrectionists got the people used to the streets and taught them to defy the police, the military, the cavalry. We learn how in the villages secret organizations, the jacques, set fire to the barns of the lord of the manor, destroyed his crops or his game, murdered him himself, threatened the collection or payment of rent with death. He sets forth to us how then, one day, the storehouses were broken into, the trains of wagons were stopped on the highway, the toll-gates were burned and the officials killed, the tax-lists and the account-books and the city archives went up in flames, and the revolution broke out on all sides.†

"What conclusions are to be drawn from this "‡

---

* Kr." *Paroles* " pp. 285-8.   † *Ib.* pp. 293-304.   ‡ *Ib.* p. 292.

Kropotkin does not think it necessary to explain. He contents himself with characterizing as " a precious instruction for us "* the facts which he reports.

---

* Kr. " *Paroles* " p. 304.

CHAPTER VIII

TUCKER'S TEACHING

1.—GENERAL

Benjamin R. Tucker was born in 1854 at South
Dartmouth, near New Bedford, Massachusetts. From
1870 to 1872 he studied technology in Boston; there
he made the acquaintance of Josiah Warren* in 1872.
In 1874 he traveled in England, France, and Italy.
In 1877 Tucker took the temporary editorship of
the " Word," published at Princeton, Massachusetts.
In 1878 he published the quarterly " The Radical
Review " in New Bedford; but only four numbers appeared. In 1881, in Boston, he founded the semi-
monthly paper " Liberty," of which there also appeared for a short time a German edition under the
title " Libertas "; in Boston, also, he was for ten years
one of the editorial staff of the " Globe." Since 1892
he has lived in New York, and " Liberty " has
appeared there as a weekly.†

2. Tucker's teaching about law, the State, and
property is contained mainly in his articles in
" Liberty." He has published a collection‡ of these
articles under the title " Instead of a Book. By a
Man Too Busy to Write One. A fragmentary exposition of philosophical Anarchism " (1893).

---

* [Recognized by Tucker as the originator of Anarchism, so far as any
man can claim this title. See Bailie's life of Warren.]
† [At present (1908) a bi-monthly magazine.]
‡ [Or rather a selection.]

3. Tucker calls his teaching "Anarchism." "Circumstances have combined to make me somewhat conspicuous as an exponent of the theory of Modern Anarchism."* "Anarchy does not mean simply opposed to the *archos,* or political leader. It means opposed to *archē.* Now, *archē,* in the first instance, means *beginning, origin.* From this it comes to mean *a first principle, an element;* then *first place, supreme power, sovereignty, dominion, command, authority;* and finally *a sovereignty, an empire, a realm, a magistracy, a governmental office.* Etymologically, then, the word anarchy may have several meanings. But the word Anarchy as a philosophical term and the word Anarchist as the name of a philosophical sect were first appropriated in the sense of opposition to dominion, to authority, and are so held by right of occupancy, which fact makes any other philosophical use of them improper and confusing."†

2.—BASIS

Tucker considers that the law which has supreme validity for every one of us is self-interest; and from this he derives the law of equal liberty.

1. For every man self-interest is the supreme law. "The Anarchists are not only utilitarians, but egoists in the farthest and fullest sense."‡

What does self-interest mean? My interest is everything that serves my purposes.§ It takes in not only the lowest but also "the higher forms of selfishness."‖ Thus, in particular, the interest of society is

---

* Tucker p. 21.   † *Ib.* p. 112.   ‡ *Ib.* p. 24.
§ *Ib.* pp. 24, 64.   ‖ *Ib.* p. 64.

at the same time that of every individual: "its life is inseparable from the lives of individuals; it is impossible to destroy one without destroying the other."*

Self-interest is the supreme law for man. "The Anarchists totally discard the idea of moral obligation, of inherent rights and duties."† "So far as inherent right is concerned, might is its only measure. Any man, be his name Bill Sykes or Alexander Romanoff, and any set of men, whether the Chinese highbinders or the Congress of the United States, have the right, if they have the power, to kill or coerce other men and to make the entire world subservient to their ends."‡ "The Anarchism of to-day affirms the right of society to coerce the individual and of the individual to coerce society so far as either has the requisite power."§

2. From this supreme law Tucker derives "the law of equal liberty."‖ The law of equal liberty is based on every individual's self-interest. For "liberty is the chief essential to man's happiness, and therefore the most important thing in the world, and I want as much of it as I can get."¶ On the other hand, "human equality is a necessity of stable society,"** and the life of society "is inseparable from the lives of

---

*Tucker p. 35. [This passage refers merely to what it mentions, the alleged intent utterly to destroy society. As to identity of interests, I believe Tucker's position is that the interest of society is that of *almost* every individual.]
† *Ib.* p. 24.   ‡ *Ib.* p. 24.   § *Ib.* p. 132.
‖ *Ib.* p. 42. [Eltzbacher does not seem to perceive that Tucker uses this as a ready-made phrase, coined by Herbert Spencer and designating Spencer's well-known formula that in justice "every man has freedom to do all that he wills, provided he infringes not the equal freedom of any other man."]
¶ *Ib.* p. 41.   ** *Ib.* p. 64.

individuals."* Consequently every individual's self-interest demands the equal liberty of all.

" Equal liberty means the largest amount of liberty compatible with equality and mutuality of respect, on the part of individuals living in society, for their re-spective spheres of action."† "' Mind your own business ' is the only moral law of the Anarchistic scheme."‡ " It is our duty to respect others' rights, assuming the word ' right' to be used in the sense of the limit which the principle of equal liberty logically places upon might."§—On the law of equal liberty is founded " the distinction between invasion and resistance, between government and defence. This distinction is vital: without it there can be no valid philosophy of politics."‖

" By ' invasion ' I mean the invasion of the individual sphere, which is bounded by the line inside of which liberty of action does not conflict with others' liberty of action."¶ This boundary-line is in part unmistakable; for instance, a threat is not an invasion if the threatened act is not an invasion, " a man has a right to threaten what he has a right to execute."** But the boundary-line may also be dubious; for instance, " we cannot clearly identify the maltreatment of child by parent as either invasive or non-invasive of the liberty of third parties."†† " Additional ex-

---

* Tucker p. 35. [This citation is again irrelevant, but Eltzbacher's misapplication of it does not misrepresent Tucker's views.]
† Ib. p. 65. ‡ Ib. p. 15.
§ Ib. p. 59. [It should be understood that a great part of " Instead of a Book " is made up of the reprints of discussions with various opponents whose language is quoted and alluded to.]
‖ Ib. p. 23. ¶ Ib. p. 67. ** Ib. p. 153.
†† Ib. p. 135. [Since the publication of " Instead of a Book " Tucker has had a notable discussion of the child question in " Liberty," which, while

perience is continually sharpening our sense of what
constitutes invasion. Though we still draw the line
by rule of thumb, we are drawing it more clearly
every day."* "The nature of such invasion is not
changed, whether it is made by one man upon another
man, after the manner of the ordinary criminal, or by
one man upon all other men, after the manner of an
absolute monarch, or by all other men upon one man,
after the manner of a modern democracy."†

"On the other hand, he who resists another's attempt to control is not an aggressor, an invader, a
governor, but simply a defender, a protector."‡
"The individual has the right to repel invasion of his
sphere of action."§ "Anarchism justifies the application of force to invasive men,"‖ "violence is advisable
when it will accomplish the desired end and inadvis-
able when it will not."¶ And "defensive associations
acting on the Anarchistic principle would not only
demand redress for, but would prohibit, all clearly invasive acts. They would not, however, prohibit non-
invasive acts, even though these acts create additional
opportunity for invasive persons to act invasively: for
instance, the selling of liquor."** "And the nature
of such resistance is not changed whether it be offered
by one man to another man, as when one repels a
criminal's onslaught, or by one man to all other men,
as when one declines to obey an oppressive law, or by

---

developing much disagreement on this point among Tucker's friends, has at
least brought definiteness into the judgments passed upon it.]
  *Tucker p. 78.   † Ib. p. 23.   ‡ Ib. p. 23.
  § Ib. p. 59.   [The wording of this clause is so thoroughly Eltzbacher's own
that his quotation-marks appear unjustifiable; but the doctrine is
Tucker's.]
  ‖ Ib. p. 81.   ‖ Ib. p. 80.   ** Ib. p. 167.

all other men to one man, as when a subject people rises against a despot, or as when the members of a community voluntarily unite to restrain a criminal."*

3.—LAW

According to Tucker, from the standpoint of every one's self-interest and the equal liberty of all there is no objection to law. Legal norms are to obtain: that is, norms that are based on a general will† and to which obedience is enforced, if necessary, by every means,‡ even by prison, torture, and capital punishment.§ But the law is to be "so flexible that it will shape itself to every emergency and need no alteration. And it will then be regarded as *just* in proportion to its flexibility, instead of as now in proportion to its rigidity."‖ The means to this end is that "juries will judge not only the facts, but the law";¶ machinery

---

* Tucker p. 23.   † *Ib.* pp. 60, 52, 158, 104, 167.   ‡ *Ib.* p. 25.
§ *Ib.* p. 60.   [But see below, page 200, where Tucker's page 60 is quoted *verbatim.*]
‖ *Ib.* p. 312.
¶ *Ib.* p. 312.   [Tucker is not likely to think that he is fairly represented without a fuller quotation : " not only the facts, but the law, the justice of the law, its applicability to the given circumstances, and the penalty or damage to be inflicted because of its infraction." He would emphasize " the justice of the law "—a juryman will disregard a law that he disapproves. Tucker here prefixes " All rules and laws will be little more than suggestions for the guidance of juries." Nevertheless the juryman is to be guided by norm and not by caprice : see " Liberty," Sept. 7, 1895, where he says : " I am asked by a correspondent if I would ' passively see a woman throw her baby into the fire as a man throws his newspaper '. It is highly probable that I would interfere in such a case. But it is as probable, and perhaps more so, that I would personally interfere to prevent the owner of a masterpiece by Titian from applying the torch to the canvas. My interference in the former case no more invalidates the mother's property right in her child than my interference in the latter case would invalidate the property right of the owner of the painting. If I interfere in either case, I am an invader, acting in obedience to my injured feelings. As such I deserve to be punished. I consider that it would be the duty of a policeman in the service of the defence association to arrest me for assault. On my arraignment I should plead guilty, and it would be the duty of the jury to impose a penalty on me. I might ask for a light sentence on the strength of the extenuating circumstances, and I believe that my prayer would be

for altering the law is then unnecessary.*—In particular, there are to be recognized the following legal norms, whose correctness Tucker tries to deduce from the law of equal liberty:

First, a legal norm by which the person is secured against hurt. " We are the sternest enemies of invasion of the person, and, although chiefly busy in destroying the causes thereof, have no scruples against such heroic treatment of its immediate manifestations as circumstances and wisdom may dictate."† Capital punishment is quite compatible with the protection of the person against hurt, for its essence is not that of an act of hurting, but of an act of defence.‡

Next, there is to be recognized a legal norm by virtue of which " ownership on a basis of labor "§ exists. " This form of property secures each in the possession of his own products, or of such products of others as he may have obtained unconditionally without the use of fraud or force." || " It will be seen from this definition that Anarchistic property concerns only products. But anything is a product upon which human labor has been expended. It should be stated, however, that in the case of land, or of any other material the supply of which is so limited that all cannot hold it in unlimited quantities, Anarchism undertakes to protect no titles except such as are based on actual occupancy and use."¶ Against in-

heeded. But, if such invasions as mine were persisted in, it would become the duty of the jury to impose penalties sufficiently severe to put a stop to them."]
  * Tucker p. 312.   † *Ib.* p. 52.
  ‡ *Ib.* pp. 156-7. [Compare the exact words of this passage as quoted on page 200 below.]
  § *Ib.* p. 131. [Not *verbatim.*] || *Ib.* p. 60.   ¶ *Ib,* p. 61.

jury to property, as well as against injury to the person, Anarchism has no scruples against "such heroic treatment as circumstances and wisdom may dictate."*
Furthermore, there is to be recognized the legal norm that contracts must be lived up to. Obligation comes into existence when obligations are "consciously and voluntarily assumed"; † and the other party thus acquires "a right."‡ To be sure, the obligatory force of contract is not without bounds. " Contract is a very serviceable and most important tool, but its usefulness has its limits; no man can employ it for the abdication of his manhood "; § therefore " the constituting of an association in which each member waives the right of secession would be a mere *form*." ‖
Furthermore, no one can employ it for the invasion of third parties; therefore a promise " whose fulfilment would invade third parties "¶ would be invalid.—" I deem the keeping of promises such an important matter that only in the extremest cases would I approve their violation. It is of such vital consequence that associates should be able to rely upon each other that it is better never to do anything to weaken this confidence except when it can be maintained only at the expense of some consideration of even greater importance."** " The man who has received a promise is defrauded by its non-fulfilment, invaded, deprived of a portion of his liberty against his will."†† " I have no doubt of the right of any man to whom, for a consideration, a promise has been made, to insist, even

---

* Tucker p. 52.   † *Ib.* p. 24.   ‡ *Ib.* pp. 146, 350.
§ *Ib.* p. 48.   ‖ *Ib.* p. 48.   ¶ *Ib.* p. 158.
** *Ib.* p. 51.   †† *Ib.* p. 158.

by force, upon the fulfilment of that promise, provided the promise be not one whose fulfilment would
invade third parties. And, if the promisee has a
right to use force himself for such a purpose, he has a
right to secure such co-operative force from others as
they are willing to extend. These others, in turn,
have a right to decide what sort of promises, if any,
they will help him to enforce. When it comes to the
determination of this point, the question is one of
policy solely; and very likely it will be found that the
best way to secure the fulfilment of promises is to
have it understood in advance that the fulfilment is
not to be enforced."*

4.—THE STATE

I. *With regard to every man's self-interest, especially on the basis of the law of equal liberty, Tucker
rejects the State; and that universally, not merely for
special circumstances determined by place and time.*
For the State is " the embodiment of the principle of
invasion."†

1. " Two elements are common to all the institutions to which the name 'State' has been applied:
first, aggression."‡ " Aggression, invasion, government, are interconvertible terms."§ " This is the
Anarchistic definition of government: the subjection
of the non-invasive individual to an external will."‖
And " second, the assumption of authority over a
given area and all within it, exercised generally for
the double purpose of more complete oppression of its

---

* Tucker pp. 157-8.   † *Ib.* p. 25.   ‡ *Ib.* p. 22.
§ *Ib.* p. 23.   ‖ *Ib.* p. 23.

subjects and extension of its boundaries."* Therefore "this is the Anarchistic definition of the State: the embodiment of the principle of invasion in an individual, or a band of individuals, assuming to act as representatives or masters of the entire people within a given area."†

"Rule is evil, and it is none the better for being majority rule."‡ "The theocratic despotism of kings or the democratic despotism of majorities "§ are alike condemnable. "What is the ballot? It is neither more nor less than a paper representative of the bayonet, the billy, and the bullet. It is a labor-saving device for ascertaining on which side force lies and bowing to the inevitable. The voice of the majority saves bloodshed, but it is no less the arbitrament of force than is the decree of the most absolute of despots backed by the most powerful of armies."‖

2. "In the first place, all the acts of governments are indirectly invasive, because dependent upon the primary invasion called taxation."¶ "The very first act of the State, the compulsory assessment and collection of taxes, is itself an aggression, a violation of equal liberty, and, as such, vitiates every subsequent act, even those acts which would be purely defensive if paid for out of a treasury filled by voluntary contributions. How is it possible to sanction, under the law of equal liberty, the confiscation of a man's earnings to pay for protection which he has not sought and does not desire? "**

---

* Tucker p. 22.   † *Ib.* p. 23.   ‡ *Ib.* p. 169.
§ *Ib.* p. 115.   [The words are Lucien V. Pinney's, but Tucker quotes them approvingly.]
‖ *Ib.* pp. 426-7.   ¶ *Ib.* p. 57.   ** *Ib.* p. 25.

" And, if this is an outrage, what name shall we give to such confiscation when the victim is given, instead of bread, a stone, instead of protection, oppression? To force a man to pay for the violation of his own liberty is indeed an addition of insult to injury. But that is exactly what the State is doing."* For " in the second place, by far the greater number of their acts are directly invasive, because directed, not to the restraint of invaders, but to the denial of freedom to the people in their industrial, commercial, social, domestic, and individual lives."†

" How thoughtless, then, to assert that the existing political order is of a purely defensive character! "‡

" Defence is a service, like any other service. It is labor both useful and desired, and therefore an economic commodity subject to the law of supply and demand. In a free market this commodity would be furnished at the cost of production. The production and sale of this commodity are now monopolized by the State. The State, like almost all monopolists, charges exorbitant prices. Like almost all monopolists, it supplies a worthless, or nearly worthless, article. Just as the monopolist of a food product often furnishes poison instead of nutriment, so the State takes advantage of its monopoly of defence to furnish invasion instead of protection. Just as the patrons of the one pay to be poisoned, so the patrons of the other pay to be enslaved. And the State exceeds all its fellow-monopolists in the extent of its villany because it enjoys the unique privilege of compelling all people to buy its product whether they want it or not."§

---

* Tucker pp. 25-6.   † *Ib.* p. 57.   ‡ *Ib.* p. 26.   § *Ib.* p. [32-]33.

3. It cannot be alleged in favor of the State that it is necessary as a means for combating crime.* "The State is itself the most gigantic criminal extant. It manufactures criminals much faster than it punishes them."† "Our prisons are filled with criminals which our virtuous State has made what they are by its iniquitous laws, its grinding monopolies, and the horrible social conditions that result from them. We enact many laws that manufacture criminals, and then a few that punish them."‡

No more can the State be defended on the ground that it is wanted for the relief of suffering. "The State is rendering assistance to the suffering and starving victims of the Mississippi inundation. Well, such work is better than forging new chains to keep the people in subjection, we allow; but is not worth the price that is paid for it. The people cannot afford to be enslaved for the sake of being insured. If there were no other alternative, they would do better, on the whole, to take Nature's risks and pay her penalties as best they might. But Liberty supplies another alternative, and furnishes better insurance at cheaper rates. Mutual insurance, by the organization of risk, will do the utmost that can be done to mitigate and equalize the suffering arising from the accidental destruction of wealth."§

II. *Every man's self-interest, and equal liberty particularly, demands, in place of the State, a social human life on the basis of the legal norm that contracts must be lived up to.* The "voluntary associa-

---

* Tucker p. 54.   † *Ib.* p. 53.
‡ *Ib.* pp. 26-7.   § *Ib.* pp. 158-9.

tion of contracting individuals "* is to take the place
of the State.

1. "The Anarchists have no intention or desire to
abolish society. They know that its life is inseparable
from the lives of individuals; that it is impossible to
destroy one without destroying the other."† "Society
has come to be man's dearest possession. Pure air is
good, but no one wants to breathe it long alone. Independence is good, but isolation is too heavy a price
to pay for it."‡

But men are not to be held together in society by a
concrete supreme authority, but solely by the legally
binding force of contract.§ The form of society is to
be " voluntary association,"‖ whose " constitution "¶
is nothing but a contract.

2. But what is to be the nature of the voluntary
association in detail?

In the first place, it cannot bind its members for
life. "The constituting of an association in which
each member waives the right of secession would be a
mere *form*, which every decent man who was a party
to it would hasten to violate and tread under foot as
soon as he appreciated the enormity of his folly. To
indefinitely waive one's right of secession is to make
one's self a slave. Now, no man can make himself so
much a slave as to forfeit the right to issue his own
emancipation proclamation."**

In the next place, the voluntary association, as

---

* Tucker p. 44. [See my note below, page 195.]
† *Ib.* p. 35.   ‡ *Ib.* p. 321.   § *Ib.* p. 32.
‖ *Ib.* p. 44.   [Or rather p. 167, and sundry other passages ; on p. 44 see my
note below, page 195.]
¶ *Ib.* p. 342.   ** *Ib.* p. 48.

such, can have no dominion over a territory. "Certainly such voluntary association would be entitled to enforce whatever regulations the contracting parties might agree upon within the limits of whatever territory, or divisions of territory, had been brought into the association by these parties as individual occupiers thereof, and no non-contracting party would have a right to enter or remain in this domain except upon such terms as the association might impose. But if, somewhere between these divisions of territory, had lived, prior to the formation of the association, some individual on his homestead, who for any reason, wise or foolish, had declined to join in forming the association, the contracting parties would have had no right to evict him, compel him to join, make him pay for any incidental benefits that he might derive from proximity to their association, or restrict him in the exercise of any previously-enjoyed right to prevent him from reaping these benefits. Now, voluntary association necessarily involving the right of secession, any seceding member would naturally fall back into the position and upon the rights of the individual above described, who refused to join at all. So much, then, for the attitude of the individual toward any voluntary association surrounding him, his support thereof evidently depending upon his approval or disapproval of its objects, his view of its efficiency in attaining them, and his estimate of the advantages and disadvantages involved in joining, seceding, or abstaining."*

---

* Tucker pp. 44-5. [All this is a discussion of the characteristics which the State of to-day would have to possess if it were to deserve to be charac-

For the members of the voluntary association numerous obligations arise from their membership. The association may require, as a condition of membership, the agreement to perform certain services,— for instance, "jury service."* And " inasmuch as Anarchistic associations recognize the right of secession, they may utilize the ballot, if they see fit to do so. If the question decided by ballot is so vital that the minority thinks it more important to carry out its own views than to preserve common action, the minority can withdraw. In no case can a minority, however small, be governed without its consent."† The voluntary association is entitled to compel its members to live up to their obligations. " If a man makes an agreement with men, the latter may combine to hold him to his agreement "; ‡ therefore a voluntary association is " entitled to enforce whatever regulations the contracting parties may agree upon."§ To be sure, one must bear in mind that " very likely the best way to secure the fulfilment of promises is to have it understood in advance that the fulfilment is not to be enforced." ‖

Of especial importance among the obligations of the members of a voluntary association is the duty of paying taxes; but the tax is voluntary by virtue of the fact that it is based on contract.¶ " Voluntary

---

terized as a voluntary association. The same conditions must of course be fulfilled by any future voluntary association ; but it does not follow that all the points mentioned are such as Anarchistic associations would have most occasion to contemplate.]
*Tucker p. 56.   † *Ib*. pp. 56-7.   ‡ *Ib*. p. 24.
§ *Ib*. p. 44. [For context and limitations see page 195 of the present book.]   ‖ *Ib*. p. 158.
¶ *Ib*. p. 32. [It is not necessary that taxation exist, though it may be altogether presumable that it will. Still less is it necessary that the taxation be considerable in amount.]

taxation, far from impairing the association's credit, would strengthen it "; * for, in the first place, because of the simplicity of its functions, the association seldom or never has to borrow; in the second place, it cannot, like the present State upon its basis of compulsory taxation, repudiate its debts and still continue business; and, in the third place, it will necessarily be more intent on maintaining its credit by paying its debts than is the State which enforces taxation.† And furthermore, the voluntariness of the tax has this advantage, that " the defensive institution will be steadily deterred from becoming an invasive institution through fear that the voluntary contributions will fall off; it will have this constant motive to keep itself trimmed down to the popular demand."‡

" Ireland's true order: the wonderful Land League, the nearest approach, on a large scale, to perfect Anarchistic organization that the world has yet seen. An immense number of local groups, scattered over large sections of two continents separated by three thousand miles of ocean; each group autonomous, each free; each composed of varying numbers of individuals of all ages, sexes, races, equally autonomous and free; each inspired by a common, central purpose; each supported entirely by voluntary contributions; each obeying its own judgment; each guided in the formation of its judgment and the choice of its conduct by the advice of a central council of picked men, having no power to enforce its orders except that inherent in the convincing logic of the reasons on which the orders are based; all co-ordi-

---

* Tucker pp. 36-7. † *Ib.* p. 37. ‡ *Ib.* p. 43.

nated and federated, with a minimum of machinery
and without sacrifice of spontaneity, into a vast working unit, whose unparalleled power makes tyrants
tremble and armies of no avail."*

3. Among the prominent associations of the new
society are mutual insurance societies and mutual
banks,† and, especially, defensive associations.

"The abolition of the State will leave in existence a
defensive association "‡ which will give protection
against those " who violate the social law by invading
their neighbors."§　To be sure, this need will be only
transitory. " We look forward to the ultimate disappearance of the necessity of force even for the purpose of repressing crime."‖　" The necessity for defence against individual invaders is largely and perhaps, in the end, wholly due to the oppressions of the
invasive State.　When the State falls, criminals will
begin to disappear."¶

A number of defensive associations may exist side
by side.　" There are many more than five or six insurance companies in England, and it is by no means
uncommon for members of the same family to insure
their lives and goods against accident or fire in different companies.　Why should there not be a considerable number of defensive associations in England, in
which people, even members of the same family, might

---

* Tucker p. 414.
　† *Ib.* p. 159.　[Tucker himself would assuredly have given the emphasis of
" especially " to the mutual banks.　The defensive associations receive
especially frequent mention because of the need of incessantly answering
the objection "If we lose the State, who will protect us against ruffians? "
but Tucker certainly expects that the defensive association will from the
start fill a much smaller sphere in every respect than the present police.
See *e. g.* " Instead of a Book " p. 40.]
　‡ *Ib.* p. 25.　§ *Ib.* p. 25.　‖ *Ib.* p. 52.　¶ *Ib.* p. 40.

insure their lives and goods against murderers or
thieves? Defence is a service, like any other
service."* "Under the influence of competition the
best and cheapest protector, like the best and cheapest
tailor, would doubtless get the greater part of the
business. It is conceivable even that he might get the
whole of it. But, if he should, it would be by his
virtue as a protector, not by his power as a tyrant.
He would be kept at his best by the possibility of
competition and the fear of it; and the source of
power would always remain, not with him, but with
his patrons, who would exercise it, not by voting him
down or by forcibly putting another in his place, but
by withdrawing their patronage."† But, if invader
and invaded belong to different defensive associations,
will not a conflict of associations result? " Anticipa-
tions of such conflicts would probably result in
treaties, and even in the establishment of federal tri-
bunals, as courts of last resort, by the co-operation of
the various associations, on the same voluntary principle in accordance with which the associations themselves were organized." ‡

" Voluntary defensive associations acting on the
Anarchistic principle would not only demand redress
for, but would prohibit, all clearly invasive acts."§
To fulfil this function they may choose any appropriate means, without thereby exercising a govern-

---

* Tucker p. 32.   † Ib. pp. 326-7.   ‡ Ib. p. 36.
§ Ib. p. 167. [But the restraint of aggressions against those with whom
the association has no contract, and also the possible refusal to pay any
attention to some particular class of aggressions which it may be thought
best to let alone, are optional ; in these respects the association will do
what seems best to serve the interests (including the pleasure, altruistic or
other) of its members ; those who do not approve the policy adopted mav
quit the association if they like.]

ment. " Government is the subjection of the *non-in-vasive* individual to a will not his own. The subjection of the *invasive* individual is not government, but resistance to and protection from government."*— " Anarchism recognizes the right to arrest, try, convict, and punish for wrong doing."† " Anarchism will take enough of the invader's property from him to repair the damage done by his invasion."‡ " If it can find no better instrument of resistance to invasion, Anarchism will use prisons."§ It admits even capital punishment. " The society which inflicts capital punishment does not commit murder. Murder is an offensive act. The term cannot be applied legitimately to any defensive act. There is nothing sacred in the life of an invader, and there is no valid principle of human society that forbids the invaded to protect themselves in whatever way they can."‖ " It is allowable to punish invaders by torture. But, if the ' good ' people are not fiends, they are not likely to defend themselves by torture until the penalties of death and tolerable confinement have shown themselves destitute of efficacy."¶—" All disputes will be submitted to juries."** " Speaking for myself, I think the jury should be selected by drawing twelve names by lot from a wheel containing the names of all

---

*Tucker p. 39.
† *Ib*. p. 55 [where Tucker explicitly refuses to approve this statement unless he is allowed to add the caveat " if by the words wrong doing is meant invasion "].
‡ *Ib*. p. 56.   § *Ib*. p. 56.
‖ *Ib*. pp. 156-7. [But accompanied by a disapproval of the ordinary practice of capital punishment.]
¶ *Ib*. p. 60 [where the particular torture under discussion is failure to " feed, clothe, and make comfortable " the prisoners].
** *Ib*. p. 312. [But " Anarchism, as such, neither believes nor disbelieves in jury trial ; it is a matter of expediency," pp. 55-6.]

the citizens in the community."* "The juries will judge not only the facts, but the law, the justice of the law, its applicability to the given circumstances, and the penalty or damage to be inflicted because of its infraction."†

5.—PROPERTY

I. *According to Tucker, from the standpoint of every one's self-interest and the equal liberty of all there is no objection to property.* Tucker rejects only the distribution of property on the basis of monopoly, as it everywhere and always exists in the State. That the State is essentially invasion appears in the laws which "not only prescribe personal habits, but, worse still, create and sustain monopolies "‡ and thereby make usury possible.§

1. Usury is the taking of surplus value.‖ "A laborer's product is such portion of the value of that which he delivers to the consumer as his own labor has contributed."¶ The laborer does not get this product, "at least not as laborer; he gains a bare subsistence by his work."** But, "somebody gets the surplus wealth. Who is the somebody?"††
"The usurer."‡‡

"There are three forms of usury: interest on money, rent of land and houses, and profit in exchange. Whoever is in receipt of any of these is a usurer. And who is not? Scarcely any one. The

---

* Tucker p. 56.   † *Ib.* p. 312.   ‡ *Ib.* p. 26.   § *Ib.* p. 178.
‖ *Ib.* pp. 178, 177.   ¶ *Ib.* p. 241.
** *Ib.* p. 177.   [This is given as an answer to the question here quoted next, about "surplus wealth."]
†† *Ib.* p. 177.   [Quoted from N. Y. "Truth."]
‡‡ *Ib.* p. 178.

banker is a usurer; the manufacturer is a usurer; the merchant is a usurer; the landlord is a usurer; and the workingman who puts his savings, if he has any, out at interest, or takes rent for his house or lot, if he owns one, or exchanges his labor for more than an equivalent,—he too is a usurer. The sin of usury is one under which all are concluded, and for which all are responsible. But all do not benefit by it. The vast majority suffer. Only the chief usurers accumulate: in agricultural and thickly settled countries, the landlords; in industrial and commercial countries, the bankers. Those are the Somebodies who swallow up the surplus wealth."*

2. " And where do they get their power? From monopoly maintained by the State. Usury rests on this."† And "of the various monopolies that now prevail, four are of principal importance."‡

" First in the importance of its evil influence they [the founders of Anarchism] considered the money monopoly, which consists of the privilege given by the government to certain individuals, or to individuals holding certain kinds of property, of issuing the circulating medium, a privilege which is now enforced in this country by a national tax of ten per cent. upon all other persons who attempt to furnish a circulating medium, and by State laws making it a criminal offence to issue notes as currency. It is claimed that holders of this privilege control the rate of interest, the rate of rent of houses and buildings, and the

---

* Tucker p. 178.
† Ib. p. 178. [Not verbatim.]
‡ Ib. p. 11.

prices of goods,—the first directly, and the second and third indirectly. For, if the business of banking were made free to all, more and more persons would enter into it until the competition should become sharp enough to reduce the price of lending money to the labor cost, which statistics show to be less than three-fourths of one per cent."* "Then down will go house-rent. For no one who can borrow capital at one per cent. with which to build a house of his own will consent to pay rent to a landlord at a higher rate than that."† Finally, " down will go profits also. For merchants, instead of buying at high prices on credit, will borrow money of the banks at less than one per cent., buy at low prices for cash, and correspondingly reduce the prices of their goods to their customers."‡

" Second in importance comes the land monopoly, the evil effects of which are seen principally in exclusively agricultural countries, like Ireland. This monopoly consists in the enforcement by government of land-titles which do not rest upon personal occupancy and cultivation."§ " Ground-rent exists only because the State stands by to collect it and to protect land-titles rooted in force or fraud."‖ " As soon as individuals should no longer be protected in anything but personal occupancy and cultivation of land, ground-rent would disappear, and so usury have one less leg to stand on."¶

---

*Tucker p. 11.   † *Ib.* p. 12.   ‡ *Ib.* p. 12.
§ *Ib.* p. 12.   ‖ *Ib.* p. 178.
¶ *Ib.* p. 12. [This is given as the view of Proudhon and Warren ; the next sentence states Tucker's belief that for perfect correctness it should be modified by admitting that a small fraction of ground-rent, tending con-

The third and fourth places are occupied by the tariff and patent monopolies.* "The tariff monopoly consists in fostering production at high prices and under unfavorable conditions by visiting with the penalty of taxation those who patronize production at low prices and under favorable conditions. The evil to which this monopoly gives rise might more properly be called *mis*usury than usury, because it compels labor to pay, not exactly for the use of capital, but rather for the misuse of capital."† "The patent monopoly protects inventors and authors against competition for a period long enough to enable them to extort from the people a reward enormously in excess of the labor measure of their services,—in other words, it gives certain people a right of property for a term of years in laws and facts of nature, and the power to exact tribute from others for the use of this natural wealth, which should be open to all."‡ It is on the tariff and patent monopolies, next to the money monopoly, that profit in exchange is based. If they were done away along with the money monopoly, it would disappear.§

II. *Every one's self-interest, and particularly the equal liberty of all, demands a distribution of property in which every one is guaranteed the product of his labor.*‖

1. "Equal liberty, in the property sphere, is such a balance between the liberty to take and the liberty to keep that the two liberties may coexist without con-

---

stantly to a minimum, would persist even then, but would be no cause for "serious alarm."]
*Tucker pp. 12-13.   †*Ib.* p. 12.   ‡*Ib.* p. 13.
§*Ib.* pp. 12-13, 178.   ‖*Ib.* pp. 59-60.

flict or invasion."* "Nearly all Anarchists consider labor to be the only basis of the right of ownership in harmony with that law "; † "the laborers, instead of having only a small fraction of the wealth in the world, should have all the wealth."‡ This form of property "secures each in the possession of his own products, or of such products of others as he may have obtained unconditionally without the use of fraud or force, and in the realization of all titles to such products which he may hold by virtue of free contract with others."§

"It will be seen from this definition that Anarchistic property concerns only products. But anything is a product upon which human labor has been expended, whether it be a piece of iron or a piece of land. (It should be stated, however, that in the case of land, or of any other material the supply of which is so limited that all cannot hold it in unlimited quantities, Anarchism undertakes to protect no titles except such as are based on actual occupancy and use.)"||

2. A distribution of property in which every one is guaranteed the product of his labor presupposes merely that equal liberty be applied in those spheres which are as yet dominated by State monopoly.¶

"Free money first."** "I mean by free money the utter absence of restriction upon the issue of all money not fraudulent"; †† "making the issue of money as free as the manufacture of shoes."‡‡

---

* Tucker p. 67.   † Ib. p. 131.
‡ Ib. p. 185. [Quoted, with express approval, from A. B. Brown.]
§ Ib. p. 60. || Ib. p. 61.   ¶ Ib. p. 178.
** Ib. p. 273.   †† Ib. p. 274.   ‡‡ Ib. p. 374.

Money is here understood in the broadest sense, it
means both " commodity money and credit money,"*
by no means coin alone; " if the idea of the royalty
of gold and silver could once be knocked out of the
people's heads, and they could once understand that
no particular kind of merchandise is created by nature
for monetary purposes, they would settle this question
in a trice."† " If they only had the liberty to do so,
there are enough large and small property-holders
willing and anxious to issue money, to provide a far
greater amount than is needed."‡ " Does the law of
England allow citizens to form a bank for the issue of
paper money against any property that they may see
fit to accept as security; said bank perhaps owning no
specie whatever; the paper money not redeemable in
specie except at the option of the bank; the customers
of the bank mutually pledging themselves to accept
the bank's paper in lieu of gold or silver coin of the
same face value; the paper being redeemable only at
the maturity of the mortgage notes, and then simply
by a return of said notes and a release of the mort-
gaged property,—is such an institution, I ask, allowed by the law of England? If it is, then I have
only to say that the working people of England are
very great fools not to take advantage of this in-
estimable liberty."§ Then " competition would reduce the rate of interest on capital to the mere cost of
banking, which is much less than one per cent.,"‖ for
"capitalists will not be able to lend their capital at interest when people can get money at the bank without

---

*Tucker p. 272.   †*Ib.* p. 198.   ‡*Ib.* p. 248.
§*Ib.* p. 226.   ‖*Ib.* p. 474.

interest with which to buy capital outright."[*]
Likewise the charge of rent on buildings "would be
almost entirely and directly abolished,"[†] and "profits
fall to the level of the manufacturer's or merchant's
proper wage,"[‡] "except in business protected by
tariff or patent laws."[§] "This facility of acquiring
capital will give an unheard-of impetus to business"; [||]
"if free banking were only a picayunish attempt to
distribute more equitably the small amount of wealth
now produced, I would not waste a moment's energy
on it."[¶]

Free land is needed in the second place.[**] "'The
land for the people,' according to 'Liberty', means
the protection of all people who desire to cultivate
land in the possession of whatever land they personally cultivate, without distinction between the existing classes of landlords, tenants, and laborers, and
the positive refusal of the protecting power to lend its
aid to the collection of any rent whatsoever."[††] This
"system of occupying ownership, accompanied by no
legal power to collect rent, but coupled with the abolition of the State-guaranteed monopoly of money, thus
making capital readily available,"[‡‡] would "abolish
ground-rent"[§§] and "distribute the increment natur-
ally and quietly among its rightful owners."[||||]

In the third and fourth place, free trade and freedom of intellectual products are necessary.[¶¶] If they
were added to freedom in money, "profit on merchan-

---

[*] Tucker p. 287.   [†] *Ib.* pp. 274-5.   [‡] *Ib.* p. 287.
[§] *Ib.* p. 178.   [||] *Ib.* p. 11.   [¶] *Ib.* p. 243.   [**] *Ib.* p. 275.
[††] *Ib.* p. 299.   [‡‡] *Ib.* p. 325.   [§§] *Ib.* p. 275.
[||||] *Ib.* p. 325. [Meaning, of course, John Stuart Mill's "unearned incre-
ment" in the value of land.]
[¶¶] *Ib.* pp. 12-13.

dise would become merely the wages of mercantile labor."* Free trade " would result in a great reduction in the prices of all articles taxed."† And " the abolition of the patent monopoly would fill its beneficiaries with a wholesome fear of competition which would cause them to be satisfied with pay for their services equal to that which other laborers get for theirs."‡

If equal liberty is realized in these four spheres, its realization in the sphere of property follows of itself: that is, a distribution of property in which every one is guaranteed the product of his labor.§ " Economic privilege must disappear as a result of the abolition of political tyranny."‖ In a society in which there is no more government of man by man, there can be no such things as interest, rent, and profits;¶ every one is guaranteed the ownership of the product of his labor. " Socialism does not say: ' Thou shalt not steal! ' It says: ' When all men have Liberty, thou wilt not steal.' "**

3. " Liberty will abolish all means whereby any laborer can be deprived of any of his product; but it will not abolish the limited inequality between one laborer's product and another's."†† " There will remain the slight disparity of products due to superiority of soil and skill. But even this disparity will soon develop a tendency to decrease. Under the new economic conditions and enlarged opportunities resulting

---

* Tucker pp. 474, 178. † *Ib.* p. 12. ‡ *Ib.* p. 13.
§ *Ib.* p. 403. ‖ *Ib.* p. 403. ¶ *Ib.* p. 470.
** *Ib.* p. 362. [" Socialism " is here used as including Anarchism ; and Tucker prefers so to use the word.]
†† *Ib.* p. [347-]348.

from freedom of credit and land classes will tend to disappear; great capacities will not be developed in a few at the expense of stunting those of the many; freedom of locomotion will be vastly increased; the toilers will no longer be anchored in such large numbers in the present commercial centres, and thus made subservient to the city landlords; territories and resources never before utilized will become easy of access and development; and under all these influences the disparity above mentioned will decrease to a minimum."*

" Probably it will never disappear entirely."‡

" Now, because liberty has not the power to bring this about, there are people who say: We will have no liberty, for we must have absolute equality. I am not of them. If I can go through life free and rich, I shall not cry because my neighbor, equally free, is richer. Liberty will ultimately make all men rich; it will not make all men equally rich. Authority may (and may not) make all men equally rich in purse; it certainly will make them equally poor in all that makes life best worth living."†

6.—REALIZATION

According to Tucker, the manner in which the change called for by every one's self-interest takes place is to be that those who have recognized the truth shall first convince a sufficient number of people how necessary the change is to their own interests, and that then they all of them, by refusing obedience, abolish

---

*Tucker pp. 332-3.   † *Ib.* p. 333.   ‡ *Ib.* p. 348.

the State, transform law and property, and thus bring about the new condition.

I. First a sufficient number of men are to be convinced that their own interests demand the change.

1. " A system of Anarchy in actual operation implies a previous education of the people in the principles of Anarchy."* " The individual must be penetrated with the Anarchistic idea and taught to rebel."† " Persistent inculcation of the doctrine of equality of liberty, whereby finally the majority will be made to see in regard to existing forms of invasion what they have already been made to see in regard to its obsolete forms,—namely, that they are not seeking equality of liberty at all, but simply the subjection of all others to themselves."‡ " The Irish Land League failed because the peasants were acting, not intelligently in obedience to their wisdom, but blindly in obedience to leaders who betrayed them at the critical moment. Had the people realized the power they were exercising and understood the economic situation, they would not have resumed the payment of rent at Parnell's bidding, and to-day they might have been free. The Anarchists do not propose to repeat their mistake. That is why they are devoting themselves entirely to the inculcation of principles, especially of economic principles. In steadfastly pursuing this course regardless of clamor, they alone are laying a sure foundation for the success of the revolution."§

2. In particular, according to Tucker, appropriate means for the inculcation of the Anarchistic idea are

---

* Tucker p. 104. † *Ib.* p. 114.
‡ *Ib.* pp. 77-8. § *Ib.* p. 416.

"speech and the press."*—But what if the freedom of speech and of the press be suppressed? Then force is justifiable.†

But force is to be used only as a "last resort."‡ "When a physician sees that his patient's strength is being exhausted so rapidly by the intensity of his agony that he will die of exhaustion before the medical processes inaugurated have a chance to do their curative work, he administers an opiate. But a good physician is always loth to do so, knowing that one of the influences of the opiate is to interfere with and defeat the medical processes themselves. It is the same with the use of force, whether of the mob or of the State, upon diseased society; and not only those who prescribe its indiscriminate use as a sovereign remedy and a permanent tonic, but all who ever propose it as a cure, and even all who would lightly and unnecessarily resort to it, not as a cure, but as an expedient, *are social quacks.*"§

Therefore violence "should be used against the oppressors of mankind only when they have succeeded in hopelessly repressing all peaceful methods of agitation."‖ "Bloodshed in itself is pure loss. When we must have freedom of agitation, and when nothing but bloodshed will secure it, then bloodshed is wise."¶

"As long as freedom of speech and of the press is not struck down, there should be no resort to physical force in the struggle against oppression. It must not be inferred that, because ' Libertas ' thinks it may become

---

* Tucker pp. 397, 413.   † *Ib.* p. 413.   ‡ *Ib.* p. 397.   § *Ib.* p. 428.
‖ *Ib.* p. 428 [where the subject is not "violence " of all sorts great and small, but "terrorism and assassination "].
¶ *Ib.* p. 439.

advisable to use force to secure free speech, it would therefore sanction a bloody deluge as soon as free speech had been struck down in one, a dozen, or a hundred instances. Not until the gag had become completely efficacious would ' Libertas ' advise that last resort, the use of force."* " Terrorism is expedient in Russia and inexpedient in Germany and England."†—In what form is violence to be used? " The days of armed revolution have gone by. It is too easily put down."‡ " Terrorism and assassination "§ are necessary, but they " will have to consist of a series of acts of individual dynamiters."‖

3. But, besides speech and the press, there are yet other methods of " propagandism."¶

Such a method is " isolated individual resistance to taxation."** " Some year, when an Anarchist feels exceptionally strong and independent, when his conduct can impair no serious personal obligations, when on the whole he would a little rather go to jail than not, and when his property is in such shape that he can successfully conceal it, let him declare to the assessor property of a certain value, and then defy the collector to collect. Or, if he have no property, let him decline to pay his poll tax. The State will then be put to its trumps. Of two things one,—either it will let him alone, and then he will tell his neighbors all about it, resulting the next year in an alarming disposition on their part to keep their own money in

---

*Tucker p. 397.   †*Ib.* p. 428.   ‡*Ib.* p. 440.
§*Ib.* p. 428 [with limiting context quoted above, page 211].
‖*Ib.* p. 440.   ¶*Ib.* p. 45.
**Ib.* p. 45 [where nothing is said as to whether the work is the better or the worse for being " isolated "].

their own pockets; or else it will imprison him, and then by the requisite legal processes he will demand and secure all the rights of a civil prisoner and live thus a decently comfortable life until the State shall get tired of supporting him and the increasing number of persons who will follow his example. Unless, indeed, the State, in desperation, shall see fit to make its laws regarding imprisonment for taxes more rigorous, and then, if our Anarchist be a determined man, we shall find out how far a republican government, 'deriving its just powers from the consent of the governed,' is ready to go to procure that 'consent,'— whether it will stop at solitary confinement in a dark cell or join with the czar of Russia in administering torture by electricity. The farther it shall go the better it will be for Anarchy, as every student of the history of reform well knows. Who shall estimate the power for propagandism of a few cases of this kind, backed by a well-organized force of agitators outside the prison walls?"*

Another method of propaganda consists in "a practical test of Anarchistic principles."† But this cannot take place in isolated communities, but only "in the very heart of existing industrial and social life."‡ "In some large city fairly representative of the varied interests and characteristics of our heterogeneous civilization let a sufficiently large number of earnest and intelligent Anarchists, engaged in nearly all the different trades and professions, combine to carry on their production and distribution on the cost principle, and,"§ "setting at defiance the national and State

---

* Tucker p. 412.   † *Ib.* p. 423.   ‡ *Ib.* p. 423.   § *Ib.* p. 423.

banking prohibitions,"* " to start a bank through
which they can obtain a non-interest-bearing currency
for the conduct of their commerce and dispose their
steadily accumulating capital in new enterprises, the
advantages of this system of affairs being open to all
who should choose to offer their patronage,—what
would be the result?   Why, soon the whole composite
population, wise and unwise, good, bad, and indifferent, would become interested in what was going on
under their very eyes, more and more of them would
actually take part in it, and in a few years, each man
reaping the fruit of his labor and no man able to live
in idleness on an income from capital, the whole city
would become a great hive of Anarchistic workers,
prosperous and free individuals."†

II. If a sufficient number of persons are convinced
that their self-interest demands the change, then the
time is come to abolish the State, transform law and
property, and bring about the new condition, by
"the Social Revolution,"‡ *i. e.* by as general a refusal of obedience as possible.   The State "is sheer
tyranny, and has no rights which any individual is
bound to respect; on the contrary, every individual
who understands his rights and values his liberties will
do his best to overthrow it."§

1. Many believe "that the State cannot disappear
until the individual is perfected.

" In saying which, Mr. Appleton joins hands with
those wise persons who admit that Anarchy will be
practicable when the millennium arrives.   No doubt
it is true that, if the individual could perfect himself

---

* Tucker p. 27.   † *Ib.* pp. 423-4.   ‡ *Ib.* pp. 416, 439.   § *Ib.* p. 45.

while the barriers to his perfection are standing, the
State would afterwards disappear. Perhaps, too, he
could go to heaven, if he could lift himself by his
boot-straps."*   " ' Bullion ' thinks that ' civilization
consists in teaching men to govern themselves and
then letting them do it.' A very slight change
suffices to make this stupid statement an entirely accurate one, after which it would read: ' Civilization
consists in teaching men to govern themselves by letting them do it.' "†   Therefore it is necessary to
" abolish the State "‡ by " the impending social
revolution."§
    2. Others have the " fallacious idea that Anarchy
can be inaugurated by force."‖
    In what way it is to be inaugurated is solely a
question of " expediency."¶   " To brand the policy
of terrorism and assassination as immoral is ridicu-
lously weak. ' Liberty ' does not assume to set any
limit on the right of an invaded individual to choose
his own methods of defence. The invader, whether
an individual or a government, forfeits all claim to
consideration from the invaded. This truth is independent of the character of the invasion. It makes no
difference in what direction the individual finds his
freedom arbitrarily limited; he has a right to vindi-
cate it in any case, and he will be justified in vindicat-
ing it by whatever means are available."**
    " The right to resist oppression by violence is be-
yond doubt. But its exercise would be unwise unless
the suppression of free thought, free speech, and a

---

*Tucker p. 114.   † Ib. p. 158.   ‡ Ib. p. 114.   § Ib. p. 487.
‖ Ib. p. 427.   ¶ Ib. p. 429.   ** Ib. pp. 428-9.

free press were enforced so stringently that all other means of throwing it off had become hopeless."* "If government should be abruptly and entirely abolished to-morrow, there would probably ensue a series of physical conflicts about land and many other things, ending in reaction and a revival of the old tyranny. But, if the abolition of government shall take place gradually, it will be accompanied by a constant acquisition and steady spreading of social truth."†

3. The social revolution is to come about by passive resistance; that is, refusal of obedience.‡

"Passive resistance is the most potent weapon ever wielded by man against oppression."§ "'Passive resistance,' said Ferdinand Lassalle, with an obtuseness thoroughly German, 'is the resistance which does not resist.' Never was there a greater mistake. It is the only resistance which in these days of military discipline meets with any result. There is not a tyrant in the civilized world to-day who would not do anything in his power to precipitate a bloody revolution rather than see himself confronted by any large fraction of his subjects determined not to obey. An insurrection is easily quelled, but no army is willing or able to train its guns on inoffensive people who do not even gather in the street but stay at home and stand back on their rights."‖

"Power feeds on its spoils, and dies when its victims refuse to be despoiled, They can't persuade it to death; they can't vote it to death; they can't shoot

---

* Tucker p. 439.
† *Ib.* p. 329 [where the course it must take is somewhat more precisely described].
† *Ib.* p. 413.   § *Ib.* p. 415.   ‖ *Ib.* p. 413.

it to death; but they can always starve it to death.
When a determined body of people, sufficiently strong
in numbers and force of character to command respect
and make it unsafe to imprison them, shall agree to
quietly close their doors in the faces of the tax-col-
lector and the rent-collector, and shall, by issuing
their own money in defiance of legal prohibition, at
the same time cease paying tribute to the money-lord,
government, with all the privileges which it grants
and the monopolies which it sustains, will go by the
board."*

Consider " the enormous and utterly irresistible
power of a large and intelligent minority, comprising
say one-fifth of the population in any given locality,"
refusing to pay taxes.† " I need do no more than
call attention to the wonderfully instructive history of
the Land League movement in Ireland, the most
potent and instantly effective revolutionary force the
world has ever known so long as it stood by its
original policy of ' Pay No Rent,' and which lost
nearly all its strength the day it abandoned that
policy. But it was pursued far enough to show that
the British government was utterly powerless before
it; and it is scarcely too much to say, in my opinion,
that, had it been persisted in, there would not to-day
be a landlord in Ireland. It is easier to resist taxes in
this country than it is to resist rent in Ireland; and
such a policy would be as much more potent here than
there as the intelligence of the people is greater, providing always that you can enlist in it a sufficient
number of earnest and determined men and women.

---

* Tucker pp. 415-16. † *Ib.* p. 412.

If one-fifth of the people were to resist taxation, it would cost more to collect their taxes, or try to collect them, than the other four-fifths would consent to pay into the treasury."*

---

*Tucker pp. 412-13. [This chapter should be completed by a mention of Tucker's doctrine that we must expect Anarchy to be established by gradually getting rid of one oppression after another till at last all the domination of violence shall have disappeared. See, for instance, " Liberty " for December, 1900: " The fact is that Anarchist society was started thousands of years ago, when the first glimmer of the idea of liberty dawned upon the human mind, and has been advancing ever since,—not steadily advancing, to be sure, but fitfully, with an occasional reversal of the current. Mr. Byington looks upon the time when a jury of Anarchists shall sit, as a point not far from the beginning of the history of Anarchy's growth, whereas I look upon that time as a point very near the end of that history. The introduction of more Anarchy into our economic life will have made marriage a thing of the past long before the first drawing of a jury of Anarchists to pass upon any contract whatever." Also " Instead of a Book " p. 104: " Anarchists work for the abolition of the State, but by this they mean not its overthrow, but, as Proudhon put it, its dissolution in the economic organism. This being the case, the question before us is not, as Mr. Donisthorpe supposes, what measures and means of interference we are justified in instituting, but which ones of those already existing we should first lop off." Tucker has lately been laying more emphasis on this view than on the more programme-like propositions cited by Eltzbacher, which date from the first six years of the publication of " Liberty." Indeed, I am sure I remember that somewhere lately, being challenged as to the feasibility of some of the latter, he admitted that those precise forms of action might perhaps not be adequate to bring the State to its end, and added that the end of the State is at present too remote to allow us to specify the processes by which it must ultimately be brought about. All this, however, does not mean that Tucker's faith in passive resistance as the most potent instrument discoverable both for propaganda and for the practical winning of liberty has grown weaker; he has no more given up this principle than he has given up the plan of propaganda by discussion.]

CHAPTER IX

TOLSTOI'S TEACHING

1.—GENERAL

I. Lef Nikolayevitch Tolstoi was born in 1828 at
Yasnaya Polyana, district of Krapivna, government of
Tula. From 1843 to 1846 he studied in Kazan at
first oriental languages, then jurisprudence; from
1847 to 1848, in St. Petersburg, jurisprudence.
After a lengthy stay at Yasnaya Polyana, he entered
an artillery regiment in the Caucasus, in 1851; he became an officer, remained in the Caucasus till 1853,
then served in the Crimean war, and left the army
in 1855.

Tolstoi now lived at first in St. Petersburg. In
1857 he took a lengthy tour in Germany, France,
Italy, and Switzerland. After his return he lived
mostly in Moscow till 1860. In 1860-1861 he traveled in Germany, France, Italy, England, and Belgium; in Brussels he made the acquaintance of
Proudhon.

Since 1861 Tolstoi has lived almost uninterruptedly
at Yasnaya Polyana, as at once agriculturist and
author.

Tolstoi has published numerous works; his works
up to 1878 are mostly stories, among which the two
novels "War and Peace" and "Anna Karenina" are
notable; his later works are mostly of a philosophical
nature.

2. Of special importance for Tolstoï's teaching about law, the State, and property are his works "My Confession" (1879), "The Gospel in Brief" (1880), "What I Believe" (1884) [also known in English as "My Religion"], "What Shall We Do Then?" (1885), "On Life" (1887), "The Kingdom of God is Within You; or, Christianity not a mystical doctrine, but a new life-conception" (1893).

3. Tolstoï does not call his teaching about law, the State, and property "Anarchism." He designates as "Anarchism" the teaching which sets up as its goal a life without government and wishes to see this realized by the application of force.*

2.—BASIS

According to Tolstoï our supreme law is love; from this he derives the commandment not to resist evil by force.

1. Tolstoï designates "Christianity"† as his basis; but by Christianity he means not the doctrine of one of the Christian churches, neither the Orthodox nor the Catholic nor that of any of the Protestant bodies,‡ but the pure teaching of Christ.§

"Strange as it may sound, the churches have always been not merely alien but downright hostile to the teaching of Christ, and they must needs be so. The churches are not, as many think, institutions that are based on a Christian origin and have only erred a little from the right way; the churches as such, as es-

---

*To. "Kingdom" pp. 244-5, 280, 315, 325.
† *Ib.* pp. 263, 285-6, To. "Gospel" p. 25, "Religion and Morality" p. 14.
‡ To. "What I Believe " p. 251.
§ To. "Gospel" pp. 13-14, 16-17.

sociations that assert their infallibility, are anti-Christian institutions. The Christian churches and Christianity have no fellowship except in name; nay, the two are utterly opposite and hostile elements. The churches are arrogance, violence, usurpation, rigidity, death; Christianity is humility, penitence, submissiveness, progress, life."* The church has " so transformed Christ's teaching to suit the world that there no longer resulted from it any demands, and that men could go on living as they had hitherto lived. The church yielded to the world, and, having yielded, followed it. The world did everything that it chose, and left the church to hobble after as well as it could with its teachings about the meaning of life. The world led its life, contrary to Christ's teaching in each and every point, and the church contrived subtleties to demonstrate that in living contrary to Christ's law men were living in harmony with it. And it ended in the world's beginning to lead a life worse than the life of the heathen, and the church's daring not only to justify such a life but even to assert that this was precisely what corresponded to Christ's teaching."†

Particularly different from Christ's teaching is the church " creed,"‡—that is, the totality of the utterly incomprehensible and therefore useless " dogmas."§
" Of a God, external creator, origin of all origins, we know nothing "; ‖ " God is the spirit in man,"¶ " his conscience,"** " the knowledge of life "; †† " every man recognizes in himself a free rational spirit inde-

*To. "Kingdom " p. 96-7.   † To. " What I Believe " pp. 247-8.
‡ To. " Reason and Dogma " p. 5.   § To. " What I Believe " p. 196.
‖ To. " Gospel " pp. 51, 29-30.   ¶ Ib. p. 47.
** To. " Patriotism " p. 118.   †† To. " Gospel " p. 29.

pendent of the flesh: this spirit is what we call God."*
Christ was a man,† "the son of an unknown father;
as he did not know his father, in his childhood he
called God his father"; ‡ and he was a son of God
as to his spirit, as every man is a son of God,§ he em-
bodied "Man confessing his sonship of God."‖
Those who "assert that Christ professed to redeem
with his blood mankind fallen by Adam, that God is
a trinity, that the Holy Spirit descended upon the
apostles and that it passes to the priest by the laying
on of hands, that seven mysteries are necessary to salvation, and so forth,"¶ "preach doctrines utterly alien
to Christ."** "Never did Christ with a single word
attest the personal resurrection and the immortality of
man beyond the grave,"†† which indeed is "a very
low and coarse idea"; ‡‡ the Ascension and the Resurrection are to be counted among "the most objection-
able miracles."§§

Tolstoi accepts Christ's teaching as valid not on the
ground of faith in a revelation, but solely for its
rationality. Faith in a revelation "was the main
reason why the teaching was at first misunderstood
and later mutilated outright."‖‖ Faith in Christ is
"not a trusting in something related to Christ, but the
knowledge of the truth."¶¶

"'There is a law of evolution, and therefore one
must live only his own personal life and leave the rest

---

* To. "Gospel" p. 50 ; To. " Religion and Morality " p. 27.
† To. " On Life " p. 214.   ‡ To. " Gospel " p. 31.
§ *Ib.* pp. 32 31, 40, 112.   ‖ To. " What I Believe " p. 164.
¶ To. " Gospel " p. 21.   ** *Ib.* p. 21.
†† To. " What I Believe " pp. 160, 174.   ‡‡ *Ib.* p. 166.
§§ To. " Confession " p. 92.   ‖‖ To. " Kingdom " pp. 75-7, 79.
¶¶ To. " What I Believe " pp. 195, 272, " Kingdom " pp. 72-3, " Gospel "
p. 5.

to the law of evolution,' is the last word of the refined culture of our day, and, at the same time, of that obscuration of consciousness to which the cultured classes are a prey."* But "human life, from getting up in the morning to going to bed at night, is an unbroken series of actions; man must daily choose out from hundreds of actions possible to him those actions which he will perform; therefore, man cannot live without something to guide the choice of his actions."† Now, reason alone can offer him this guide. "Reason is that law, recognized by man, according to which his life is to be accomplished."‡ "If there is no higher reason,—and such there is not, nor can anything prove its existence,—then my reason is the supreme judge of my life."§ "The ever-increasing subjugation "‖ "of the bestial personality to the rational consciousness "¶ is "the true life,"** is "life "†† as opposed to mere "existence."‡‡

"It used to be said, 'Do not argue, but believe in the duty that we have prescribed to you; reason will deceive you; faith alone will bring you the true happiness of life.' And the man exerted himself to believe, and he believed. But intercourse with other men showed him that in many cases these believed something quite different, and asserted that this other faith bestowed the highest happiness. It has become unavoidable to decide the question which of the many faiths is the right one; and only reason can decide this."§§ "If the Buddhist who has learned to know

* To. " Kingdom " p. 234.   † To. " On Life " p. 48.
‡ Ib. pp. 72, 66.   § To. "Confession " p. 54.
‖ To. " On Life " p. 101.   ¶ Ib. p. 100.   ** Ib. p. 100.
†† Ib. pp. 160, 101.   ‡‡ Ib. pp. 160, 101.   §§ Ib. pp. 262-3.

Islam remains a Buddhist, he is no longer a Buddhist in faith but in reason. As soon as another faith comes up before him, and with it the question whether to reject his faith or this other, reason alone can give him an answer. If he has learned to know Islam and has still remained a Buddhist, then rational conviction has taken the place of his former blind faith in Buddha."* " Man recognizes truth only by reason, not by faith."†

" The law of reason reveals itself to men gradually."‡ " Eighteen hundred years ago there appeared in the midst of the pagan Roman world a remarkable new teaching, which was not comparable to any that had preceded it, and which was ascribed to a man called Christ."§ This teaching contains " the very strictest, purest, and completest "‖ apprehension of the law of reason to which " the human mind has hitherto raised itself."¶ Christ's teaching is " reason itself"; ** it must be accepted by men because it alone gives those rules of life " without which no man ever has lived or can live, if he would live as a man,—that is, with reason."†† Man has, " on the basis of reason, no right to refuse allegiance to it."‡‡

2. Christ's teaching sets up love as the supreme law for us.

What is love? " What men who do not understand life call ' love ' is only the giving to certain conditions of their personal comfort a preference over any

---

* To. "On Life " p. 263.   † Ib. p. 263.
‡ To. " Religion and Morality " pp. 21-2.
§ To. " Kingdom " p. 71.   ‖ To. " Gospel " p. 25.
¶ Ib. p. 25.   ** To. " What I Believe " pp. 138-9
†† Ib. p. 268.   ‡‡ Ib. p. 148.

others. When the man who does not understand life
says that he loves his wife or child or friend, he means
by this only that his wife's, child's, or friend's presence
in his life heightens his personal comfort."*
"True love is always renunciation of one's personal
comfort "† for a neighbor's sake. True love "is a
condition of wishing well to all men, such as commonly characterizes children but is produced in grown
men only by self-abnegation."‡   "What living man
does not know the happy feeling, even if he has felt it
only once and in most cases only in earliest childhood,
of that emotion in which one wishes to love everybody,
neighbors and father and mother and brothers and
bad men and enemies and dog and horse and grass;
one wishes only one thing, that it were well with all,
that all were happy; and still more does one wish that
he were himself capable of making all happy, one
wishes he might give himself, give his whole life, that
all might be well off and enjoy themselves.   Just this,
this alone, is that love in which man's life consists."§
     True love is "an ideal of full, infinite, divine per-
fection."‖   "Divine perfection is the asymptote of
human life, toward which it constantly strives, to
which it draws nearer and nearer, but which can be
attained only at infinity."¶   "True life, according to
previous teachings, consists in the fulfilling of commandments, the fulfilling of the law; according to
Christ's teaching it consists in the maximum approach
to the divine perfection which has been exhibited, and
which is felt in himself by every man."**

---

* To. "On Life " pp. 159-60.   † *Ib.* p. 165.   ‡ *Ib.* p. 164.
§ *Ib.* pp. 170-71.   ‖ To. "Kingdom " p. 140.
¶ *Ib.* p. 139.   ** *Ib.* p. 138.

According to the teaching of Christ, love is our highest law. "The commandment of love is the expression of the inmost heart of the teaching."* There are "three conceptions of life, and only three: first the personal or bestial, second the social or heathenish,"† "third the Christian or divine."‡ The man of the bestial conception of life, "the savage, acknowledges life only in himself; the mainspring of his life is personal enjoyment. The heathenish, social man recognizes life no longer in himself alone, but in a community of persons, in the tribe, the family, the race, the State; the mainspring of his life is reputation. The man of the divine conception of life acknowledges life no longer in his person, nor yet in a community of persons, but in the prime source of eternal, never-dying life—in God; the mainspring of his life is love."§

That love is our supreme law according to Christ's teaching means nothing else than that it is such according to reason. As early as 1852 Tolstoi gives utterance to the thought "That love and beneficence are truth is the only truth on earth,"‖ and much later, in 1887, he calls love "man's only rational activity,"¶ that which "resolves all the contradictions of human life."** Love abolishes the insensate activity directed to the filling of the bottomless tub of our bestial personality,†† does away with the foolish fight between beings that strive after their own happiness,‡‡

---

* To. "Kingdom" p. 142, "What I Believe" p. 17.
† To. "Kingdom" p. 123.   ‡ To. "Religion and Morality" p. 12.
§ To. "Kingdom" pp. 124-5.   ‖ To. "Morning" pp. 70-71.
¶ To. "On Life" p. 148.   ** Ib. pp. 147, 148.
†† Ib. pp. 122, 133-5, 174, 176.   ‡‡ Ib. pp. 121, 174.

gives a meaning independent of space and time to life, which without it would flow off without meaning in the face of death.*

3. From the law of love Christ's teaching derives the commandment not to resist evil by force. " 'Resist not evil' means 'never resist the evil man ', that is, 'never do violence to another', that is, 'never commit an act that is contrary to love'."†

Christ expressly derived this commandment from the law of love. He gave numerous commandments, among which five in the Sermon on the Mount are notable; " these commandments do not constitute the teaching, they only form one of the numberless stages of approach to perfection "; ‡ they " are all negative, and only show "§ what " at mankind's present age "‖ we "have already the full possibility of not doing, along the road by which we are striving to reach perfection."¶ The first of the five commandments of the Sermon on the Mount reads " Keep the peace with all, and if the peace is broken use every effort to restore it "; ** the second says " Let the man take only one woman and the woman only one man, and let neither forsake the other under any pretext "; †† the third, " make no vows "; ‡‡ the fourth, " endure injury, return not evil for evil "; §§ the fifth, " break not the peace to benefit thy people."‖‖ Among these commandments the fourth is the most important; it is enunciated in the fifth chapter of Matthew, verses

---

*To. " On Life " pp. 26, 122-3, 196, 206.
† To. " What I Believe " p. 17. ‡ To. " Kingdom " p. 144.
§ Ib. pp. 142-3. ‖ Ib. p. 160. ¶ Ib. p. 144.
** To. " What I Believe " p. 122. †† Ib. p. 123.
‡‡ Ib. p. 123. §§ Ib. p. 123. ‖‖ Ib. p. 123.

38-9: "Ye have heard that it was said, Eye for eye, and tooth for tooth. But I say to you, Resist not evil."* Tolstoi tells how to him this passage "became the key of the whole."† "I needed only to take these words simply and downrightly, as they were spoken, and at once everything in Christ's whole teaching that had seemed confused to me, not only in the Sermon on the Mount but in the Gospels altogether, was comprehensible to me, and everything that had been contradictory agreed, and the main gist appeared no longer useless but a necessity; everything formed a whole, and the one confirmed the other past a doubt, like the pieces of a shattered column that one has rightly put together."‡ The principle of non-resistance binds together "the entire teaching into a whole; but only when it is no mere dictum but a peremptory rule, a law."§ "It is really the key that opens everything, but only when it goes into the inmost of the lock."‖

We must necessarily derive the commandment not to resist evil by force from the law of love. For this demands that either a sure, indisputable criterion of evil be found, or all violent resistance to evil be abandoned.¶ "Hitherto it has been the business now of the pope, now of an emperor or king, now of an assembly of elected representatives, now of the whole nation, to decide what was to be rated as an evil and combated by violent resistance. But there have always been men, both without and within the State, who have not acknowledged as binding upon them

---

* To. "What I Believe" p. 12.   † *Ib.* p. 12.   ‡ *Ib.* p. 15.
§ *Ib.* pp. 21-2.   ‖ *Ib.* p. 22.   ¶ To. "Kingdom" pp. 68-9.

either the decisions that were given out as divine commandments or the decisions of the men who were clothed with sanctity or the institutions that were supposed to represent the will of the people; men who regarded as good what to the powers that be appeared evil, and who, in opposition to the force of these powers, likewise made use of force. The men who were clothed with sanctity regarded as an evil what appeared good to the men and institutions that were clothed with secular authority, and the combat grew ever sharper and sharper. Thus it came to what it has come to to-day, to the complete obviousness of the fact that there is not and cannot be a generally binding external definition of evil."* But from this follows the necessity of accepting the solution given by Christ.†

According to Tolstoi, the precept of non-resistance must not be taken " as if it forbade every combat against evil."‡ It forbids only the combating of evil by force.§ But this it forbids in the broadest sense. It refers, therefore, not only to evil practised against ourselves, but also to evil practised against our fellowmen; ‖ when Peter cut off the ear of the high priest's servant, he was defending " not himself but his beloved divine Teacher, but Christ forbade him outright and said ' All who take the sword will perish by the sword.' "¶ Nor does the precept say that only a part of men are under obligation " to submit without a

* To. " Kingdom " pp. 269-70.   † Ib. p. 282.   ‡ Ib. p. 63.
§ To. " What I Believe " pp. 17, 20 ; " Kingdom " p. 268.   [Has Tolstoi compared in a Greek concordance the other occurrences of the word translated " resist "?]
‖ To. " Kingdom " pp. 49-50.   ¶ Ib. p. 50.

contest to what is prescribed to them by certain authorities,"* but it forbids " everybody, therefore even those in whom power is vested, and these especially, to use force in any case against anybody."†

3.—LAW

I. *For love's sake, particularly on the ground of the commandment not to resist evil by force, Tolstoi rejects law; not unconditionally, indeed, but as an institution for the more highly developed peoples of our time.* To be sure, he speaks only of enacted laws; but he means all law,‡ for he rejects on principle every norm based on the will of men,§ upheld by human force,‖ especially by courts,¶ capable of deviating from the moral law,** of being different in different territories,†† and of being at any time arbitrarily changed.‡‡

Perhaps once upon a time law was better than its non-existence. Law is " upheld by violence "; §§ on the other hand, it guards against violence of individuals to each other; ‖‖ perhaps there was once a time when the former violence was less than the latter .¶¶ Now, at any rate, this time is past for us; manners have grown milder; the men of our time " acknowledge the commandments of philanthropy, of sympathy with one's neighbor, and ask only the possibility of quiet, peaceable life."***

---

* To. " Kingdom " pp. 268-9.   † *Ib.* p. 269.
‡ [" He speaks only of the *Gesetz*, but he means all *Recht* "; see footnote on page 145 of the present book.]
§ To. " Kingdom " pp. 268, 300-301.   ‖ *Ib.* pp. 361-2.
¶ To. " What I Believe " pp. 29, 32.
** To. " Kingdom " pp. 361-2, 172.   †† *Ib.* p. 172.   ‡‡ *Ib.* p. 300.
§§ *Ib.* p. 361.   ‖‖ *Ib.* p. 241.   ¶¶ *Ib.* p. 240.   *** *Ib.* p. 256.

Law offends against the commandment not to resist evil by force.* Christ declared this. The words "Judge not, that ye be not judged " (Matt. 7.1), "Condemn not, and ye shall not be condemned " (Luke 6.37), "mean not only ' do not judge your neighbor in words,' but also ' do not condemn him by act; do not judge your neighbor according to your human laws by your courts.' "† Christ here speaks not merely " of every individual's personal relation to the court,"‡ but rejects "the administration of law itself."§ "He says, 'You believe that your laws better the evil; they only make it greater; there is only one way to check evil, and this consists in returning good for evil, doing good to all without discrimination.' "‖ And "my heart and my reason "¶ say to me the same as Christ says.

But this is not the only objection to be made against law. " Authority condemns in the rigid form of law only what public opinion has in most cases long since disallowed and condemned; withal, public opinion disallows and condemns all actions that are contrary to the moral law, but the law condemns and prosecutes only the actions included within certain quite definite and very narrow limits, and thereby, in a measure, justifies all similar actions that do not come within these limits. Ever since Moses's day public opinion has regarded selfishness, sensuality, and cruelty as evils and has condemned it; it has repudiated and condemned every form of selfishness, not only the appropriation of others' property by force,

---

* To. " What I Believe " p. 29.   † Ib. pp. 28-9.   ‡ Ib. p. 32.
§ Ib. p. 32.   ‖ Ib. pp. 45-6.   ¶ Ib. p. 29.

fraud, or guile, but exploitation altogether; it has condemned every sort of unchastity, be it with a concubine, a slave, a divorced woman, or even with one's own wife; it has condemned all cruelty, as it finds expression in the ill-treating, starving, and killing not only of men but of animals too. But the law prosecutes only particular forms of selfishness, like theft and fraud, and only particular forms of unchastity and cruelty, like marital infidelity, murder, and mayhem; therefore, in a measure, it permits all the forms of selfishness, unchastity, and cruelty that do not come under its narrow definitions inspired by a false conception."*

"The Jew could easily submit to his laws, for he did not doubt that they were written by God's finger; likewise the Roman, as he thought they originated from the nymph Egeria; and man in general so long as he regarded the princes who gave him laws as God's anointed, or believed that the legislating assemblies had the wish and the capacity to make the best laws."† But "as early as the time when Christianity made its appearance men were beginning to comprehend that human laws were written by men; that men, whatever outward splendor may enshroud them, cannot be infallible, and that erring men do not become infallible even by getting together and calling themselves 'Senate' or something else."‡ "We know how laws are made; we have all been behind the scenes; we all know that the laws are products of selfishness, deception, partisanship, that true justice does not and cannot dwell in them."§ Therefore

---

* To. " Kingdom " pp. 361-2.   † *Ib.* p. 172.   ‡ *Ib.* p. 268.   § *Ib.* p. 172.

"the recognition of any special laws is a sign of the crassest ignorance."*

II. *Love requires that in place of law it itself be the law for men.* From this it follows that instead of law Christ's commandments should be our rule of action.† But this is "the Kingdom of God on earth."‡ "When the day and the hour of the Kingdom of God appear, depends on men themselves alone."§ "Each must only begin to do what we must do, and cease to do what we must not do, and the near future will bring the promised Kingdom of God."‖ "If only everybody would bear witness, in the measure of his strength, to the truth that he knows, or at least not defend as truth the untruth in which he lives, then in this very year 1893 there would take place such changes toward the setting up of truth on earth as we dare not dream of for centuries to come."¶ "Only a little effort more, and the Galilean has won."**

The Kingdom of God is "not outside in the world, but in man's soul."†† "The Kingdom of God cometh not with outward show; neither will men say, 'Lo here!' or, 'There!' for, behold, the kingdom of God is within you (Luke 17.20)."‡‡ The Kingdom of God is nothing else than the following of Christ's commandments, especially the five commandments of the Sermon on the Mount,§§ which tell us how we must act in our present stage in order to correspond to the ideal of love as much as possible,‖‖ and which

* To. "What I Believe" p. 120.   † *Ib.* pp. 180, 235.
‡ *Ib.* pp. 235, 180.   § To. "Kingdom" p. 393, "What I Believe" p. 121.
‖ To. "Kingdom" pp. 393-4.   ¶ *Ib.* pp. 486-7.
** To. "Persecutions" p. 47.   †† To. "Gospel" p. 50.
‡‡ To. "Kingdom" p. 523.   §§ To. "What I Believe" p. 121.
‖‖ To. "Kingdom" pp. 142-3, 144.

command us to keep the peace and do everything for
its restoration when it is broken, to remain true to one
another as man and wife, to make no vows, to forgive
injury and not return evil for evil, and, finally, not to
break the peace with anybody for our people's sake.*

But what form will outward life take in the Kingdom of God? "The disciple of Christ will be poor;
that is, he will not live in the city but in the country;
he will not sit at home, but work in wood and field,
see the sunshine, the earth, the sky, and the beasts; he
will not worry over what he is to eat to tempt his
appetite, and what he can do to help his digestion,
but will be hungry three times a day; he will not roll
on soft cushions and think upon deliverance from in-
somnia, but sleep; he will be sick, suffer, and die like
all men—the poor who are sick and die seem to have
an easier time of it than the rich—"; † he "will live
in free fellowship with all men "; ‡ "the Kingdom of
God on earth is the peace of men with each other;
thus it appeared to the prophets, and thus it appears
to every human heart."§

4.—THE STATE

II. *Together with law Tolstoi necessarily has to reject also, for the more highly developed nations of our
time, the legal institution of the State.*

"Perhaps there was once a time when, in a low
state of morality with a general inclination of men to
mutual violence, the existence of a power limiting this
violence was advantageous—that is, in which the

---

*To. "What I Believe " pp. 122-3, 179, 124, 219-20 ; "Gospel " pp. 59-60 ;
" Kingdom " pp. 143-4.
† To. "What I Believe " p. 225.   ‡ *Ib.* p. 225.   § *Ib.* p. 121.

State violence was less than that of individuals against each other. But such an advantage of State violence over its non-existence could not last; the more the individuals' inclination to violence decreased and manners grew milder, and the more the governments degenerated by having nothing to check them, the more worthless did State violence grow. In this change— in the moral evolution of the masses on the one hand and the degeneration of the governments on the other —lies the whole history of the last two thousand years."* "I cannot prove either the general necessity of the State or its general perniciousness,"† "I know only that on the one hand the State is no longer necessary for me, and that on the other hand I can no longer do the things that are necessary for the existence of the State."‡

"Christianity in its true significance abolishes the State,"§ annihilates all government.‖ The State offends against love, particularly against the commandment not to resist evil by force.¶ And not only this; in founding a dominion** the State furthermore offends against the principle that for love "all men are God's sons and there is equality among them all";†† it is therefore to be rejected even aside from the violence on which it is based as a legal institution. "That the Christian teaching has an eye only to the redemption of the individual, and does not relate to public questions and State affairs, is a bold and unfounded assertion."‡‡ "To every honest, earnest

---

* To. "Kingdom" pp. 240-41.   † Ib. p. 336.   ‡ Ib. pp. 335-6.   § Ib. p. 332.
‖ Ib. p. 211.   ¶ To. "What I Believe" p. 21; "Persecutions" p. 46.
** To. "Kingdom" pp. 209-10.   †† Ib. pp. 167, 164.
‡‡ To. "What I Believe" p. 25.

man in our time it must be clear that true Christianity
—the doctrine of humility, forgiveness, love—is incompatible with the State and its haughtiness, its
deeds of violence, its capital punishments and wars."*
" The State is an idol"; † its objectionableness is independent of its form, be this " absolute monarchy, the
Convention, the Consulate, the empire of a first or
third Napoleon or yet of a Boulanger, constitutional
monarchy, the Commune, or the republic."‡—Tolstoi
carries this out into detail.

1. The State is the rule of the bad, raised to the
highest pitch.

The State is rule. Government in the State is " an
association of men who do violence to the rest."§
" All governments, the despotic and the liberal alike,
have in our time become what Herzen has so aptly
called a Jenghis Khan with telegraphs." ‖ The men
in whom the power is vested " practise violence not in
order to overcome evil, but solely for their advantage
or from caprice; and the other men submit to the violence not because they believe that it is practised for
their good,—that is, in order to liberate them from
evil,—but only because they cannot free themselves
from it."¶ " If Nice is united with France, Lorraine
with Germany, Bohemia with Austria, if Poland is
divided, if both Ireland and India are subjected to the
English dominion, if people fight with China, kill the
Africans, expel the Chinese from America, and persecute the Jews in Russia, it is not because this is good

---

* To. "Kingdom " p. 332. † To. " What I Believe " p. 50.
‡ To. "Kingdom " pp. 429-30, 244, § Ib. pp. 209-10.
‖ Ib. p. 274. ¶ Ib. pp. 271-2.

or necessary or useful for men and the opposite would be evil, but only because it so pleases those in whom the power is vested."[*]

The State is the rule of the bad.[†] " ' If the State power were to be annihilated, the wicked would rule over the less wicked,' say the defenders of State rule."[‡] But has the power, when it has passed from some men to some others in the State, really always come to the better men? " When Louis the Sixteenth, Robespierre, Napoleon, came to power, who ruled then, the better or the worse? When did the better rule, when the power was vested in the Versaillese or in the Communards, when Charles the First or Cromwell stood at the head of the government? When Peter the Third was czar, and then when after his murder the authority of czar was exercised in one part of Russia by Catharine and in another by Pugatcheff, who was wicked then and who was good? All men who find themselves in power assert that their power is necessary in order that the wicked may not do violence to the good, and regard it as self-evident that they are the good and are giving the rest of the good protection against the bad."[§] But in reality those who grasp and hold the power cannot possibly be the better.[||] " In order to obtain and retain power, one must love it. But the effort after power is not apt to be coupled with goodness, but with the opposite qualities, pride, craft, and cruelty. Without exalting self and abasing others, without hypocrisy, lying, prisons, fortresses, penalties, killing, no power can

---

* To. "Kingdom " p. 271.   † Ib. pp. 341, 339.   ‡ Ib. p. 340.
§ Ib. p. 340. || Ib. p. 339.

arise or hold its own."*   " It is downright ridiculous
to speak of Christians in power."†   To this it is to be
added " that the possession of power depraves men."‡
" The men who have the power cannot but misuse it;
they must infallibly be unsettled by such frightful authority."§   " However many means men have invented to hinder the possessors of power from subordinating the welfare of the whole to their own advantage, hitherto not one of these means has worked.
Everybody knows that those in whose hands is the
power—be they emperors, ministers, chiefs of police,
or common policemen—are, just because the power is
in their hands, more inclined to immorality, to the
subordinating of the general welfare to their advantage, than those who have no power; nor can it
be otherwise."‖

The State is the rule of the bad, raised to the highest pitch.   We shall always find " that the scheming
of the possessors of authority—nay, their unconscious
effort—is directed toward weakening the victims of
their authority as much as possible; for, the weaker
the victim is, the more easily can he be held down."¶
" To-day there is only one sphere of human activity
left that has not been conquered by the authority of
government: the sphere of the family, of housekeep-
ing, private life, labor.   And even this sphere, thanks
to the fighting of the Communists and Socialists, the
governments are already beginning to invade, so that
soon, if the reformers have their way, work and rest,

---

* To. " Kingdom " pp. 339-40.
† Ib. p. 342.   ‡ Ib. p. 243.   § To. " Patriotism " p. 91.
‖ To. " Kingdom " p. 23).   ¶ Ib. p. 243.

housing, clothing, and food, will likewise be fixed and regulated by the governments."* "The most fearful band of robbers is not so horrible as a State organization. Every robber chief is at any rate limited by the fact that the men who make up his band retain at least a part of human liberty, and can refuse to commit acts which are repugnant to their consciences."† But in the State there is no such limit; " no crime is so horrible that it will not be committed by the officials and the army at the will of him—Boulanger, Pugatcheff, Napoleon—who accidentally stands at the head."‡

2. The rule in the State is based on physical force.

Every government has for its prop the fact that there are in the State armed men who are ready to execute the government's will by physical force, a class "educated to kill those whose killing the authorities command."§ Such men are the police‖ and especially the army.¶ The army is nothing else than a collectivity of " disciplined murderers ",** its training is "instruction in murdering ",†† its victories are " deeds of murder."‡‡ " The army has always formed the basis of power, and does to this day. The power is always in the hands of those who command the army, and, from the Roman Cæsars to the Russian and German emperors, all possessors of power have always cared first and foremost for their armies."§§

In the first place, the army upholds the govern-

---

* To. " Kingdom " p. 281.   † Ib. p. 442.   ‡ Ib. p. 442.
§ To. " Persecutions " p. 41.   ‖ To. " Kingdom " p. 327.
¶ Ib. p. 238.   ** To. " Patriotism " p. 120.
†† To. " Kingdom " p. 443.   ‡‡ To. " Patriotism " p. 119.
§§ To. " Kingdom " p. 238.

ment's rule against external assaults. It protects it against having the rule taken from it by another government.* War is nothing but a contest of two or more governments for the rule over their subjects. It is "impossible to establish international peace in a rational way, by treaty or arbitration, so long as the insensate and pernicious subjection of nations to governments continues to exist."† In consequence of this importance of armies " every State is compelled to increase its army to face the others, and this increase has the effect of a contagion, as Montesquieu observed a hundred and fifty years since."‡

But, if one thinks armies are kept by governments only for external defence, he forgets " that governments need armies particularly to protect them against their oppressed and enslaved subjects."§ " In the German Reichstag lately, in reply to the question why money was needed in order to increase the pay of the petty officers, the chancellor made the direct statement that reliable petty officers were necessary for the combating of Socialism. Caprivi merely said out loud what everybody knows, carefully as it is concealed from the peoples,—the reason why the French kings and the popes kept Swiss and Scots, why in Russia the recruits are so introduced that the interior regiments get their contingents from the frontiers and the frontier regiments theirs from the interior. Caprivi told, by accident, what everybody knows or at least feels,—to wit, that the existing order exists not because it must exist or because the people wills its

---

*To. " Kingdom " pp. 248-9. † To. " Patriotism " p. 91.
‡ To. " Kingdom " p. 249. § Ib. p. 245.

existence, but because the government's force, the army with its bribed petty-officers and officers and generals, keeps it up."*

3. The rule in the State is based on the physical force of the ruled.

It is peculiar to government that it demands from the citizens the very force on which it is based, and that consequently in the State " all the citizens are their own oppressors."† The government demands from the citizens both force and the supporting of force. Here belongs the obligation, general in Russia, to take an oath at the czar's accession to the throne, for by this oath one vows obedience to the authorities,—that is, to men who are devoted to violence; likewise the obligation to pay taxes, for the taxes are used for works of violence, and the compulsory use of passports, for by taking out a passport one acknowledges his dependence on the State's institution of violence; withal the obligation to testify in court and to take part in the court as juryman, for every court is the fulfilment of the commandment of revenge; furthermore, the obligation to police service which in Russia rests upon all the country people, for this service demands that we do violence to our brother and torment him; and above all the general obligation to military service,—that is, the obligation to be executioners and to prepare ourselves for service as executioners.‡ The unchristianness of the State comes to light most plainly in the general obligation to military service: " every man has to take in hand

* To. " Kingdom " p. 246-7.   † Ib. pp. 250, 423-4.
‡ Ib. pp. 314-28.

deadly weapons, a gun, a knife; and, if he does not have to kill, at least he does have to load the gun and sharpen the knife,—that is, be ready for killing."* But how comes it that the citizens fulfil these demands of the government, though the government is based on this very fulfilment, and so mutually oppress each other? This is possible only by "a highly artificial organization, created with the help of scientific progress, in which all men are bewitched into a circle of violence from which they cannot free themselves. At present this circle consists of four means of influence; they are all connected and hold each other, like the links of a chain."† The first means is "what is best described as the hypnotization of the people."‡ This hypnotization leads men to "the erroneous opinion that the existing order is unchangeable and must be upheld, while in reality it is unchangeable only by its being upheld."§ The hypnotization is accomplished "by fomenting the two forms of superstition called religion and patriotism"; ‖ it "begins its influence even in childhood, and continues it till death."¶ With reference to this hypnotization one may say that State authority is based on the fraudulent misleading of public opinion.** The second means consists in "bribery; that is, in taking from the laboring populace its wealth, by money taxes, and dividing this among the officials, who, for this pay, must maintain and strengthen the enslavement of the people."†† The officials "more or less believe in the

* To. "What I Believe" pp. 26-7.   † To. "Kingdom" p. 274.
‡ Ib. p. 276.   § Ib. p. 422.   ‖ Ib. p. 277.   ¶ Ib. p. 276.
** To. "Patriotism" pp. 40-41, 100-102 ; "Kingdom" pp. 429-32.
†† To. "Kingdom" p. 275.

unchangeability of the existing order, mainly because it benefits them."* With reference to this bribery one may say that State authority is based on the selfishness of those to whom it guarantees profitable positions.† The third means is "intimidation. It consists in setting down the present State order—of whatever sort, be it a free republican order or be it the most grossly despotic—as something sacred and unchangeable, and imposing the most frightful penalties upon every attempt to change it."‡ Finally, the fourth means is to "separate a certain part of all the men whom they have stupefied and bewitched by the three first means, and subject these men to special stronger forms of stupefaction and bestialization, so that they become will-less tools of every brutality and cruelty that the government sees fit to resolve upon."§ This is done in the army, to which, at present, all young men belong by virtue of the general obligation to military service.‖ "With this the circle of violence is made complete. Intimidation, bribery, hypnosis, bring men to enlist as soldiers. The soldiers, in turn, afford the possibility of punishing men, plundering them in order to bribe officials with the money, hypnotizing them, and thus bringing them into the ranks of the very soldiers on whom the power for all this is based.¶"

II. *Love requires that a social life based solely on its commandments take the place of the State.* "To-day every man who thinks, however little, sees the impossibility of keeping on with the life hitherto lived,

*To. "Kingdom " p. 422.   † *Ib.* pp. 275-6, 420-22, 444-5.
‡ *Ib.* p. 278.   § *Ib.* p. 278.   ‖ *Ib.* p. 279.   ¶ *Ib.* p. 279.

and the necessity of determining new forms of life."*
" The Christian humanity of our time must unconditionally renounce the heathen forms of life that it
condemns, and set up a new life on the Christian bases
that it recognizes."†

1. Even after the State is done away, men are to
live in societies. But what is to hold them together
in these societies?

Not a promise, at any rate. Christ commands us
to make " no vows,"‡ to " promise men nothing."§
" The Christian cannot promise that he will do or not
do a particular thing at a particular hour, because he
cannot know what the law of love, which it is the
meaning of his life to obey, will demand of him at
that hour."‖ And still less can he "give his word to
fulfil somebody's will, without knowing what the substance of this will is to be ";¶ by the mere fact of
such a promise he would " make it manifest that the
inward divine law is no longer the sole law of his
life ";** " one cannot serve two masters."††

Men are to be held together in societies in future
by the mental influence which the men who have made
progress in knowledge exert upon the less advanced.
" Mental influence is such a way of working upon a
man that by it his wishes change and coincide with
what is wanted of him; the man who yields to a
mental influence acts according to his own wishes."‡‡
Now, the force "by which men can live in societies "§§
is found in the mental influence which the men who

---

*To. " Kingdom " p. 511 ; " Patriotism " p. 117.
†To. " Kingdom " p. 189.   ‡To. " What I Believe " p. 123.
§To. " Kingdom " pp. 143-4.   ‖ *Ib.* pp. 300-301.   ¶ *Ib.* p. 300.
** *Ib.* p. 301.   †† *Ib.* p. 301.   ‡‡ *Ib.* p. 236.   §§ *Ib.* p. 461.

have made progress in knowledge exert upon the less advanced, in the " characteristic of little-thinking men, that they subordinate themselves to the directions of those who stand on a higher level of knowledge."* In consequence of this characteristic " a body of men put themselves under the same rational principles, the minority consciously, because the principles agree with the demands of their reason, and the majority unconsciously, because the principles have become public opinion."† " In this subordination there is nothing irrational or self-contradictory."‡

2. But in the future societary condition how shall the functions which the State at present performs be performed? Here people usually have three things in mind.§

First, protection against the bad men in our midst.|| " But who are the bad men among us? If there once were such men three or four centuries ago, when people still paraded warlike arts and equipments and looked upon killing as a brilliant deed, they are gone to-day anyhow; nobody any longer carries weapons, everybody acknowledges the commands of philanthropy. But, if by the men from whom the State must protect us we mean the criminals, then we know that they are not special creatures like the wolf among the sheep, but just such men as all of us, who like committing crimes as little as we do; we know that the activity of governments with their cruel forms of punishment, which do not correspond to the present stage of morality, their prisons, tortures, gal-

---

* To. "Kingdom " p. 461.   † Ib. pp. 461-2.   ‡ Ib. p. 461.
§ Ib. p. 255. || Ib. p. 255.

lows, guillotines, contributes more to the barbarizing
of the people than to their culture, and hence rather
to the multiplication than to the diminution of such
criminals."* If we are Christians and start from the
principle that " what our life exists for is the serving
of others, then no one will be foolish enough to rob
men that serve him of their means of support or to
kill them. Miklucho-Maclay settled among the wild-
est so-called ' savages', and they not only left him
alive but loved him and submitted to his authority,
solely because he did not fear them, asked nothing of
them, and did them good."†

Secondly, the question is asked how in the future
societary condition we can find protection against external enemies.‡ But we do know " that the nations
of Europe profess the principles of liberty and frater-
nity, and therefore need no protection against each
other; but, if it were a protection against the bar-
barians that was meant, a thousandth part of the
armies that are now kept up would suffice. State
authority not merely leaves in existence the danger of
hostile attacks, but even itself provokes this danger."§
But, " if there existed a community of Christians who
did evil to nobody and gave to others all the superfluous products of their labor, then no enemy, neither
the German nor the Turk nor the savage, would kill
or vex such men; all one could do would be to take
from them what they were ready to give voluntarily
without distinguishing between Russians, Germans,

---

* To. " Kingdom " pp. 255-6.
† To. " What I Believe " p. 290.
‡ To. " Kingdom " pp. 255, 258.   § *Ib.* p. 258.

Turks, and savages."*

Thirdly, the question is asked how in the future societary condition institutions for education, popular culture, religion, commerce, etc. are to be possible.†

"Perhaps there was once a time when men lived so far apart, when the means for coming together and exchanging thoughts were so undeveloped, that people could not, without a State centre, discuss and agree on any matter either of trade and economy or of culture. But to-day this separation no longer exists; the means of intercourse have developed extraordinarily; for the forming of societies, associations, corporations, for the gathering of congresses and the creation of economic and political institutions, governments are not needed; nay, in most cases they are rather a hindrance than a help toward the attainment of such ends."‡

3. But what form will men's life together in the future societary condition take in detail? "The future will be as circumstances and men shall make it."§ We are not at this moment able to get perfectly clear ideas of it.‖

"Men say, 'What will the new orders be like, that are to take the place of the present ones? So long as we do not know what form our life will take in future, we will not go forward, we will not stir from this spot.'"¶ "If Columbus had gone to making such observations, he would never have weighed anchor. It was insanity to steer across an ocean that no man had ever yet sailed upon toward a land whose exist-

---

* To. "What I Believe" p. 289.   † To. "Kingdom" pp. 255, 257.
‡ Ib. p. 257.   § Ib. p. 510.
‖ To. "Persecutions" pp. 46-7.   ¶ To. "Kingdom" p. 372.

ence was a question. With this insanity, he discovered the New World. It would certainly be more convenient if nations had nothing to do but move out of one ready-furnished mansion into another and a better; only, by bad luck, there is nobody there to furnish the new quarters."*

But what disquiets men in their imagining of the future is " less the question ' What will be? ' They are tormented by the question ' How are we to live without all the familiar conditions of our existence, that are called science, art, civilization, culture? ' "†
" But all these, bear in mind, are only forms in which truth appears. The change that lies before us will be an approach to the truth and its realization. How can the forms in which truth appears be brought to naught by an approach to the truth? They will be made different, better, higher, but by no means will they be brought to naught. Only that which was false in the forms of its appearance hitherto will be brought to naught; what was genuine will but unfold itself the more splendidly."‡

" If the individual man's life were completely known to him when he passes from one stage of maturity to another, he would have no reason for living. So it is with the life of mankind too; if at its entrance upon a new stage of growth a programme lay before it already drawn up, this would be the surest sign that it was not alive, not progressing, but that it was sticking at one point. The details of a new order of life cannot be known to us, they have to be worked out by us ourselves. Life consists only in learning to know the

---

*To. " Kingdom " p. 510.   †Ib. p. 512.   ‡Ib. pp. 513-14.

unknown, and putting our action in harmony with the
new knowledge. In this consists the life of the individual, in this the life of human societies and of
humanity."*

5.—PROPERTY

I. *Together with law Tolstoi necessarily has to
reject also, for the more highly developed nations of
our time, the legal institution of property.*

Perhaps there was once a time when the violence
necessary to secure the individual in the possession of
a piece of goods against all others was less than the
violence which would have been practised in a general
fight for the possession of the goods, so that the existence of property was better than its non-existence.
But at any rate this time is past, the existing order
has "lived out its time"; † among the men of to-day
no wild fight for the possession of goods would break
out even if there were no property; they all "profess
allegiance to the commands of philanthropy," ‡ each
of them "knows that all men have equal rights in the
goods of the world,"§ and already we see "many a
rich man renounce his inheritance from a specially
delicate sense of germinant public opinion."‖

Property offends against love, especially against the
commandment not to resist evil by force.¶ But not
only this; in founding a dominion of possessors over
non-possessors it also offends against the principle that
for love "all men are God's sons and there is equality

---

*To. "Kingdom" pp. 372-3.   † *Ib.* p. 518.
‡ *Ib.* p. 256.   § *Ib.* p. 164.   ‖ *Ib.* p. 376.
¶ To. "What I Believe" p. 21 ; "What Shall We Do" pp. 157-8.

among them all "; * and it is therefore to be rejected, even aside from the violence on which it is based as a legal institution. The rich are under "guilt by the very fact that they are rich."† It is "a crime "‡ that tens of thousands of "hungry, cold, deeply degraded human beings are living in Moscow, while I with a few thousand others have tenderloin and sturgeon for dinner and cover horses and floors with blankets and carpets."§ I shall be "an accomplice in this unending and uninterrupted crime so long as I still have a superfluous bit of bread while another has no bread at all, or still possess two garments while another does not possess even one." ‖—Tolstoi carries this out into detail.

1. Property means the dominion of the possessors over the non-possessors.

Property is the exclusive right to use some things, whether one actually uses them or not.¶ "Many of the men who called me their horse," Tolstoi makes the horse Linen-Measurer say, "did not ride me; quite different men rode me. Nor did they feed me; quite different men fed me. Nor was it those who called me their horse that did me kindnesses, but coachmen, veterinary surgeons, strangers altogether. Later, when the circle of my observations grew wider, I convinced myself that the idea 'mine,' which has no other basis than men's low and bestial propensity which they call 'sense of ownership' or 'right of property,' finds application not only with respect to us horses.

---

*To. "Kingdom" pp. 167, 164.   † *Ib.* p. 273.
‡ To. "What Shall We Do" p. 19.   § *Ib.* pp. 18-19.   ‖ *Ib.* p. 19.
¶ To. "Money" p. 18.

A man says ' this house is mine ' and never lives in it, he only attends to the building and repair of the house. A merchant says ' my store, my dry-goods store,' and his clothing is not of the best fabrics he has in his store. There are men who call a piece of land ' mine ' and have never seen this piece of land nor set foot on it. What men aim at in life is not to do what they think good, but to call as many things as possible ' mine.' "*

But the significance of property consists in the fact that the poor man who has no property is dependent on the rich man who has property; in order to come by the things which he needs for his living, but which belong to another, he must do what this other wills— in particular, he must work for him. Thus property divides men into " two castes, an oppressed laboring caste that famishes and suffers and an idle oppressing caste that enjoys and lives in superfluity."† " We are all brothers, and yet every morning my brother or my sister carries out my dishes. We are all brothers, but every morning I have to have my cigar, my sugar, my mirror, and other such things, in whose production healthy brothers and sisters, people like me, have sacrificed and are sacrificing their health."‡ " I spend my whole life in the following way: I eat, talk, and listen; eat, write, and read—that is, talk and listen again; eat and play; eat, talk, and listen again; eat and go to bed; and so it goes on, one day like another. I cannot do, do not know how to do, anything beyond this. And, that I may be able to

---

* To. "Linen-Measurer " pp. 602-3.
† To. "Kingdom " p. 164.   ‡ *Ib.* p. 168.

do this, the porter, the farmer, the cook, the cook's maid, the lackey, the coachman, the laundress, must work from morning till night, not to speak of the work of other men which is necessary in order that those coachmen, cooks, lackeys, and so on may have all that they need when they work for me—the axes, barrels, brushes, dishes, furniture, likewise the wax, the blacking, the kerosene, the hay, the wood, the beef. All of them have to work day by day, early and late, that I may be able to talk, eat, and sleep."[*]

This significance of property makes itself especially felt in the case of the things that are necessary for the producing of other things, and so most notably in the case of land and tools.[†] "There can be no farmer without land that he tills, without scythes, wagons, and horses; no shoemaker is possible without a house built on the earth, without water, air, and tools"; [‡] but property means that in many cases "the farmer possesess no land, no horses, no scythe, the shoemaker no house, no water, no awl: that somebody is keeping these things back from them."[§] This leads to the consequence "that for a large fraction of the workers the natural conditions of production are deranged, that this fraction is necessitated to use other people's stock,"[||] and may by the owner of the stock be compelled "to work not on their own account, but for an employer."[¶] Consequently the workman works "not for himself, to suit his own wish, but under compulsion, to suit the whim of some idle persons who live in superfluity, for the benefit of some rich man, the pro-

---

[*] To. "What Shall We Do" p. 143.   [†] To. "Money" p. 18.
[‡] Ib. p. 13.   [§] Ib. p. 13.   [||] Ib. p. 16.   [¶] Ib. p. 15.

prietor of a factory or other industrial plant."*
Thus property means the exploitation of the laborer
by those to whom the land and tools belong; it means
"that the products of human labor pass more and
more out of the hands of the laboring masses into the
hands of the unlaboring."†
Furthermore, the significance of property as making
the poor dependent on the rich becomes especially
prominent in the case of money.   " Money is a value
that remains always equal, that always ranks as correct and legal."‡   Consequently, as the saying is,
" he who has money has in his pocket those who have
none."§   " Money is a new form of slavery, distinguished from the old solely by its impersonality, by
the lack of any human relation between the master
and the slave "; ‖ for " the essence of all slavery consists in drawing the benefit of another's labor-force by
compulsion, and it is quite immaterial whether the
drawing of this benefit is founded upon property in
the slave or upon property in money which is indispensable to the other man."¶   " Now, honestly, of
what sort is my money, and how have I come by it?
I got part for the land that I inherited from my
father.   The peasant sold his last sheep, his last cow,
to pay me this money.   Another part of my assets
consists of the sums which I have received for my
literary productions, my books.   If my books are
harmful, then by them I have seduced the purchasers
to evil and have acquired the money by bad means.

---

* To. " Kingdom " p. 166.   † To. " What Shall We Do " p. 139.
‡ Ib. p. 152.   § To. " Money " p. 6.
‖ To. " What Shall We Do " pp. 151-2.   ¶ Ib. p. 160.

If, on the contrary, my books are useful to people, the
case is still worse; I have not given them without
ceremony to those who had a use for them, but have
said ' Give me seventeen rubles and you shall have
them,' and, as in the other case the peasant sold his
last sheep, so here the poor student or teacher, and
many another poor person, have denied themselves the
plainest necessities to give me the money. And thus
I have piled up a quantity of such money, and what
do I do with it? I bring it to the city and give it to
the poor here on condition that they satisfy all my
whims, that they come after me into the city to clean
the sidewalks for me, and to make me lamps, shoes,
and so forth, in the factories. With my money I take
all their products to myself, and I take pains to give
them as little as possible and get from them as much
as possible for it. And then all at once, quite unexpectedly, I begin to distribute to the poor this same
money gratis—not to all, but arbitrarily to any whom
I happen to take up at random "; * that is, I take
from the poor thousands of rubles with one hand, and
with the other I distribute to some of them a few
kopeks.†

2. The dominion which property involves, of possessors over non-possessors, is based on physical force.

" If the vast wealth that the laborers have piled up
ranks not as the property of all, but only as that of
an elect few,—if the power of raising taxes from labor
and using them at pleasure is reserved to some men,—
this is not based on the fact that the people want to
have it so or that by nature it must be so, but on the

---

* To. " What Shall We Do " pp. 134-5.   † *Ib.* p. 135.

fact that the ruling classes see their advantage in it
and determine it so by virtue of their power over
men's bodies "; * it is based on " violence and slaying
and the threat thereof."† " If men hand over the
greatest part of the product of their labor to the
capitalist or landlord, though they, as do all laborers
now, hold this to be unjust,"‡ they do it " only because they know they will be beaten and killed if they
do not."§ "One may even say outright that in our
society, in which to every well-to-do man living an
aristocratic life there are ten weary, ravenous, envious
laborers, probably pining away with wife and children
too, all the privileges of the rich, all their luxury
and their abundance, are acquired and secured only
by chastisement, imprisonment, and capital
punishment." ||

Property is upheld by the police¶ and the army.**
" We may act as if we did not see the policeman
walking up and down before the window with loaded
revolver to protect us while we eat a savory meal or
look at a new play, and as if we had no inkling of the
soldiers who are every moment ready to go with rifle
and cartridges where any one tries to infringe on our
property. Yet we well know, if we can finish our
meal and see the new play in peace, if we can drive
out or hunt or attend a festival or a race undisturbed,
we have to thank for this only the policeman's bullet
and the soldier's weapon, which are ready to pierce
the poor victim of hunger who looks upon our enjoyments from his corner with grumbling stomach, and

---

* To. " Kingdom " pp. 247-8. † Ib. p. 406. ‡ Ib. p. 407.
§ Ib. p. 407. || Ib. p. 409. ¶ Ib. p. 492. ** Ib. pp. 247, 447.

who would at once disturb them if the policeman with his revolver went away, or if in the barracks there were no longer any soldiers standing ready to appear at our first call."*

3. The dominion which property involves, of the possessors over the non-possessors, is based on the physical force of the ruled.

Those very men of the non-possessing classes who through property are dependent on the possessing classes must do police duty, serve in the army, pay the taxes out of which police and army are kept up, and in these and other ways either themselves exercise or at least support the physical force by which property is upheld.† "If there did not exist these men who are ready to discipline or kill any one whatever at the word of command, no one would dare assert what the non-laboring landlords now do all of them so confidently assert,—that the soil which surrounds the peasants who die off for lack of land is the property of a man who does not work on it"; ‡ it would "not come into the head of the lord of the manor to take from the peasants a forest that has grown up under their eyes"; § nor would any one say "that the stores of grain accumulated by fraud in the midst of a starving population must remain unscathed that the merchant may have his profit."‖

II. *Love requires that a distribution based solely on its commandments take the place of property.* "The impossibility of continuing the life that has hitherto been led, and the necessity of determining new forms

---

* To. "Kingdom" pp. 492-3.   † *Ib.* pp. 314-28.
‡ *Ib.* pp. 424-5.   § *Ib.* p. 425.   ‖ *Ib.* p. 425.

of life,"* relate to the distribution of goods as well as
to other things. "The abolition of property,"† and
its replacement by a new kind of distribution of
goods, is one of the " questions now in order."‡

According to the law of love, every man who works
as he has strength should have so much—but only so
much—as he needs.

1. That every man who works as he has strength
should have so much as he needs and no more is a
corollary from two precepts which follow from the law
of love.

The first of these precepts says, Man shall " ask no
work from others, but himself devote his whole life to
work for others. ' Man lives not to be served but to
serve.' "§ Therefore, in particular, he is not to keep
accounts with others about his work, or think that he
" has the more of a living to claim, the greater or
more useful his quantum of work done is."‖ Following this precept provides every man with what he
needs. This is true primarily of the healthy adult.
" If a man works, his work feeds him. If another
makes use of this man's work for himself, he will feed
him for the very reason that he is making use of his
work."¶ Man assures himself of a living " not by
taking it away from others, but by making himself
useful and necessary to others. The more necessary
he is to others, the more assured is his existence."**
But the following of the precept to serve others also
provides the sick, the aged, and children with their

---

* To. " Kingdom " p. 511. † To. " What I Believe " p. 249.
‡ *Ib.* p. 249. § *Ib.* p. 228. ‖ *Ib.* pp. 227-8.
¶ *Ib.* p. 227. ** *Ib.* p. 229.

living. Men " do not stop feeding an animal when it falls sick; they do not even kill an old horse, but give it work appropriate to its strength; they bring up whole families of little lambs, pigs, and puppies, because they expect benefit from them. How, then, should they not support the sick man who is necessary to them? How should they not find appropriate work for old and young, and bring up human beings who will in turn work for them?"*

The second precept that follows from the law of love, and of which a corollary is that every man who works as he has strength should have as much as he needs and no more, bids us "Share what you have with the poor; gather no riches."† "To the question of his hearers, what they were to do, John the Baptist gave the short, clear, simple answer, ' He who hath two coats, let him share with him who hath none; and he who hath food let him do likewise ' (Luke 3.10-11). And Christ too made the same declaration several times, only still more unambiguously and clearly. He said, ' Blessed are the poor, woe to the rich.' He said that one could not serve God and Mammon at once. He not only forbade his disciples to take money, but also to have two garments. He told the rich young man that because he was rich he could not enter into the Kingdom of God, and that a camel should sooner go through a needle's eye than a rich man come into heaven. He said that he who did not forsake everything—house, children, lands—to follow him could not be his disciple. He told his hearers the parable of the rich man who did

---

* To. " What I Believe " p. 230.   † To. " Kingdom " p. 520.

nothing bad except that he—like our rich men—
clothed himself in costly apparel and fed himself on
savory food and drink, and who plunged his soul into
perdition by this alone, and of the poor Lazarus who
did nothing good and who entered into the Kingdom
of Heaven only because he was a beggar."*

2. But what form can such a distribution of goods
take in detail?

This is best shown us by "the Russian colonists.
These colonists arrive on the soil, settle, and begin to
work, and no one of them takes it into his head that
any one who does not begin to make use of the land
can have any right to it; on the contrary, the colonists regard the ground *a priori* as common property, and consider it altogether justifiable that
everybody plows and reaps where he chooses. For
working the fields, for starting gardens, and for building houses, they procure implements; and here too it
does not suggest itself to them that these could of
themselves produce any income—on the contrary, the
colonists look upon any profit from the means of
labor, any interest for grain lent, etc., as an injustice.
They work on masterless land with their own means
or with means borrowed free of interest, either each
for himself or all together on joint account."†

" In talking of such fellowship I am not setting
forth fancies, but only describing what has gone on at
all times, what is even at present taking place not
only among the Russian colonists but everywhere
where man's natural condition is not yet deranged by
some circumstances or other. I am describing what

---

* To. " What Shall We Do " pp. 157-8.   † To. " Money " p. 10.

seems to everybody natural and rational. The men settle on the soil and go each one to work, make their implements, and do their labor. If they think it advantageous to work jointly, they form a labor company."* But, in individual business as well as in collective industry, " neither the water nor the ground nor the garments nor the plow can belong to anybody save him who drinks the water, wears the garments, and uses the plow; for all these things are necessary only to him who puts them to use."† One can call " only his labor his own ";‡ by it one has as much as one needs.§

6.—REALIZATION

The way in which the change required by love is to take place, according to Tolstoi, is that those men who have learned to know the truth are to convince as many others as possible how necessary the change is for love's sake, and that they, with the help of the refusal of obedience, are to abolish law, the State, and property, and bring about the new condition.

I. The prime necessity is that the men who have learned to know the truth should convince as many others as possible that love demands the change.

1. " That an order of life corresponding to our knowledge may take the place of the order contrary to it, the present antiquated public opinion must first be replaced by a new and living one."‖

It is not deeds of all sorts that bring to pass the grandest and most significant changes in the life of

---

* To. " Money " p. 11.   † *Ib.* pp. 11-12.
‡ " Kernel " p.89.   § *Ib.* p. 89.   ‖ " Patriotism " p. 116.

humanity, " neither the fitting out of armies a million strong nor the construction of roads and engines, neither the organization of expositions nor the formation of trade-unions, neither revolutions, barricades, and explosions nor inventions in aerial navigation—but the changes of public opinion, and these alone."* Liberation is possible only " by a change in our conception of life "; † " everything depends on the force with which each individual man becomes conscious of Christian truth"; ‡ " know the truth and the truth shall make you free."§   Our liberation must necessarily take place by " the Christian's recognizing the law of love, which his Master has revealed to him, as entirely sufficient for all human relations, and his perceiving the superfluousness and illegitimateness of all violence."‖

The bringing about of this revolution in public opinion is in the hands of the men who have learned to know the truth.¶   " A public opinion does not need hundreds and thousands of years to arise and spread; it has the quality of working by contagion and swiftly seizing a great number of men."**   " As a jarring touch is enough to change a fluid saturated with salts to crystals in a moment, so now the slightest effort may perhaps suffice to cause the unveiled truth to seize upon hundreds, thousands, millions of men so that a public opinion corresponding to knowledge shall be established and that hereby the whole order of life shall become other than it is.   It is in our

---

* To. " Patriotism " pp. 108-9.   † To. " Kingdom " p. 301.
‡ Ib. p. 474.   § Ib. p. 302.   ‖ Ib. p. 301.
¶ To. " Patriotism " pp. 116-17.   ** To. " Kingdom " p. 358.

hands to make this effort."*

2. The best means for bringing about the necessary revolution in public opinion is that the men who have learned to know the truth should testify to it by deed. "The Christian knows the truth only in order to testify to it before those who do not know it,"† and that "by deed."‡ "The truth is imparted to men by deeds of truth, deeds of truth illuminate every man's conscience, and thus destroy the force of deceit."§ Hence you ought properly, "if you are a landlord, to give your land at once to the poor, and, if you are a capitalist, to give your money or your factory to the workingmen; if you are a prince, a cabinet minister, an official, a judge, or a general, you ought at once to resign your position, and, if you are a soldier, you ought to refuse obedience without regard to any danger."‖ But, to be sure, "it is very probable that you are not strong enough to do this; you have connections, dependents, subordinates, superiors, the temptations are powerful, and your force gives out."¶

3. But there is still another means, though a less effective one, for bringing about the necessary revolution in public opinion, and this "you can always "** employ. It is that the men who have learned to know the truth should "speak it out frankly."††

"If men—yes, if even a few men—would do this, the antiquated public opinion would at once fall of itself, and a new, living, present-day one would arise."‡‡ "Not billions of rubles, not millions of

---

* To. "Kingdom" p. 508.   † To. "What I Believe" p. 290.
‡ Ib. p. 290.   § Ib. p. 293.   ‖ To. "Kingdom" p. 523.
¶ Ib. p. 523.   ** Ib. p. 523.
†† To. "Patriotism" p. 116.   ‡‡ Ib. p. 109.

soldiers, no institutions, wars, or revolutions, have so much power as the simple declaration of a free man that he considers something to be right or wrong. If a free man speaks out honestly what he thinks and feels, in the midst of thousands who in word and act stand for the very contrary, one might think he must remain isolated. But usually it is otherwise; all, or most, have long been privately thinking and feeling in the same way; and then what to-day is still an individual's new opinion will perhaps to-morrow be already the general opinion of the majority."* " If we would only stop lying and acting as if we did not see the truth, if we would only testify to the truth that summons us and boldly confess it, it would at once turn out that there are hundreds, thousands, millions, of men in the same situation as ourselves, that they see the truth like us, are afraid like us of remaining isolated if they confess it, and are only waiting, like us, for the rest to testify to it."†

II. To bring about the change and put the new condition in the place of law, the State, and property, it is further requisite that the men who have learned to know the truth should conform their lives to their knowledge, and, in particular, that they should refuse obedience to the State.

1. Men are to bring about the change themselves. They are " no longer to wait for somebody to come and help them, be it Christ in the clouds with the sound of the trumpet, be it a historic law or a differential or integral law of forces. Nobody will help us

---

* To. " Patriotism " pp. 112-13.
† To. " Kingdom " p. 509.

if we do not help ourselves."*

" I have been told a story that happened to a courageous commissary of police. He came into a village where they had applied for soldiers on account of an outbreak among the peasants. In the spirit of Nicholas the First he proposed to make an end of the rising by his personal presence alone. He had a few cart-loads of sticks brought, gathered all the peasants in a barn, and shut himself in with them. By his shouts he succeeded in so cowing the peasants that they obeyed him and began to beat each other at his command. So they beat each other till there was found a simple-minded peasant who did not obey, and who called out to his fellows that they should not beat each other either. Only then did the beating cease, and the official made haste to get away. The advice of this simple-minded peasant " should be followed by the men of our time.†

2. But it is not by violence that men are to bring about the change. " Revolutionary enemies fight the government from outside; Christianity does not fight at all, but wrecks its foundations from within."‡

" Some assert that liberation from force, or at least its diminution, can be effected by the oppressed men's forcibly shaking off the oppressing government; and many do in fact undertake to act on this doctrine. But they deceive themselves and others: their activity only enhances the despotism of governments, and the attempts at liberation are welcomed by the governments as pretexts for strengthening their power."§

---

* To. " What I Believe " pp. 147-8. † To. " Kingdom " pp. 306-7.
‡ *Ib.* p. 326. § *Ib.* pp. 279-80.

However, suppose that by the favor of circumstances (as, for instance, in France in 1870) they succeed in overthrowing a government, the party which had won by force would be compelled, " in order to remain at the helm and introduce its order into life, not only to employ all existing violent methods, but to invent new ones in addition. It would be other men that would be enslaved, and they would be coerced into other things, but there would exist not merely the same but a still more cruel condition of violence and enslavement; for the combat would have fanned the flames of hatred, strengthened the means of enslavement, and evolved new ones. Thus it has been after all revolutions, insurrections, and conspiracies, after all violent changes of government. Every fight only puts stronger means of enslavement in the hands of the men who at a given time are in power."[*]

3. Men are to bring about the change by conforming their lives to their knowledge. " The Christian frees himself from all human authority by recognizing as sole plumb-line for his life and the lives of others the divine law of love that is implanted in man's soul and has been brought into consciousness by Christ."[†]

This means that one is to return good for evil,[‡] give to one's neighbor all that one has that is superfluous and take away from him nothing that one does not need,[§] especially acquire no money and get rid of the money one has,[||] not buy nor rent,[¶] and, without shrinking from any form of work, satisfy one's needs

---

[*] To. " Kingdom " pp. 280-81.   [†] *Ib.* p. 298.
[‡] To. " What I Believe " p. 292.
[§] To. " What Shall We Do " p. 164; " What I Believe " p. 291.
[||] To. " What Shall We Do " p. 162.   [¶] *Ib.* p. 161.

with one's own hands; * and particularly does it mean
that one is to refuse obedience to the unchristian demands of State authority.†

That obedience to these demands is refused we see
in many cases in Russia at present. Men are refusing
the payment of taxes, the general oath, the oath in
court, the exercise of police functions, action as jury-
men, and military service.‡ " The governments find
themselves in a desperate situation as they face the
Christians' refusals."§ They " can chastise, put to
death, imprison for life, and torture, any one who tries
to overthrow them by force; they can bribe and
smother with gold the half of mankind; they can
bring into their service millions of armed men who
are ready to annihilate all their foes. But what can
they do against men who do not destroy anything, do
not set up anything either, but only, each for himself,
are unwilling to act contrary to the law of Christ, and
therefore refuse to do what is most necessary for the
governments?"‖ " Let the State do as it will by such
men, inevitably it will contribute only to its own annihilation,"¶ and therewith to the annihilation of law
and property and to the bringing in of the new order
of life. " For, if it does not persecute people like the
Dukhobors, the Stundists, etc., the advantages of their
peaceable Christian way of living will induce others to
join them—and not only convinced Christians, but
also such as want to get clear of their obligations to
the State under the cloak of Christianity. If, on the

---

* To. " What Shall We Do " p. 161.   † To. " Kingdom " p. 314.
‡ Ib. pp. 327-8.   § Ib. p. 330.   ‖ Ib. p. 328.
¶ To. " Persecutions " p. 44.

other hand, it deals cruelly with men against whom there is nothing except that they have endeavored to live morally, this cruelty will only make it still more enemies, and the moment must at last come when there can no longer be found any one who is ready to back up the State with instrumentalities of force."*

4. In the conforming of life to knowledge the individual must make the beginning. He must not wait for all or many to do it at the same time with him.

The individual must not think it will be useless if he alone conforms his life to Christ's teaching.†

" Men in their present situation are like bees that have left their hive and are hanging on a twig in a great mass. The situation of the bees on the twig is a temporary one, and absolutely must be changed. They must take flight and seek a new abode. Every bee knows that, and wishes to make an end of its own suffering condition and that of the others; but this cannot be done by one so long as the others do not help. But all cannot rise at once, for one hangs over another and hinders it from letting go; therefore all remain hanging. One might think that there was no way out of this situation for the bees ";‡ and really there would be none, were it not that each bee is an independent living being. But it is only needful " that one bee spread its wings, rise and fly, and after it the second, the third, the tenth, the hundredth, for the immobile hanging mass to become a freely flying swarm of bees. Thus it is only needful that one man

---

*To. " Persecutions " p. 44.
†To. " Kingdom " p. 293.　　‡ *Ib.* pp. 302-3.

comprehend life as Christianity teaches it, and take hold of it as Christianity teaches him to, and then that a second, a third, a hundredth follow him, and the magic circle from which no escape seemed possible is destroyed."*

Neither may the individual let himself be deterred by the fear of suffering. " ' If I alone,' it is commonly said, ' fulfil Christ's teaching in the midst of a world that does not follow it, give away my belongings, turn my cheek without resistance, yes, and refuse the oath and military service, then I shall have the last bit taken from me, and, if I do not die of hunger, they will beat me to death, and, if they do not beat me to death, they will jail me or shoot me; and I shall have given all the happiness of my life, nay, my life itself, for nothing.' "† Be it so. " I do not ask whether I shall have more trouble, or die sooner, if I follow Christ's teaching. That question can be asked only by one who does not see how meaningless and miserable is his life as an individual life, and who imagines that he shall ' not die '. But I know that a life for the sake of one's own happiness is the greatest folly, and that such an aimless life can be followed only by an aimless death. And therefore I fear nothing. I shall die like everybody, like even those who do not fulfil Christ's teaching, but my life and my death will have a meaning for me and for others. My life and my death will contribute to the rescue and life of others—and that is just what Christ taught."‡

---

*To. " Kingdom " pp. 303-4.
† " What I Believe " p. 148.   ‡ Ib. pp. 179-80.

If once enough individuals have conformed their lives to their knowledge, the multitude will soon follow. "The passage of men from one order of life to another does not take place steadily, as the sand in the hour-glass runs out, one grain after another from the first to the last, but rather as a vessel that has been sunk into water fills itself. At first the water gets in only on one side, slowly and uniformly; but then its weight makes the vessel sink, and now the thing takes in, all at once, all the water that it can hold."* Thus the impulse given by individuals will provoke a movement that goes on faster and faster, wider and wider, avalanche-like, suddenly sweeps along the masses, and brings about the new order of life.† Then the time is come "when all men are filled with God, shun war, beat their swords into plowshares and their spears into pruning-hooks; that is, in our language, when the prisons and fortresses are empty, when the gallows, rifles, and cannon are out of use. What seemed a dream has found its fulfilment in a new form of life."‡

---

*To. "Kingdom" p. 353.   † *Ib.* p. 356.   ‡ *Ib.* p. 392.

CHAPTER X

THE ANARCHISTIC TEACHINGS

1.—GENERAL

We have now gained the standpoint that permits us to view comprehensively the entire body of Anarchistic teachings.

This comprehensive view is possible only as follows: first we have to look and see what the seven recognized Anarchistic teachings here presented have in common, and what specialties are to be found among them; next we must consider how far that which is common to the seven teachings may be equated to that which the entire body of Anarchistic teachings have in common, and, in addition, how far the specialties represented among the seven teachings may be equated to the specialties represented in the entire body of Anarchistic teachings.

To characterize those qualities of the Anarchistic teachings to which attention is to be paid, words already existing are here used as far as has been found practicable. Where such were totally lacking, the need of a concise formula has of necessity overcome repugnance to neologisms.

2.—BASIS

I. As to their basis the seven teachings here presented have nothing in common.

1. In part they recognize as the supreme law of

human procedure merely a natural law, which, as
such, does not tell us what ought to take place but
what really will take place; these teachings may be
called *genetic*. The other part of them regard as the
supreme law of human procedure a norm, which, as
such, tells us what ought to take place, even if it
never really will take place; these teachings may be
characterized as *critical*. Genetic are the teachings of
Bakunin and Kropotkin: the supreme law of human
procedure is for Bakunin the evolutionary law of mankind's progress from a less perfect existence to an existence as perfect as possible, and for Kropotkin that
of mankind's progress from a less happy existence to
an existence as happy as possible. Critical are the
teachings of Godwin, Proudhon, Stirner, Tucker, and
Tolstoi.

2. The critical teachings, again, are partly such as
set up a duty as the supreme law of human procedure,
the duty being itself the ultimate purpose,—these
teachings may be characterized as *idealistic*,—and
partly such as set up happiness as the supreme law of
human procedure, all duty being only a means to
happiness,—these may take the name of *eudemonistic*.
Idealistic are the teachings of Proudhon and Tolstoi:
Proudhon sets up as the supreme law of human procedure the duty of justice, Tolstoi the duty of love.
Eudemonistic are the teachings of Godwin, Stirner,
and Tucker.

3. The eudemonistic teachings, finally, regard as
the supreme law of human procedure either the happiness of mankind as a whole, which the individual is
accordingly to further without regard to his own

happiness,—these teachings may be characterized as *altruistic*,—or the happiness of the individual, which he is accordingly to further without regard to the welfare of mankind as a whole,—these teachings may be called *egoistic*. Altruistic is Godwin's teaching, egoistic Stirner's and Tucker's.

II. With regard to what they have in common in their basis, the seven recognized Anarchistic teachings here presented may be taken as equivalent to the entire body of recognized Anarchistic teachings. They have in their basis nothing in common with each other; all the more is it impossible, therefore, that the entire body of recognized Anarchistic teachings should have in their basis anything in common.

Furthermore, as regards the specialties that they exhibit in respect to their basis the teachings here presented may be taken as equivalent to the entire body of Anarchistic teachings without limitation. For the specialties represented among them can be arranged as a system that has no room left for any more coordinate specialties, but only for subordinate. No Anarchistic teaching, therefore, can have any specialty that will not be subordinate to these specialties.

Therefore, what is true of the seven teachings here presented is true of Anarchistic teachings altogether. In their basis they have nothing in common, and are to be divided with respect to its differences as shown in the table on page 273.

3.—LAW

I. In their relation to law—that is, to those norms which are based on men's will to have a certain pro-

cedure generally observed within a circle which includes themselves—the seven teachings here presented
have nothing in common.

1. A part of them negate law for our future; these
teachings may be called *anomistic*.   The other part

Genetic Teachings	*Critical Teachings*		
	Idealistic	*Eudemonistic*	
		Altruistic	Egoistic
Bakunin Kropotkin	Proudhon Tolstoi	Godwin	Stirner Tucker

of them affirm it for our future; these teachings may
be characterized as *nomistic*.   Anomistic are the
teachings of Godwin, Stirner, Tolstoi; nomistic those
of Proudhon, Bakunin, Kropotkin, and Tucker.

There cannot be given a more precise definition of
what is common to the anomistic teachings on the one
hand and to the nomistic on the other, and what is
peculiar to the one group as against the other, than
has here been given.   For both the negation and the
affirmation of law for our future have totally different
meanings in the different teachings.

The negation of law for our future means in the
cases of Godwin and Stirner that they reject law unconditionally, and so for our fnture as well as everywhere else: Godwin because it is always and everywhere contrary to the general happiness, Stirner because it is always and everywhere contrary to the

individual's happiness.

In Tolstoi's case the meaning of the negation of law for our future is that he rejects law, though not unconditionally, yet for our future, because it is, though not at all times and in all places, yet under our circumstances, in a higher degree repugnant to love than its non-existence.

The affirmation of law for our future means in the cases of Proudhon and Tucker that they approve law as such (though certainly not every particular form of law) unconditionally, and hence for our future as well as elsewhere: Proudhon because law as such never and nowhere offends against justice, Tucker because law as such never and nowhere impairs the individual's happiness.*

In the cases of Bakunin and Kropotkin, finally, the affirmation of law for our future has the meaning that they foresee that the progress of evolution will in our future leave in existence law as such, even though not the present particular form of law: Bakunin meaning by this the progress of mankind from a less perfect existence to an existence as perfect as possible, and Proudhon its progress from a less happy existence to an existence as happy as possible.

2. The anomistic teachings part company again in regard to what they (in the same different senses in which they negate law for our future) affirm for our future in contrast to the law.

According to Godwin, in future the general happi-

---

* [I shall not indorse this statement till I understand it, and I doubt if Tucker will. Perhaps Eltzbacher might have been content with saying " is in no case more injurious to the happiness of most individuals than its non-existence."]

ness ought to be men's controlling principle in the place of law.

According to Stirner, in future the happiness of self ought to be men's controlling principle in the place of law.

According to Tolstoi, in future love ought to be men's controlling principle in the place of law.

3. On the other part, the nomistic teachings part company in regard to the particular form of law that they affirm for our future.

According to Tucker, even in future there ought to exist enacted law, in which the will that creates the law is expressly declared,* as well as unenacted law, in which such an express declaration of this will is not present.

According to Bakunin and Kropotkin, in future only unenacted law will exist.

According to Proudhon, there ought to exist in future only the single legal norm that contracts must be lived up to.†

II. With regard to what they have in common in their relation to law, the seven recognized Anarchistic teachings here presented may be taken as equivalent to the entire body of recognized Anarchistic teachings. In their relation to law they have nothing in common. Much less, therefore, can the entire body of recognized Anarchistic teachings have anything in common in

---

* [This, if interpreted by Eltzbacher's quotations from Tucker, must refer to the right of a voluntary association of any sort to make rules for its own members. But in this sense it seems in the highest degree doubtful whether Eltzbacher is justified in denying the same to all the other six, who have omitted to mention this point (perhaps regarding it as self-evident) while they were talking against laws in the sense of laws compulsorily binding everybody in the land.]

† [But see on Proudhon and Stirner my notes on pages 80 and 97.]

their relation to law.

Furthermore, as regards the specialties that they exhibit in their relation to law the teachings here presented may be taken as equivalent to the entire body of Anarchistic teachings without limitation. For the specialties represented among them can be arranged as a system in which there is no room left for any more co-ordinate specialties, but only for subordinate. No Anarchistic teaching, therefore, can have any specialty that will not be subordinate to these specialties.

Therefore, what is true of the seven teachings here presented is true of Anarchistic teachings altogether. In their relation to law they have nothing in common, and are to be divided as follows with respect to the differences of this relation:

Anomistic Teachings	Nomistic Teachings
Godwin	Proudhon
Stirner	Bakunin
Tolstoi	Kropotkin
	Tucker

4.—THE STATE

I. In their relation to the State—that is, to the legal relation by virtue of which a supreme authority exists in a territory—the seven teachings here presented have something in common.

1. They have this in common, that they negate the State for our future.

There cannot be given a more precise definition of

what the teachings here presented have in common in
their relation to the State than has here been given.
For the negation of the State for our future has
totally different meanings in them.

In the cases of Godwin, Stirner, Tucker, and
Proudhon, the negation of the State for our future
means that they reject the State unconditionally, and
hence for our future as well as everywhere else: Godwin because the State always and everywhere impairs
the general happiness, Stirner and Tucker because it
always and everywhere impairs the individual's happiness, Proudhon because at all times and in all places
the State offends against justice.

In Tolstoi's case the negation of the State for our
future means that he rejects the State, though not unconditionally, yet for our future, because the State is,
though not always and everywhere. yet under our
circumstances, more repugnant to love than its
non-existence.

Finally, in the cases of Bakunin and Kropotkin the
negation of the State for our future has the meaning
that they foresee that in our future the progress of
evolution will abolish the State: Bakunin meaning
mankind's progress from a less perfect existence to
one as perfect as possible, Kropotkin its progress from
a less happy existence to one as happy as possible.

2. As to what they affirm for our future in contrast
to the State (in the same different senses in which
they negate the State for our future) the seven teachings here presented have nothing in common.

One part of them affirm for our future, in contrast
to the State, a social human life in a voluntary legal

relation—to wit, under the legal norm that contracts must be lived up to; these teachings may take the name of *federalistic.* The other part of them affirm for our future, in contrast to the State, a social human life without any legal relation—to wit, under the same controlling principle that they affirm for our future in contrast to law; these teachings may be characterized as *spontanistic.* Federalistic are the teachings of Proudhon, Bakunin. Kropotkin, and Tucker; spontanistic those of Godwin,* Stirner, and Tolstoi.

3. The spontanistic teachings in turn part company in respect to the non-legal controlling principle which they affirm in contrast to the State as the basis of the social human life for our future.

According to Godwin, the place of the State ought to be taken by a social human life based on the principle that the general happiness should be every one's rule of action.

According to Stirner, the place of the State ought to be taken by a social human life based on the principle that each one's own happiness should be his rule of action.

According to Tolstoi, the place of the State ought to be taken by a social human life based on the prin-

---

*[It will be seen by consulting the footnotes on pages 46, 47, and 48 that the warrants for this statement about Godwin are drawn exclusively from the first one-fifth of his book, contrary to Eltzbacher's profession at the top of page 41; that the passages quoted *verbatim* are not in Godwin's second edition; and that the quotations which are not *verbatim* are of doubtful correctness by the second edition. This makes it appear that Godwin's sweeping rejection of the principle of contract was one of those over-hasty propositions about which he changed his mind even before they were published (see his words quoted on page 40, and the preface to his second edition). Yet I am not prepared to assert that Godwin would at any time have made contract the basis of his civil order.]

ciple that love should be every one's rule of action.

II. With regard to what they have in common in their relation to the State, the seven recognized Anarchistic teachings here presented may be taken as equivalent to the entire body of recognized Anarchistic teachings. In their relation to the State they have only this one thing in common, that they negate the State for our future—and in very different senses at that. But this is common to all recognized Anarchistic teachings: observation of any recognized Anarchistic teaching shows that in one sense or another it negates the State for our future.

Furthermore, as regards the specialties that they exhibit in their relation to the State the teachings here presented may be taken as equivalent to the entire body of Anarchistic teachings without limitation. For the specialties represented among them can be arranged as a system which affords no room for any more co-ordinate specialties, but only for subordinate. No Anarchistic teaching, therefore, can have any specialty that will not be subordinate to these specialties.

Therefore, what is true of the seven teachings here presented is true of the Anarchistic teachings altogether, In their relation to the State they have in common their negating the State for our future; and with regard to the differences in what they affirm for our future in contrast to the State they are to be divided as shown in the table on page 280.

Federalistic Teachings	*Spontanistic Teachings*
Proudhon Bakunin Kropotkin Tucker	Godwin Stirner Tolstoi

5.—PROPERTY

I. In their relation to property—that is, to that legal relation by virtue of which some one has within a certain group of men the exclusive privilege of ultimately disposing of a thing—the seven teachings here presented have nothing in common.

1. One part of them negate property for our future; these teachings may be characterized as *indominstic*. The other part affirm it for our future; these teachings may be called *dominstic*. Indominstic are the teachings of Godwin, Proudhon, Stirner, and Tolstoi; dominstic the teachings of Bakunin, Kropotkin, and Tucker.

There cannot be given a more precise definition of what is common to the indominstic teachings on the one hand and to the dominstic on the other, and what is peculiar to the one group as against the other, than has here been given. For both the affirmation and the negation of property for our future have totally different meanings in the different teachings.

In the cases of Godwin, Stirner, and Proudhon, the negation of property for our future means that they reject property unconditionally, and so for our future as well as elsewhere: Godwin because it is always and everywhere contrary to the general happiness, Stirner because it is always and everywhere contrary to the individual's happiness, Proudhon because it always and everywhere offends against justice.

In Tolstoi's case the meaning of the negation of property for our future is that he rejects property, though not absolutely, yet for our future, because it is, though not at all times and in all places, yet under our circumstances, in a higher degree repugnant to love than is its non-existence.

In Tucker's case the affirmation of property for our future means that he approves property as such (though certainly not every particular form of property) unconditionally, and hence for our future as well as elsewhere, because property as such is never and nowhere contrary to the individual's happiness.*

Finally, in the cases of Bakunin and Kropotkin the affirmation of property for our future is as much as to say that they foresee that in our future the progress of evolution will leave in existence property as such, even though not the present particular form of property: Bakunin meaning mankind's progress from a less perfect existence to one as perfect as possible, Kropotkin its progress from a less happy existence to one as happy as possible.

2. The indominal teachings part company again as to what they affirm for our future (in the same different senses in which they negate property for our future) in contrast to property.

According to Proudhon, a distribution of goods determined by a voluntary legal relation, and based

---

* [On Proudhon, Stirner, Tucker, see my notes on pages 80, 97, 274.]

on the legal norm that contracts ought to be lived up to, ought to take the place of property.

According to Godwin, Stirner, and Tolstoi, the place of property ought to be taken by a distribution without any legal relation, based rather on the same rule of action that is affirmed by them in contrast to law.

According to Godwin, therefore, that distribution of goods which is to take the place of property ought to be based on what is prescribed to each one by the general happiness.

According to Stirner it ought to be based on what is prescribed to each one by his own happiness.

According to Tolstoi it ought to be based on what is prescribed to each one by love.

3. The doministic teachings on their side part company again as to the particular form of property that they affirm for our future.

According to Tucker there ought to exist in future, as at present, both property of the individual and property of the collectivity, in all things indiscriminately.* This teaching may be called *individualistic.*

According to Bakunin, in future there will exist property of the individual and of the entire community only in goods for consumption, indiscriminately, while in the materials and instruments of production there will be solely property of the collectivity. This teaching may be characterized as *collectivistic.*

---

*[We are getting into an ambiguity of language here. The " collectivity " in which Kropotkin vests property is, as I understand, the entire population; the only " collectivity " which Tucker could recognize as owning property would be a voluntary association, whose membership, whether large or small, would in general be limited by the arbitrary choice of men.]

According to Kropotkin, in future there will exist solely property of the collectivity in all things indiscriminately. This teaching may be called *communistic*.

II. With regard to what they have in common in their relation to property, the seven Anarchistic teachings here presented may be taken as equivalent to the entire body of recognized Anarchistic teachings. They have nothing in common in their relation to property. All the more is it impossible, therefore, that the entire body of recognized Anarchistic teachings should in their relation to property have anything in common.

Furthermore, in regard to the specialties that they exhibit in their relation to property the teachings here presented may be taken as equivalent to the entire body of Anarchistic teachings without limitation. For the specialties represented among them can be arranged as a system in which there is no room left for any more co-ordinate specialties, but only for subordinate. No Anarchistic teaching, therefore, can have any specialty that will not be subordinate to these specialties.

Therefore, what is true of the seven teachings here presented is true of Anarchistic teachings altogether. They have nothing in common in their relation to property, and are to be divided with respect to the differences of this relation as shown in the table on page 284.

Indominstic Teachings	Dominstic Teachings		
	Individualistic	Collectivistic	Communistic
Godwin Proudhon Stirner Tolstoi	Tucker	Bakunin	Kropotkin

6.—REALIZATION

I. With regard to the manner in which they conceive their realization—that is, the transition from the negated condition to the affirmed condition—as taking place, the seven teachings here presented have nothing in common.

1. The one part of them conceive their realization as taking place without breach of law: they have in mind a transition from the negated to the affirmed condition merely by the application of legal norms of the negated condition; these teachings may be characterized as *reformatory*. Reformatory are the teachings of Godwin and Proudhon. The other part conceive their realization as a breach of law: they have in mind a transition from the negated to the affirmed condition with violation of legal norms of the negated condition; these teachings may be called *revolutionary*. Revolutionary are the teachings of Stirner, Bakunin, Kropotkin, Tucker, and Tolstoi.

There cannot be given a more precise definition of what is common to the reformatory teachings on the one hand, to the revolutionary on the other, and what is peculiar to the one group as against the other, than has here been given. For the conceiving the transition from a negated to an affirmed condition as taking place in any given way has totally different meanings in the different teachings.

If Godwin, Proudhon, Stirner, Tucker, and Tolstoi conceive the transition from a negated to an affirmed condition as taking place in any given way, this is as much as to say that they demand that we should in a given way first prepare for, and then effect, the transition from a disapproved to an approved condition.

If, on the contrary, Bakunin and Kropotkin conceive the transition from a negated to an affirmed condition as taking place in any given way, this means that they foresee that in the progress of evolution the transition from a disappearing to a newly-appearing condition will of itself take place in a given way, and that they only demand that we should make a certain sort of preparation for this transition.

2. The revolutionary teachings part company again as to the fashion in which they conceive of the breach of law that helps in the transition from the negated to the affirmed condition.

Some of them conceive of the breach of law as taking place without the employment of force; these teachings may be characterized as *renitent*. Renitent are the teachings of Tucker and Tolstoi: Tucker conceiving the breach of law chiefly as a refusal to pay taxes and rent and an infringement of the banking monopoly, Tolstoi especially as a refusal to do military, police, or jury service, and also to pay taxes.

The other revolutionary teachings conceive of the

breach of law that helps in the transition from the
negated to the affirmed condition as taking place with
the employment of force; these teachings may take
the name of *insurgent*. Insurgent are the teachings
of Stirner, Bakunin, and Kropotkin: Stirner and
Bakunin conceiving only of the transition itself as attended with the use of violence, but Kropotkin also of
preparation for it by such acts (propaganda of
deed).

II. With regard to what they have in common in
respect of the conceived manner of realization, the
seven recognized Anarchistic teachings which have
been presented may be taken as equivalent to the
entire body of recognized Anarchistic teachings. In
respect of the conceived manner of realization they
have nothing in common. Much less, therefore, can
the entire body of recognized Anarchistic teachings
have anything in common in this respect.

Furthermore, as regards the specialties that they
exhibit in respect of the conceived manner of realization the teachings here presented may be taken as
equivalent to the entire body of Anarchistic teachings
without limitation. For the specialties represented
among them can be arranged as a system in which
there is no room left for any more co-ordinate specialties, but only for subordinate. No Anarchistic teaching, therefore, can have any specialty that will not be
subordinate to these specialties.

Therefore, what is true of the seven teachings here
presented is true of the Anarchistic teachings altogether. In respect of the conceived manner of realization they have nothing in common, and are to be

arranged as follows with reference to the differences
therein:

Reformatory Teachings	*Revolutionary Teachings*	
	Renitent	*Insurgent*
Godwin Proudhon	Tucker Tolstoi	Stirner Bakunin Kropotkin

CHAPTER XI

ANARCHISM AND ITS SPECIES

I.—ERRORS ABOUT ANARCHISM AND ITS SPECIES

It has now become possible to set aside some of the numerous errors about Anarchism and its species.

I. It is said that Anarchism has abolished morality and bases itself upon scientific materialism,* that its ideal of society is determined by its peculiar conception of the way things come to pass in history.† If this were correct, the teachings of Godwin, Proudhon, Stirner, Tucker, Tolstoi, and very many other recognized Anarchistic teachings, would have to be regarded as not Anarchistic.

2. It is asserted that Anarchism sets up the happiness of the individual as final goal,‡ that it appraises every human action from the abstract view-point of the unlimited right of the individual,§ that to it the supreme law is not the general welfare but every individual's free preference.‖ Were this really the case, we should have to look upon the teachings of Godwin, Proudhon, Bakunin, Kropotkin, Tolstoi, and a multitude of other recognized Anarchistic teachings, as not Anarchistic.

3. The moral law of justice is set down as Anarchism's supreme law.¶ Were this assertion correct,

---

* "*Der Anarchismus und seine Träger*" pp. 127, 124, 125.
† Reichesberg p. 27.   ‡ Lenz p. 3.   § Plechanow p. 80.
‖ Rienzi p. 43.   ¶ Bernatzik pp. 2, 3.

288

the teachings of Godwin, Stirner, Bakunin, Kropotkin, Tucker, Tolstoi, and numerous other recognized Anarchistic teachings, could not rank as
Anarchistic.

4. It is said that Anarchism culminates in the negation of every programme,* that it has only a negative goal.† If this were in accordance with truth, the
teachings of Godwin, Proudhon, Stirner, Bakunin,
Kropotkin, Tucker, Tolstoi, and well-nigh all other
recognized Anarchistic teachings, would not admit of
being regarded as Anarchistic.

5. It is asserted that Anarchism rejects law,‡ the
compulsion of law.§ If this were so, the teachings of
Proudhon, Bakunin, Kropotkin, Tucker, and very
many other recognized Anarchistic teachings, could
not rank as Anarchistic.

6. It is declared that Anarchism rejects society,‖
that its ideal consists in wiping out society to make a
fresh start,¶ that for it fellowship exists only to be
combated.** Were this correct, we should have to
look upon the teachings of Godwin, Proudhon,
Stirner, Bakunin, Kropotkin, Tucker, Tolstoi, and
pretty nearly all other recognized Anarchistic teachings, as not Anarchistic.

7. It is said that Anarchism demands the abolition
of the State,†† wills to destroy the State off the face of
the earth,‡‡ wills to have the State in no form at
all,§§ wills to have no government.‖‖ If this were
correct, the teachings of Bakunin and Kropotkin, and

---

* Lenz p. 5.   † Crispi p. 4.   ‡ Stammler pp. 2, 4, 34, 36.
§ Lenz pp. 1, 4.   ‖ Garraud p. 12, Tripels p. 253.
¶ Silió p. 145.   ** Reichesberg pp. 14, 16.   †† Bernstein p. 359.
‡‡ Lenz p. 5.   §§ Bernatzik p. 3.   ‖‖ " Hintermänner " p. 14.

all the other recognized Anarchistic teachings which only foresee the abolition of the State but do not demand it, could not rank as Anarchistic.

8. It is asserted that in Anarchism's future society the individual's consent binds him only so long as he is disposed to keep it up.* Were this really so, then the teachings of Proudhon, Bakunin, Kropotkin, Tucker, and very many other recognized Anarchistic teachings, would have to be looked upon as not Anarchistic.

9. It is said that Anarchism wills to put a federation in the place of the State,† that what it is striving for is the ordering of all public affairs by free contracts among federalistically instituted communes and societies.‡ Were this in accordance with truth, the teachings of Godwin, Stirner, Tolstoi, and very many other recognized Anarchistic teachings, would not admit of being regarded as Anarchistic, and no more would the teachings of Bakunin and Kropotkin and the rest of the recognized Anarchistic teachings that do not demand, but only foresee, a fellowship of contract.

10. It is declared that Anarchism rejects property.§ If this were correct, we should have to rate the teachings of Bakunin, Kropotkin, Tucker, and all the other recognized Anarchistic teachings that affirm property either unconditionally or at any rate in some particular form, as not Anarchistic.

11. It is asserted that Anarchism rejects private property,‖ endeavors to establish community of

* Reichesberg p. 30.   † "*Hintermänner* " p. 14.
‡ Lombroso p. 31.   § Silió p. 145, Dubois p. 213.
‖ Proal p. 50.

goods,* is necessarily communistic.† Were Anarchism necessarily communistic, then, in the first place, the teachings of Godwin, Proudhon, Stirner, Tolstoi, and all the other recognized Anarchistic teachings which negate property in every form, even as the property of society, could not rank as Anarchistic; and furthermore, neither could the teachings of Tucker and Bakunin, and such other recognized Anarchistic teachings as affirm private property either in all things or at least in goods for direct consumption. And if in addition to this it were a matter of rejection or endeavor, then not even Kropotkin's teaching, and the rest of the recognized Anarchistic teachings which do not demand, but foresee, a communistic form of property, could be regarded as Anarchistic.

12. A distinction is made between Communist, Collectivist, and Individualist Anarchism,‡ or simply between Communist and Individualist Anarchism.§ Were the first division a complete one, the teachings of Godwin, Proudhon, Stirner, Tolstoi, and all the other recognized Anarchistic teachings that do not affirm property in any form, could not rank as Anarchistic; were the second complete, these again could not, nor yet could Bakunin's teaching and such other recognized Anarchistic teachings as affirm a property in the means of production only for society, but in the supplies of consumption for individuals also.

13. It is said that Anarchism preaches crime,|| looks to a violent revolution for the initiation of the

---

* Lombroso p. 31.   † Sernicoli vol. 2 p. 67, Garraud pp. 3, 4.
‡ "*Die historische Entwickelung des Anarchismus*" p. 16 ; Zenker p. 161.
§ Rienzi p. 9 ; Stammler pp. 28-31 ; Merlino pp. 18, 27 ; Shaw p. 23.
|| Garraud p. 6 ; Lenz p. 5.

new condition,* seeks to attain its goal with the help of all agencies, even theft and murder.† If Anarchism conceived of its realization as taking place by crime, we should have to look upon the teachings of Godwin and Proudhon and very many more recognized Anarchistic teachings as not Anarchistic; and, if it conceived of its realization as taking place by criminal acts of violence, the teachings of Tucker and Tolstoi and numerous other recognized Anarchistic teachings would also have to be regarded as not Anarchistic.

14. It is asserted that Anarchism recognizes the propaganda of deed as a means toward its realization.‡ If this were correct, the teachings of Godwin, Proudhon, Stirner, Bakunin, Tucker, Tolstoi, and most of the other recognized Anarchistic teachings, could not rank as Anarchistic.

2.—THE CONCEPTS OF ANARCHISM AND ITS SPECIES

It is now possible, furthermore, to determine the common and special qualities of the Anarchistic teachings, to assign them a place in the total realm of our experience, and thus to define conceptually Anarchism and its species.

I. *The common and special qualities of the Anarchistic teachings.*

1. The Anarchistic teachings have in common only this, that they negate the State for our future. In the cases of Godwin, Proudhon, Stirner, and Tucker,

---

*Sernicoli vol. 2 p. 116 ; Garraud p. 2 ; Reichesberg p. 38 ; Van Hamel p. 113.
† Lombroso pp. 31, 35.   ‡ Garraud pp. 10-11 ; Lombroso p. 34 ; Ferri p. 257.

the negation means that they reject the State unconditionally, and so for our future as well as elsewhere;
in the case of Tolstoi it means that he rejects the
State, though not unconditionally, yet for our future;
in the cases of Bakunin and Kropotkin it means that
they foresee that in future the progress of evolution
will do away with the State.

2. As to their basis, the Anarchistic teachings are
classifiable as *genetic*, recognizing as the supreme law
of human procedure merely a law of nature (Bakunin,
Kropotkin) and *critical*, regarding a norm as the
supreme law of human procedure. The critical teachings, again, are classifiable as *idealistic*, whose supreme
law is a duty (Proudhon, Tolstoi), and *eudemonistic*,
whose supreme law is happiness. The eudemonistic
teachings, finally, are on their part further classifiable
as *altruistic*, for which the general happiness is supreme law (Godwin), and *egoistic*, for which the individual's happiness takes this rank (Stirner, Tucker).

As to what they affirm for our future in contrast to
the State, the Anarchistic teachings are either *federalistic*—that is, they affirm for our future a social
human life on the basis of the legal norm that contracts must be lived up to (Proudhon, Bakunin, Kropotkin, Tucker)—or *spontanistic*—that is, they affirm
for our future a social human life on the basis of a
non-juridical controlling principle (Godwin, Stirner,
Tolstoi).

As to their relation to law, a part of the Anarchistic teachings are *anomistic*, negating law for our
future (Godwin, Stirner, Tolstoi); the other part are
nomistic, affirming it for our future (Proudhon, Ba-

kunin, Kropotkin, Tucker).

As to their relation to property, the Anarchistic teachings are partly *indominstic*, negating property for our future (Godwin, Proudhon, Stirner, Tolstoi), partly *dominstic*, affirming it for our future. The dominstic teachings, again, are partly *individualistic*, affirming property, without limitation, for the individual as well as for the collectivity (Tucker), partly *collectivistic*, affirming as to supplies for direct consumption a property that will sometimes be the individual's, but as to the means of production a property that is only for the collectivity (Bakunin), and, finally, partly *communistic*, affirming property solely for the collectivity (Kropotkin).

As to how they conceive their realization, the Anarchistic teachings divide into the *reformatory*, which conceive the transition from the negated to the affirmed condition as without breach of law (Godwin, Proudhon), and *revolutionary*, which conceive this transition as a breach of law. The revolutionary teachings, again, divide into *renitent*, which conceive the breach of law as without the use of force (Tucker, Tolstoi) and *insurgent*, which conceive it as attended by the use of force (Stirner, Bakunin, Kropotkin).

II. *The place of the Anarchistic teachings in the total realm of our experience.*

1. There must be distinguished three lines of thought in the philosophy of law: that is, three fashions of judging law.

The first is *jurisprudential dogmatism*. It judges whether a legal institution ought to exist or not, and it judges quite unconditionally, solely by what the

institution consists of, without regard to its effect
under this or that particular set of circumstances. It
embraces, therefore, the doctrines of a *proper law*:
that is, the schools that seek to determine what law—
for instance, whether the legal institution of marriage
—is under all circumstances to be approved or to be
disapproved. Its best known form is " natural law."

The weakness of jurisprudential dogmatism lies in
its not taking account of the fact that our judgment
of legal institutions must depend on their effects, and
that one and the same legal institution has under
different circumstances altogether different effects.

The second line of thought is *jurisprudential
skepticism*. In view of the weakness of jurisprudential
dogmatism it foregoes judgment on whether a legal
institution ought to exist or not, and pronounces judgment only on whether the tendency of evolution gives
ground for expecting that a legal institution will persist or disappear, arise or remain non-existent. It embraces, therefore, the doctrines of the *evolution of law*:
that is, the schools that undertake to inform us what
sort of law is to be expected in future—for instance,
whether the legal institution of marriage has a prospect of remaining in force among us. Its best-known
forms are the historical school in the science of law,
and Marxism.

The weakness of jurisprudential skepticism consists
in its not meeting our want of a scientific basis that
shall enable us to recognize as correct or incorrect the
incessantly-appearing judgments on the value of legal
institutions, and to approve or disapprove the manifold propositions for changes in law.

The third line of thought is *jurisprudential criticism.* In view of the weakness of jurisprudential dogmatism it foregoes passing judgment, without regard to the particular circumstances under which a legal institution operates, on whether that institution ought to exist or not; but yet in view of the weakness of jurisprudential skepticism it does not forego answering the question whether a legal institution ought to exist or not. It therefore sets up a supreme governing principle by which legal institutions are to be judged with regard to the particular circumstances under which they operate, the point being whether, under the particular circumstances under which a legal institution operates, it fulfils that supreme governing principle as well as is possible under these circumstances, or at least better than any other legal institution. It embraces, therefore, the doctrines of *the propriety of law:* that is, the schools that set up fundamental principles by which it is to be determined what law—for instance, whether the legal institution of marriage—ought under any particular circumstances to exist or not to exist.

2. With respect to the State these three lines of thought in the philosophy of law may arrive at different judgments, each one from its standpoint.

First, to the *affirmation of the State.*

So far as the schools of jurisprudential dogmatism affirm the State, they approve of it unconditionally, and so for our future as well as elsewhere, without any regard to its effects under this or that particular set of circumstances.

Among the numerous affirmative doctrines of the State in the sense of jurisprudential dogmatism, the teachings of Hobbes, Hegel, and Jhering may perhaps be selected for emphasis as belonging to different sections of history.

So far as the doctrines of jurisprudential skepticism affirm the State, they foresee, looking to the course evolution is taking, that in our future the State will continue to exist.

The most notable representatives of jurisprudential skepticism, such as Puchta and Merkel, have offered no teaching regarding the State; but affirmative doctrines of the State in the sense of jurisprudential skepticism may be found, for instance, in Montaigne and Bernstein.

Finally, so far as the doctrines of jurisprudential criticism affirm the State, they commend it for our future in consideration of the particular circumstances that at present prevail in our case.

Jurisprudential criticism has thus far been most clearly set forth by Stammler, who, however, has offered no teaching with regard to the State; but, for instance, Spencer's teaching may rank as an affirmative doctrine of the State in the sense of jurisprudential criticism.

Second, the three lines of thought in the philosophy of law may arrive at the *negation of the State*, each one from its standpoint.

So far as the doctrines of jurisprudential dogmatism negate the State, they reject it unconditionally, and so for our future as well as elsewhere, without any regard to its effects under this or that particular set of circumstances.

Negative doctrines of the State in the sense of jurisprudential dogmatism are the teachings of Godwin, Proudhon, Stirner, and Tucker.

So far as the doctrines of jurisprudential skepticism negate the State, they foresee, looking to the course evolution is taking, that in our future the State will disappear.

Negative doctrines of the State in the sense of jurisprudential skepticism are the teachings of Bakunin and Kropotkin.

So far as the doctrines of jurisprudential criticism negate the State, they reject it for our future in consideration of the particular circumstances that at present prevail in our case.

A negative doctrine of the State in the sense of jurisprudential criticism is Tolstoi's teaching.

3. Therefore, the place of the Anarchistic teachings in the total realm of our experience is defined by the fact that they, as a species of doctrine about the State in the philosophy of law,—to wit, as negative doctrines of the State,—stand in opposition to the other species of doctrine about the State, the affirmative doctrines of the State.

This may be represented as shown in the table on the following page.

III. *The concepts of Anarchism and its species.*

1. Anarchism is the negation of the State in the philosophy of law: that is, it is that species of jurisprudential doctrine of the State which negates the State.

2. An Anarchistic teaching cannot be complete without stating on what basis it rests, what condition it affirms in contrast to the State, and how it conceives

	Affirmative Doctrines of the State	*Negative Doctrines of the State*
In the sense of jurisprudential dogmatism	Hobbes Hegel Jhering	Godwin Proudhon Stirner Tucker
In the sense of jurisprudential skepticism	Montaigne Bernstein	Bakunin Kropotkin
In the sense of jurisprudential criticism	Spencer	Tolstoi

the transition to this condition as taking place. A basis, an affirmative side, and a conception of the transition to that which it affirms, are necessary constituents of any Anarchistic teaching. With regard to these constituents the following species of Anarchism may be distinguished.

First, as to basis, *genetic Anarchism*, which recognizes as supreme law of human procedure only a law of nature (Bakunin, Kropotkin), and *critical Anarchism*, which regards a norm as supreme law of human procedure; as subspecies of critical Anarchism, *idealistic Anarchism*, whose supreme law is a duty (Proudhon, Tolstoi), and *eudemonistic Anarchism*, whose supreme law is happiness; and, finally, as subspecies of eudemonistic Anarchism, *altruistic Anarchism*, for which the supreme law is the general happiness (Godwin), and *egoistic Anarchism*, for which the supreme law is the individual's happiness (Stirner, Tucker).

Second, as to the condition affirmed in contrast to the State, there may be distinguished *federalistic Anarchism*, which affirms for our future a social human life according to the legal norm that contracts must be lived up to (Proudhon, Bakunin, Kropotkin, Tucker), and *spontanistic Anarchism*, which affirms for our future a social life according to a non-juridical governing principle (Godwin, Stirner, Tolstoi).

Third, as to the conception of the transition to the affirmed condition, there may be distinguished *reformatory Anarchism*, which conceives the transition from the State to the condition affirmed in contrast thereto as taking place without breach of law (Godwin, Proudhon), and *revolutionary Anarchism*, which conceives this transition as a breach of law; as subspecies of revolutionary Anarchism, *renitent Anarchism*, which conceives the breach of law as without the use of violence (Tucker, Tolstoi), and *insurgent Anarchism*, which conceives it as attended by the use of violence (Stirner, Bakunin, Kropotkin).

3. An Anarchistic teaching may be complete without taking up a position toward law or property. Whenever, therefore, an Anarchistic teaching takes up a position toward the one or the other, it contains an accidental adjunct. The Anarchistic teachings that contain this adjunct may be classified according to its character; but, since Anarchism as such can be classified only according to the character of the necessary constituents of every Anarchistic teaching, such a classification *does not give us species of Anarchism.*

So far as the Anarchistic teachings take up a position toward law, they are either *anomistic*—that is, they negate law for our future (Godwin, Stirner, Tolstoi)—or *nomistic*—that is, they affirm it for our future (Proudhon, Bakunin, Kropotkin, Tucker).

So far as they take up a position toward property, they are either *indominstic*, negating property for our future (Godwin, Proudhon, Stirner, Tolstoi), or *dominstic*, affirming it for our future; the dominstic teachings, again, are either *individualistic*, affirming property, without limitation, for the individual as well as for the collectivity (Tucker), or *collectivistic*, affirming as to supplies for direct consumption a property which may be the individual's, but as to the means of production a property that is only for the collectivity (Bakunin), or, last of all, *communistic*, affirming property for the collectivity alone (Kropotkin).

All this is brought before the eye in the table on page 302.

☞ [The table is given as compiled by Eltzbacher. For correction of errors either certain or probable, see footnotes to pages 80, 97, 278; note also that under "condition affirmed" the distinction is excessively fine between Stirner, who would have men agree on the terms of a union which they are to stick to as long as they find it advisable, and Bakunin and Tucker, who would have them bound together by a contract limited by the inalienable right of secession.]

Doctrines of the State in the Philosophy of Law

Affirmative Doctrines of the State				Negative Doctrines of the State — ANARCHISM					Anarchistic Teachings may possibly be					
As to its basis				As to condition affirmed in contrast to the State		As to its conception of the transition to the affirmed condition			As to their attitude toward law		As to their attitude toward property			
Genetic	Critical			Federalistic	Spontanistic	Reformatory	Revolutionary		Anomistic	Nomistic	Indoministic	Doministic		
	Idealistic	Eudemonistic					Renitent	Insurgent				Individualistic	Collectivistic	Communistic
		Altruistic	Egoistic											
		Go			Go*	Go			Go		Go			
	Pr			Pr		Pr				Pr	Pr*			
			St		St*			St	St*		St*			
Ba				Ba				Ba		Ba			Ba	
Kr				Kr				Kr		Kr				Kr
			Tu	Tu			Tu			Tu		Tu		
	To				To		To		To		To			

* [See note, p. 301.]

CONCLUSION

1. The personal want that impelled us toward a scientific knowledge of Anarchism has met with some satisfaction.

The concepts of Anarchism and its species have been defined; the most important errors have been removed; the most prominent Anarchistic teachings of earlier and recent times have been presented in detail. We have become acquainted with Anarchism's armory. We have seen all that can be objected against the State from all possible standpoints. We have been shown the most diverse orders of life as destined to take the State's place in future. The transition from the State to these orders of life has been represented to us in the most manifold ways.

He who would know Anarchism still more intimately, investigate the less notable teachings as well as the most prominent, and assign to both these and those their place in the causal nexus of historical events, will now find at least the foundation laid for his work. He knows with what sorts of teachings, and what parts of these teachings, he must concern himself, and what questions he must put to each of them. In this investigation he must expect many surprises: the teaching of the unknown Pisacane will astonish him by its originality, and that of the much-talked-of Most will show itself to be only a coarsened form of Kropotkin's. But on the whole it is hardly likely that the investigation will be worth the trouble it takes: the special ideas that Anarchism has to offer are given with tolerable completeness in the seven teachings here presented.

2. The external want on account of which Anarchism had to be scientifically known may now also be satisfied.

One thing we must at any rate do with regard to Anarchism: examine its teachings, as to their soundness or unsoundness, with courage, composure, and impartiality. But success in this task can be expected only if we no longer wander about aimlessly in the night of jurisprudential skepticism, or try to light it up with the lantern of dogmatism, but rather keep our eye fixed upon the guiding star of criticism.

Whether, besides this, it is requisite to oppose Anarchism or at least one or another of its species by especial instrumentalities of power,—whether, in particular, crime committed for the realization of Anarchistic teachings is a more serious misdeed than any political or even ordinary crime,—as to this the legislators of each country must decide with a view to the special conditions existing therein.

INDEX

OF DETAILS, EXEMPLIFICATIONS, AND CATCHWORDS IN THE QUOTATIONS FROM THE SEVEN WRITERS

The following index is not a translation of Eltzbacher's, and does not index his part of the work, but only the matter quoted from the seven writers. Furthermore, it does not index such parts of their work as are readily found by consulting the table of contents and Chapter X. The reader will therefore, in general, for Justice, see the sections "Basis" and "Property" in each chapter, and the whole of Chapter IV; for Self-Interest, "Basis" in each chapter and the whole of Chapters V and VIII; for Classes, "State" and "Property" in each chapter; for Organization, "State" and "Realization"; for Government, Democracy, Tyranny, "State"; for Capitalism, Poverty, Inequality, "Property"; for Communism, Chapters VII and IX, especially "Property" and "Realization", comparing Chapter VI; for Propaganda, Social Revolution, "Realization" in each chapter; and so on. So far as general points of this nature are mentioned in the index, it is in most cases only on some incidental occasion, and does not supersede this general reference: nor could this be superseded without thereby misleading the reader. "Law" has received somewhat exceptional treatment.

The reader will of course not assume, because in the index he does not find a certain author among those who are cited on a certain topic, that this author has not mentioned it. While the index shows a wider range of topics than might have been expected in such a book, the nature of Eltzbacher's compilation forbids us to expect that it should serve as a complete Cyclopedia of Anarchism.

BOOKS REFERRED TO BY ABBREVIATED TITLES

Adler, "Handwoerterbuch" = GEORG ADLER, "Anarchismus," in *Handwoerterbuch der Staatswissenschaften*, 2d ed. (Jena 1898), vol. 1 pp. 296-327.

Adler, "Nord und Sued" = GEORG ADLER, "Die Lehren der Anarchisten," in *Nord und Sued* (Breslau) vol. 32 (1885) pp. 371-83.

Ba. "Articles" = "Articles écrits par Bakounine dans l'Egalité de 1869," in *Mémoire présenté par la fédération jurassienne de l'Association internationale des travailleurs à toutes les fédérations de l'Internationale* (Sonvillier, n. d.), "Pièces justificatives" pp. 68-114.

Ba. "Briefe" = "Briefe Bakunins," in Dragomanoff (see below) pp. 1-272.

Ba. "Dieu" = MICHEL BAKOUNINE, *Dieu et l'Etat,* 2d ed. (Paris 1892).

Ba. "Dieu" Œuvres = "Dieu et l'Etat," in MICHEL BAKOUNINE, *Œuvres*, 3d ed. (Paris 1895), pp. 261-326.

Ba. "Discours" = "Discours de Bakounine au congrès de Berne," in *Mémoire présenté par la fédération jurassienne de l'Association internationale des travailleurs à toutes les fédérations de l'Internationale* (Sonvillier, n. d.), "Pièces justificatives" pp. 20-38.

Ba. "Programme" = BAKOUNINE, "Programme de la section slave à Zurich," in Dragomanoff (see below) pp. 381-3.

Ba. "Proposition" = "Fédéralisme, socialisme et antithéologisme. Proposition motivée au Comité central de la Ligue de la paix et de la liberté," in MICHEL BAKOUNINE, *Œuvres,* 3d ed. (Paris 1895), pp. 1-205.

Ba. "Statuts" = "Statuts secrets de l'Alliance" and "Programme et règlement de l'Alliance publique," in "L'Alliance" (see below) pp. 118-35.

Ba. "Volkssache" = M. BAKUNIN, "Die Volkssache. Romanow, Pugatschew oder Pestel?" in Dragomanoff (see below) pp. 303-9.

Bernatzik = BERNATZIK, "Der Anarchismus," in *Jahrbuch fuer Gesetzgebung, Verwaltung und Volkswirtschaft im Deutschen Reich* (Leipzig) vol. 19 (1895) pp. 1-20.

Bernstein = EDUARD BERNSTEIN, "Die soziale Doktrin des Anarchismus," in *Die Neue Zeit* (Stuttgart) year 10 (1891-2) vol. 1 pp. 358-65, 421-8; vol. 2 pp. 589-96, 618-26, 657-66, 772-8, 813-19.

Crispi = FRANCESCO CRISPI, "The Antidote for Anarchy," in *Daily Mail* (London) no. 807 (1898) p. 4.

"Der Anarchismus und seine Traeger" = *Der Anarchismus und seine Traeger. Enthuellungen aus dem Lager der Anarchisten von* ⚠, *Verfasser der Londoner Briefe in der Koelnischen Zeitung* (Berlin 1887).

"Die historische Entwickelung des Anarchismus" = *Die historische Entwickelung des Anarchismus* (New York 1894).

Diehl=KARL DIEHL, *P. J. Proudhon. Seine Lehre und sein Leben.* (3 vol., Jena 1888-96.)

Dragomanoff = MICHAIL DRAGOMANOW, *Michail Bakunins sozialpolitischer Briefwechsel mit Alexander Iw. Herzen und Ogarjow, deutsch von Boris Minzès* (Stuttgart 1895).

Dubois = FELIX DUBOIS, *Le Péril anarchiste* (Paris 1894).

Ferri = "Discours de FERRI" in *Congrès international d'anthropologie criminelle, compte rendu des travaux de la quatrième session, tenue à Genève du 24 au 29 août 1896* (Genève 1897) pp. 254-7.

Garraud = R. GARRAUD, *L'Anarchie et la Répression* (Paris 1895).

Godwin = WILLIAM GODWIN, *An Enquiry concerning Political Justice and its Influence on General Virtue and Happiness* (2 vol., London 1793). [Bracketed references are to the "First American from the second London edition, corrected," Philadelphia, 1796.]

"Hintermaenner" = *Die Hintermaenner der Sozialdemokratie. Von einem Eingeweihten* (Berlin 1890).

Kr. "Anarchist Communism" = PETER KROPOTKINE, *Anarchist Communism: its Basis and Principles,* 2d ed. (London 1895). [Reprinted from the *Nineteenth Century*.]

Kr. "Conquête" = PIERRE KROPOTKINE, *La Conquête du pain,* 5th ed. (Paris 1895).

Kr. "L'Anarchie dans l'évolution socialiste"=PIERRE KROPOTKINE, *L'Anarchie dans l'évolution socialiste* (Paris 1892).

Kr. "L'Anarchie. Sa philosophie—son idéal = PIERRE KROPOTKINE, *L'Anarchie. Sa philosophie—son idéal* (Paris 1896).

Kr. "Morale" = PIERRE KROPOTKINE, *La Morale anarchiste* (Paris 1891).

Kr. "Paroles" = PIERRE KROPOTKINE, *Paroles d'un révolté, ouvrage publié par Elisée Réclus, nouv. éd.* (Paris, n. d.)

Kr. "Prisons " = Pierre Kropotkine, *Les Prisons* (Paris 1890).

Kr. "Siècle " = Pierre Kropotkine, *Un siècle d'attente. 1789-1889* (Paris 1893).

Kr. "Studies " = *Revolutionary Studies, translated from "La Révolte" and reprinted from "The Commonweal"* (London 1892).

Kr. "Temps nouveaux " = Pierre Kropotkine, *Les Temps nouveaux (conférence faite à Londres)* (Paris 1894).

"L'Alliance" = *L'Alliance de la démocratie socialiste et l'Association internationale des travailleurs* (Londres et Hambourg 1873).

Lenz = Adolf Lenz, *Der Anarchismus und das Strafrecht. Sonderabdruck aus der Zeitschrift fuer die gesamte Strafrechtswissenschaft, Bd. 16, Heft 1* (Berlin, n. d.).

Lombroso = C. Lombroso, *Gli Anarchici,* 2d ed. (Torino 1895).

Mackay, "Anarchisten " = John Henry Mackay, *Die Anarchisten. Kulturgemaelde aus dem Ende des 19. Jahrhunderts.* Volksausgabe (Berlin 1893).

Mackay, "Magazin " = John Henry Mackay, "Der individualistische Anarchismus: ein Gegner der Propaganda der That," in *Das Magazin fuer Litteratur* (Berlin und Weimar) vol. 67 (1898) pp. 913-15.

Mackay, "Stirner " = John Henry Mackay, *Max Stirner. Sein Leben und sein Werk* (Berlin 1898).

Merlino = F. S. Merlino, *L'Individualismo nell' anarchismo* (Roma 1895).

Pfau = "Proudhon und die Franzosen," in Ludwig Pfau, *Kunst und Kritik,* vol. 6 of *Aesthetische Schriften,* 2d ed. (Stuttgart, Leipzig, Berlin, 1888), pp. 183-236.

Plechanow = Georg Plechanow, *Anarchismus und Sozialismus* (Berlin 1894).

Pr. "Banque " = P.-J. Proudhon, *Banque du peuple, suivie du rapport de la commission des délégués du Luxembourg* (Paris 1849). (In Proudhon's *Œuvres complètes,* Paris 1866-83, this forms part of the volume "Solution.")

Pr. "Contradictions " = P.-J. Proudhon, *Système des contradictions économiques, ou philosophie de la misère* (2 vol., Paris 1846).

Pr. "Confessions " = P.-J. Proudhon, *Les Confessions d'un révolutionnaire, pour servir à l'histoire de la révolution de février* (Paris 1849).

Pr. "Droit " = P.-J. Proudhon, *Le Droit au travail et le Droit de propriété* (Paris 1848). (In the *Œuvres* this forms part of the volume "La Révolution sociale.")

Pr. " Idée " = P.-J. Proudhon, *Idée générale de la révolution au XIXe siècle (choix d'études sur la pratique révolutionnaire et industrielle)* (Paris 1851).

Pr. " Justice " = P.-J. Proudhon, *De la justice dans la révolution et dans l'Eglise. Nouveaux principes de philosophie pratique* (3 vol., Paris 1858).

Pr. " Organisation " = P.-J. Proudhon, *Organisation du crédit et de la circulation, et solution du problème social* (Paris 1848). (In the *Œuvres* this forms part of the volume " Solution.")

Pr. " Principe " = P.-J. Proudhon, *Du principe fédératif et de la nécessité de reconstituer le parti de la révolution* (Paris 1863).

Pr. " Propriété " = P.-J. Proudhon, *Qu'est-ce que la propriété? ou recherches sur le principe du droit et du gouvernement. Premier mémoire* (Paris 1841).

Pr. " Solution " = P.-J. Proudhon, *Solution du problème social* (Paris 1848).

Proal = Louis Proal, *La Criminalité politique* (Paris 1895).

Reichesberg = Naum Reichesberg, *Sozialismus und Anarchismus* (Bern und Leipzig 1895).

Rienzi = Rienzi, *L'Anarchisme, traduit du néerlandais par August Dewinne* (Bruxelles 1893).

Sernicoli = E. Sernicoli, *L'Anarchia e gli Anarchici. Studio storico e politico di E. Sernicoli* (2 vol., Milano 1894).

Shaw = George Bernard Shaw, *The Impossibilities of Anarchism* (London 1895).

Silio = Cesar Silio, " El Anarquismo y la Defensa Social," in *La Espana Moderna* (Madrid) vol. 61 (1894) pp. 141-8.

Stammler = Rudolf Stammler, *Die Theorie des Anarchismus* (Berlin 1894).

Stirner = Max Stirner, *Der Einzige und sein Eigentum* (Leipzig 1845).

Stirner " Vierteljahrsschrift " = M. St., " Rezensenten Stirners," in *Wigands Vierteljahrsschrift* (Leipzig) vol. 3 (1845) pp. 147-94.

To. " Confession " = Graf Leo Tolstoj, *Bekenntnisse. Was sollen wir denn thun? deutsch von H. von Samson-Himmelstjerna* (Leipzig 1886), pp. 1-102.

To. " Gospel " = Graf Leo N. Tolstoj, *Kurze Darlegung des Evangeliums, deutsch von Paul Lauterbach* (Leipzig, n. d.).

To. " Kernel " = " Das Korn," in Graf Leo N. Tolstoj, *Volkserzaehlungen, deutsch von Wilhelm Goldschmidt* (Leipzig, n. d.), pp. 87-9.

To. " Kingdom " = Leo N. Tolstoj, *Das Reich Gottes ist in*

euch, oder das Christentum als eine neue Lebensauffassung, nicht als mystische Lehre, deutsch von R. Loewenfeld (Stuttgart, Leipzig, Berlin, Wien, 1894).

To. " Linen-Measurer " = "Leinwandmesser. Die Geschichte eines Pferdes," in LEO N. TOLSTOJ, *Gesammelte Werke, deutsch herausgegeben von Raphael Loewenfeld,* vol. 3 (Berlin 1893) pp. 573-631.

To. "Money" = GRAF LEO TOLSTOJ, *Geld! Soziale Betrachtungen, deutsch von August Scholz* (Berlin 1891).

To. " Morning " = " Der Morgen des Gutsherrn," in LEO N. TOLSTOJ, *Gesammelte Werke, deutsch herausgegeben von Raphael Loewenfeld,* vol. 2, 2d ed. (Leipzig, n. d.), pp. 1-81.

To. " On Life " = GRAF LEO TOLSTOJ, *Ueber das Leben, deutsch von Sophie Behr* (Leipzig 1889).

To. " Patriotism " = GRAF LEO N. TOLSTOJ,*Christentum und Vaterlandsliebe, deutsch von L. A. Hauff* (Berlin n. d.).

To. "Persecutions " = *Russische Christenverfolgungen im Kaukasus. Mit einem Vor- und Nachwort von Leo Tolstoj* (Dresden und Leipzig 1896) pp. 7-8, 38-48.

To. " Reason and Dogma " = GRAF LEO N. TOLSTOJ, *Vernunft und Dogma. Eine Kritik der Glaubenslehre, deutsch von L. A. Hauff* (Berlin n. d.).

To. " Religion and Morality " = GRAF LEO TOLSTOJ, *Religion und Moral. Antwort auf eine in der " Ethischen Kultur" gestellte Frage, deutsch von Sophie Behr* (Berlin 1894).

To. " What I Believe" = GRAF LEO TOLSTOJ, *Worin besteht mein Glaube? Eine Studie, deutsch von Sophie Behr* (Leipzig 1885).

To. " What Shall We Do " = GRAF LEO TOLSTOJ, *Was sollen wir also thun? deutsch von August Scholz* (Berlin 1891).

Tripels = " Discours de Tripels," in *Congrès international d'anthropologie criminelle, compte rendu des travaux de la quatrième session, tenue à Genève du 24 au 29 août 1896* (Genève 1897) pp. 253-4.

Tucker = BENJ. R. TUCKER, *Instead of a Book. By a Man Too Busy to Write One. A fragmentary exposition of philosophical Anarchism* (New York 1893).

Van Hamel = VAN HAMEL, " L'Anarchisme et le Combat contre l'anarchisme au point de vue de l'anthropologie criminelle," in *Congrès international d'anthropologie criminelle, compte rendu des travaux de la quatrième session, tenue à Genève du 24 au 29 août 1896* (Genève 1897) pp. 254-7.

Zenker = E. V. ZENKER, *Der.Anarchismus. Kritische Geschichte der anarchistischen Theorie* (Jena 1895).

A CATALOG OF SELECTED
DOVER BOOKS
IN ALL FIELDS OF INTEREST

A CATALOG OF SELECTED DOVER
BOOKS IN ALL FIELDS OF INTEREST

CONCERNING THE SPIRITUAL IN ART, Wassily Kandinsky. Pioneering work by father of abstract art. Thoughts on color theory, nature of art. Analysis of earlier masters. 12 illustrations. 80pp. of text. 5⅜ x 8½. 23411-8

ANIMALS: 1,419 Copyright-Free Illustrations of Mammals, Birds, Fish, Insects, etc., Jim Harter (ed.). Clear wood engravings present, in extremely lifelike poses, over 1,000 species of animals. One of the most extensive pictorial sourcebooks of its kind. Captions. Index. 284pp. 9 x 12. 23766-4

CELTIC ART: The Methods of Construction, George Bain. Simple geometric techniques for making Celtic interlacements, spirals, Kells-type initials, animals, humans, etc. Over 500 illustrations. 160pp. 9 x 12. (Available in U.S. only.) 22923-8

AN ATLAS OF ANATOMY FOR ARTISTS, Fritz Schider. Most thorough reference work on art anatomy in the world. Hundreds of illustrations, including selections from works by Vesalius, Leonardo, Goya, Ingres, Michelangelo, others. 593 illustrations. 192pp. 7⅛ x 10¼. 20241-0

CELTIC HAND STROKE-BY-STROKE (Irish Half-Uncial from "The Book of Kells"): An Arthur Baker Calligraphy Manual, Arthur Baker. Complete guide to creating each letter of the alphabet in distinctive Celtic manner. Covers hand position, strokes, pens, inks, paper, more. Illustrated. 48pp. 8¼ x 11. 24336-2

EASY ORIGAMI, John Montroll. Charming collection of 32 projects (hat, cup, pelican, piano, swan, many more) specially designed for the novice origami hobbyist. Clearly illustrated easy-to-follow instructions insure that even beginning papercrafters will achieve successful results. 48pp. 8¼ x 11. 27298-2

THE COMPLETE BOOK OF BIRDHOUSE CONSTRUCTION FOR WOOD-WORKERS, Scott D. Campbell. Detailed instructions, illustrations, tables. Also data on bird habitat and instinct patterns. Bibliography. 3 tables. 63 illustrations in 15 figures. 48pp. 5¼ x 8½. 24407-5

BLOOMINGDALE'S ILLUSTRATED 1886 CATALOG: Fashions, Dry Goods and Housewares, Bloomingdale Brothers. Famed merchants' extremely rare catalog depicting about 1,700 products: clothing, housewares, firearms, dry goods, jewelry, more. Invaluable for dating, identifying vintage items. Also, copyright-free graphics for artists, designers. Co-published with Henry Ford Museum & Greenfield Village. 160pp. 8¼ x 11. 25780-0

HISTORIC COSTUME IN PICTURES, Braun & Schneider. Over 1,450 costumed figures in clearly detailed engravings–from dawn of civilization to end of 19th century. Captions. Many folk costumes. 256pp. 8⅜ x 11¾. 23150-X

STICKLEY CRAFTSMAN FURNITURE CATALOGS, Gustav Stickley and L. & J. G. Stickley. Beautiful, functional furniture in two authentic catalogs from 1910. 594 illustrations, including 277 photos, show settles, rockers, armchairs, reclining chairs, bookcases, desks, tables. 183pp. 6½ x 9¼. 23838-5

AMERICAN LOCOMOTIVES IN HISTORIC PHOTOGRAPHS: 1858 to 1949, Ron Ziel (ed.). A rare collection of 126 meticulously detailed official photographs, called "builder portraits," of American locomotives that majestically chronicle the rise of steam locomotive power in America. Introduction. Detailed captions. xi+ 129pp. 9 x 12. 27393-8

AMERICA'S LIGHTHOUSES: An Illustrated History, Francis Ross Holland, Jr. Delightfully written, profusely illustrated fact-filled survey of over 200 American lighthouses since 1716. History, anecdotes, technological advances, more. 240pp. 8 x 10¾. 25576-X

TOWARDS A NEW ARCHITECTURE, Le Corbusier. Pioneering manifesto by founder of "International School." Technical and aesthetic theories, views of industry, economics, relation of form to function, "mass-production split" and much more. Profusely illustrated. 320pp. 6⅛ x 9¼. (Available in U.S. only.) 25023-7

HOW THE OTHER HALF LIVES, Jacob Riis. Famous journalistic record, exposing poverty and degradation of New York slums around 1900, by major social reformer. 100 striking and influential photographs. 233pp. 10 x 7⅞. 22012-5

FRUIT KEY AND TWIG KEY TO TREES AND SHRUBS, William M. Harlow. One of the handiest and most widely used identification aids. Fruit key covers 120 deciduous and evergreen species; twig key 160 deciduous species. Easily used. Over 300 photographs. 126pp. 5⅜ x 8½. 20511-8

COMMON BIRD SONGS, Dr. Donald J. Borror. Songs of 60 most common U.S. birds: robins, sparrows, cardinals, bluejays, finches, more–arranged in order of increasing complexity. Up to 9 variations of songs of each species.
Cassette and manual 99911-4

ORCHIDS AS HOUSE PLANTS, Rebecca Tyson Northen. Grow cattleyas and many other kinds of orchids–in a window, in a case, or under artificial light. 63 illustrations. 148pp. 5⅜ x 8½. 23261-1

MONSTER MAZES, Dave Phillips. Masterful mazes at four levels of difficulty. Avoid deadly perils and evil creatures to find magical treasures. Solutions for all 32 exciting illustrated puzzles. 48pp. 8¼ x 11. 26005-4

MOZART'S DON GIOVANNI (DOVER OPERA LIBRETTO SERIES), Wolfgang Amadeus Mozart. Introduced and translated by Ellen H. Bleiler. Standard Italian libretto, with complete English translation. Convenient and thoroughly portable–an ideal companion for reading along with a recording or the performance itself. Introduction. List of characters. Plot summary. 121pp. 5¼ x 8½. 24944-1

TECHNICAL MANUAL AND DICTIONARY OF CLASSICAL BALLET, Gail Grant. Defines, explains, comments on steps, movements, poses and concepts. 15-page pictorial section. Basic book for student, viewer. 127pp. 5⅜ x 8½. 21843-0

THE CLARINET AND CLARINET PLAYING, David Pino. Lively, comprehensive work features suggestions about technique, musicianship, and musical interpretation, as well as guidelines for teaching, making your own reeds, and preparing for public performance. Includes an intriguing look at clarinet history. "A godsend," *The Clarinet*, Journal of the International Clarinet Society. Appendixes. 7 illus. 320pp. 5⅜ x 8½. 40270-3

HOLLYWOOD GLAMOR PORTRAITS, John Kobal (ed.). 145 photos from 1926-49. Harlow, Gable, Bogart, Bacall; 94 stars in all. Full background on photographers, technical aspects. 160pp. 8⅜ x 11¼. 23352-9

THE ANNOTATED CASEY AT THE BAT: A Collection of Ballads about the Mighty Casey/Third, Revised Edition, Martin Gardner (ed.). Amusing sequels and parodies of one of America's best-loved poems: Casey's Revenge, Why Casey Whiffed, Casey's Sister at the Bat, others. 256pp. 5⅜ x 8½. 28598-7

THE RAVEN AND OTHER FAVORITE POEMS, Edgar Allan Poe. Over 40 of the author's most memorable poems: "The Bells," "Ulalume," "Israfel," "To Helen," "The Conqueror Worm," "Eldorado," "Annabel Lee," many more. Alphabetic lists of titles and first lines. 64pp. 5³⁄₁₆ x 8¼. 26685-0

PERSONAL MEMOIRS OF U. S. GRANT, Ulysses Simpson Grant. Intelligent, deeply moving firsthand account of Civil War campaigns, considered by many the finest military memoirs ever written. Includes letters, historic photographs, maps and more. 528pp. 6⅛ x 9¼. 28587-1

ANCIENT EGYPTIAN MATERIALS AND INDUSTRIES, A. Lucas and J. Harris. Fascinating, comprehensive, thoroughly documented text describes this ancient civilization's vast resources and the processes that incorporated them in daily life, including the use of animal products, building materials, cosmetics, perfumes and incense, fibers, glazed ware, glass and its manufacture, materials used in the mummification process, and much more. 544pp. 6⅛ x 9¼. (Available in U.S. only.) 40446-3

RUSSIAN STORIES/RUSSKIE RASSKAZY: A Dual-Language Book, edited by Gleb Struve. Twelve tales by such masters as Chekhov, Tolstoy, Dostoevsky, Pushkin, others. Excellent word-for-word English translations on facing pages, plus teaching and study aids, Russian/English vocabulary, biographical/critical introductions, more. 416pp. 5⅜ x 8½. 26244-8

PHILADELPHIA THEN AND NOW: 60 Sites Photographed in the Past and Present, Kenneth Finkel and Susan Oyama. Rare photographs of City Hall, Logan Square, Independence Hall, Betsy Ross House, other landmarks juxtaposed with contemporary views. Captures changing face of historic city. Introduction. Captions. 128pp. 8¼ x 11. 25790-8

AIA ARCHITECTURAL GUIDE TO NASSAU AND SUFFOLK COUNTIES, LONG ISLAND, The American Institute of Architects, Long Island Chapter, and the Society for the Preservation of Long Island Antiquities. Comprehensive, well-researched and generously illustrated volume brings to life over three centuries of Long Island's great architectural heritage. More than 240 photographs with authoritative, extensively detailed captions. 176pp. 8¼ x 11. 26946-9

NORTH AMERICAN INDIAN LIFE: Customs and Traditions of 23 Tribes, Elsie Clews Parsons (ed.). 27 fictionalized essays by noted anthropologists examine religion, customs, government, additional facets of life among the Winnebago, Crow, Zuni, Eskimo, other tribes. 480pp. 6⅛ x 9¼. 27377-6

FRANK LLOYD WRIGHT'S DANA HOUSE, Donald Hoffmann. Pictorial essay of residential masterpiece with over 160 interior and exterior photos, plans, elevations, sketches and studies. 128pp. 9¼ x 10¾. 29120-0

THE MALE AND FEMALE FIGURE IN MOTION: 60 Classic Photographic Sequences, Eadweard Muybridge. 60 true-action photographs of men and women walking, running, climbing, bending, turning, etc., reproduced from rare 19th-century masterpiece. vi + 121pp. 9 x 12. 24745-7

1001 QUESTIONS ANSWERED ABOUT THE SEASHORE, N. J. Berrill and Jacquelyn Berrill. Queries answered about dolphins, sea snails, sponges, starfish, fishes, shore birds, many others. Covers appearance, breeding, growth, feeding, much more. 305pp. 5¼ x 8¼. 23366-9

ATTRACTING BIRDS TO YOUR YARD, William J. Weber. Easy-to-follow guide offers advice on how to attract the greatest diversity of birds: birdhouses, feeders, water and waterers, much more. 96pp. 5³/₁₆ x 8¼. 28927-3

MEDICINAL AND OTHER USES OF NORTH AMERICAN PLANTS: A Historical Survey with Special Reference to the Eastern Indian Tribes, Charlotte Erichsen-Brown. Chronological historical citations document 500 years of usage of plants, trees, shrubs native to eastern Canada, northeastern U.S. Also complete identifying information. 343 illustrations. 544pp. 6½ x 9¼. 25951-X

STORYBOOK MAZES, Dave Phillips. 23 stories and mazes on two-page spreads: Wizard of Oz, Treasure Island, Robin Hood, etc. Solutions. 64pp. 8¼ x 11. 23628-5

AMERICAN NEGRO SONGS: 230 Folk Songs and Spirituals, Religious and Secular, John W. Work. This authoritative study traces the African influences of songs sung and played by black Americans at work, in church, and as entertainment. The author discusses the lyric significance of such songs as "Swing Low, Sweet Chariot," "John Henry," and others and offers the words and music for 230 songs. Bibliography. Index of Song Titles. 272pp. 6½ x 9¼. 40271-1

MOVIE-STAR PORTRAITS OF THE FORTIES, John Kobal (ed.). 163 glamor, studio photos of 106 stars of the 1940s: Rita Hayworth, Ava Gardner, Marlon Brando, Clark Gable, many more. 176pp. 8⅜ x 11¼. 23546-7

BENCHLEY LOST AND FOUND, Robert Benchley. Finest humor from early 30s, about pet peeves, child psychologists, post office and others. Mostly unavailable elsewhere. 73 illustrations by Peter Arno and others. 183pp. 5⅜ x 8½. 22410-4

YEKL and THE IMPORTED BRIDEGROOM AND OTHER STORIES OF YIDDISH NEW YORK, Abraham Cahan. Film Hester Street based on *Yekl* (1896). Novel, other stories among first about Jewish immigrants on N.Y.'s East Side. 240pp. 5⅜ x 8½. 22427-9

SELECTED POEMS, Walt Whitman. Generous sampling from *Leaves of Grass.* Twenty-four poems include "I Hear America Singing," "Song of the Open Road," "I Sing the Body Electric," "When Lilacs Last in the Dooryard Bloom'd," "O Captain! My Captain!"—all reprinted from an authoritative edition. Lists of titles and first lines. 128pp. 5³/₁₆ x 8¼. 26878-0

THE BEST TALES OF HOFFMANN, E. T. A. Hoffmann. 10 of Hoffmann's most important stories: "Nutcracker and the King of Mice," "The Golden Flowerpot," etc. 458pp. 5⅜ x 8½. 21793-0

FROM FETISH TO GOD IN ANCIENT EGYPT, E. A. Wallis Budge. Rich detailed survey of Egyptian conception of "God" and gods, magic, cult of animals, Osiris, more. Also, superb English translations of hymns and legends. 240 illustrations. 545pp. 5⅜ x 8½. 25803-3

FRENCH STORIES/CONTES FRANÇAIS: A Dual-Language Book, Wallace Fowlie. Ten stories by French masters, Voltaire to Camus: "Micromegas" by Voltaire; "The Atheist's Mass" by Balzac; "Minuet" by de Maupassant; "The Guest" by Camus, six more. Excellent English translations on facing pages. Also French-English vocabulary list, exercises, more. 352pp. 5⅜ x 8½. 26443-2

CHICAGO AT THE TURN OF THE CENTURY IN PHOTOGRAPHS: 122 Historic Views from the Collections of the Chicago Historical Society, Larry A. Viskochil. Rare large-format prints offer detailed views of City Hall, State Street, the Loop, Hull House, Union Station, many other landmarks, circa 1904-1913. Introduction. Captions. Maps. 144pp. 9⅜ x 12¼. 24656-6

OLD BROOKLYN IN EARLY PHOTOGRAPHS, 1865-1929, William Lee Younger. Luna Park, Gravesend race track, construction of Grand Army Plaza, moving of Hotel Brighton, etc. 157 previously unpublished photographs. 165pp. 8⅞ x 11¾. 23587-4

THE MYTHS OF THE NORTH AMERICAN INDIANS, Lewis Spence. Rich anthology of the myths and legends of the Algonquins, Iroquois, Pawnees and Sioux, prefaced by an extensive historical and ethnological commentary. 36 illustrations. 480pp. 5⅜ x 8½. 25967-6

AN ENCYCLOPEDIA OF BATTLES: Accounts of Over 1,560 Battles from 1479 B.C. to the Present, David Eggenberger. Essential details of every major battle in recorded history from the first battle of Megiddo in 1479 B.C. to Grenada in 1984. List of Battle Maps. New Appendix covering the years 1967-1984. Index. 99 illustrations. 544pp. 6½ x 9¼. 24913-1

SAILING ALONE AROUND THE WORLD, Captain Joshua Slocum. First man to sail around the world, alone, in small boat. One of great feats of seamanship told in delightful manner. 67 illustrations. 294pp. 5⅜ x 8½. 20326-3

ANARCHISM AND OTHER ESSAYS, Emma Goldman. Powerful, penetrating, prophetic essays on direct action, role of minorities, prison reform, puritan hypocrisy, violence, etc. 271pp. 5⅜ x 8½. 22484-8

MYTHS OF THE HINDUS AND BUDDHISTS, Ananda K. Coomaraswamy and Sister Nivedita. Great stories of the epics; deeds of Krishna, Shiva, taken from puranas, Vedas, folk tales; etc. 32 illustrations. 400pp. 5⅜ x 8½. 21759-0

THE TRAUMA OF BIRTH, Otto Rank. Rank's controversial thesis that anxiety neurosis is caused by profound psychological trauma which occurs at birth. 256pp. 5⅜ x 8½. 27974-X

A THEOLOGICO-POLITICAL TREATISE, Benedict Spinoza. Also contains unfinished Political Treatise. Great classic on religious liberty, theory of government on common consent. R. Elwes translation. Total of 421pp. 5⅜ x 8½. 20249-6

MY BONDAGE AND MY FREEDOM, Frederick Douglass. Born a slave, Douglass became outspoken force in antislavery movement. The best of Douglass' autobiographies. Graphic description of slave life. 464pp. 5⅜ x 8½.   22457-0

FOLLOWING THE EQUATOR: A Journey Around the World, Mark Twain. Fascinating humorous account of 1897 voyage to Hawaii, Australia, India, New Zealand, etc. Ironic, bemused reports on peoples, customs, climate, flora and fauna, politics, much more. 197 illustrations. 720pp. 5⅜ x 8½.   26113-1

THE PEOPLE CALLED SHAKERS, Edward D. Andrews. Definitive study of Shakers: origins, beliefs, practices, dances, social organization, furniture and crafts, etc. 33 illustrations. 351pp. 5⅜ x 8½.   21081-2

THE MYTHS OF GREECE AND ROME, H. A. Guerber. A classic of mythology, generously illustrated, long prized for its simple, graphic, accurate retelling of the principal myths of Greece and Rome, and for its commentary on their origins and significance. With 64 illustrations by Michelangelo, Raphael, Titian, Rubens, Canova, Bernini and others. 480pp. 5⅜ x 8½.   27584-1

PSYCHOLOGY OF MUSIC, Carl E. Seashore. Classic work discusses music as a medium from psychological viewpoint. Clear treatment of physical acoustics, auditory apparatus, sound perception, development of musical skills, nature of musical feeling, host of other topics. 88 figures. 408pp. 5⅜ x 8½.   21851-1

THE PHILOSOPHY OF HISTORY, Georg W. Hegel. Great classic of Western thought develops concept that history is not chance but rational process, the evolution of freedom. 457pp. 5⅜ x 8½.   20112-0

THE BOOK OF TEA, Kakuzo Okakura. Minor classic of the Orient: entertaining, charming explanation, interpretation of traditional Japanese culture in terms of tea ceremony. 94pp. 5⅜ x 8½.   20070-1

LIFE IN ANCIENT EGYPT, Adolf Erman. Fullest, most thorough, detailed older account with much not in more recent books, domestic life, religion, magic, medicine, commerce, much more. Many illustrations reproduce tomb paintings, carvings, hieroglyphs, etc. 597pp. 5⅜ x 8½.   22632-8

SUNDIALS, Their Theory and Construction, Albert Waugh. Far and away the best, most thorough coverage of ideas, mathematics concerned, types, construction, adjusting anywhere. Simple, nontechnical treatment allows even children to build several of these dials. Over 100 illustrations. 230pp. 5⅜ x 8½.   22947-5

THEORETICAL HYDRODYNAMICS, L. M. Milne-Thomson. Classic exposition of the mathematical theory of fluid motion, applicable to both hydrodynamics and aerodynamics. Over 600 exercises. 768pp. 6⅛ x 9¼.   68970-0

SONGS OF EXPERIENCE: Facsimile Reproduction with 26 Plates in Full Color, William Blake. 26 full-color plates from a rare 1826 edition. Includes "The Tyger," "London," "Holy Thursday," and other poems. Printed text of poems. 48pp. 5¼ x 7.   24636-1

OLD-TIME VIGNETTES IN FULL COLOR, Carol Belanger Grafton (ed.). Over 390 charming, often sentimental illustrations, selected from archives of Victorian graphics—pretty women posing, children playing, food, flowers, kittens and puppies, smiling cherubs, birds and butterflies, much more. All copyright-free. 48pp. 9¼ x 12¼.   27269-9

PERSPECTIVE FOR ARTISTS, Rex Vicat Cole. Depth, perspective of sky and sea, shadows, much more, not usually covered. 391 diagrams, 81 reproductions of drawings and paintings. 279pp. 5⅜ x 8½. 22487-2

DRAWING THE LIVING FIGURE, Joseph Sheppard. Innovative approach to artistic anatomy focuses on specifics of surface anatomy, rather than muscles and bones. Over 170 drawings of live models in front, back and side views, and in widely varying poses. Accompanying diagrams. 177 illustrations. Introduction. Index. 144pp. 8⅜ x11¼. 26723-7

GOTHIC AND OLD ENGLISH ALPHABETS: 100 Complete Fonts, Dan X. Solo. Add power, elegance to posters, signs, other graphics with 100 stunning copyright-free alphabets: Blackstone, Dolbey, Germania, 97 more–including many lower-case, numerals, punctuation marks. 104pp. 8⅛ x 11. 24695-7

HOW TO DO BEADWORK, Mary White. Fundamental book on craft from simple projects to five-bead chains and woven works. 106 illustrations. 142pp. 5⅜ x 8. 20697-1

THE BOOK OF WOOD CARVING, Charles Marshall Sayers. Finest book for beginners discusses fundamentals and offers 34 designs. "Absolutely first rate . . . well thought out and well executed."–E. J. Tangerman. 118pp. 7¾ x 10⅝. 23654-4

ILLUSTRATED CATALOG OF CIVIL WAR MILITARY GOODS: Union Army Weapons, Insignia, Uniform Accessories, and Other Equipment, Schuyler, Hartley, and Graham. Rare, profusely illustrated 1846 catalog includes Union Army uniform and dress regulations, arms and ammunition, coats, insignia, flags, swords, rifles, etc. 226 illustrations. 160pp. 9 x 12. 24939-5

WOMEN'S FASHIONS OF THE EARLY 1900s: An Unabridged Republication of "New York Fashions, 1909," National Cloak & Suit Co. Rare catalog of mail-order fashions documents women's and children's clothing styles shortly after the turn of the century. Captions offer full descriptions, prices. Invaluable resource for fashion, costume historians. Approximately 725 illustrations. 128pp. 8⅜ x 11¼. 27276-1

THE 1912 AND 1915 GUSTAV STICKLEY FURNITURE CATALOGS, Gustav Stickley. With over 200 detailed illustrations and descriptions, these two catalogs are essential reading and reference materials and identification guides for Stickley furniture. Captions cite materials, dimensions and prices. 112pp. 6½ x 9¼. 26676-1

EARLY AMERICAN LOCOMOTIVES, John H. White, Jr. Finest locomotive engravings from early 19th century: historical (1804–74), main-line (after 1870), special, foreign, etc. 147 plates. 142pp. 11⅜ x 8¼. 22772-3

THE TALL SHIPS OF TODAY IN PHOTOGRAPHS, Frank O. Braynard. Lavishly illustrated tribute to nearly 100 majestic contemporary sailing vessels: Amerigo Vespucci, Clearwater, Constitution, Eagle, Mayflower, Sea Cloud, Victory, many more. Authoritative captions provide statistics, background on each ship. 190 black-and-white photographs and illustrations. Introduction. 128pp. 8⅞ x 11¾. 27163-3

LITTLE BOOK OF EARLY AMERICAN CRAFTS AND TRADES, Peter Stockham (ed.). 1807 children's book explains crafts and trades: baker, hatter, cooper, potter, and many others. 23 copperplate illustrations. 140pp. 4⅝ x 6. 23336-7

VICTORIAN FASHIONS AND COSTUMES FROM HARPER'S BAZAR, 1867–1898, Stella Blum (ed.). Day costumes, evening wear, sports clothes, shoes, hats, other accessories in over 1,000 detailed engravings. 320pp. 9⅜ x 12¼. 22990-4

GUSTAV STICKLEY, THE CRAFTSMAN, Mary Ann Smith. Superb study surveys broad scope of Stickley's achievement, especially in architecture. Design philosophy, rise and fall of the Craftsman empire, descriptions and floor plans for many Craftsman houses, more. 86 black-and-white halftones. 31 line illustrations. Introduction 208pp. 6½ x 9¼. 27210-9

THE LONG ISLAND RAIL ROAD IN EARLY PHOTOGRAPHS, Ron Ziel. Over 220 rare photos, informative text document origin (1844) and development of rail service on Long Island. Vintage views of early trains, locomotives, stations, passengers, crews, much more. Captions. 8⅞ x 11¾. 26301-0

VOYAGE OF THE LIBERDADE, Joshua Slocum. Great 19th-century mariner's thrilling, first-hand account of the wreck of his ship off South America, the 35-foot boat he built from the wreckage, and its remarkable voyage home. 128pp. 5⅜ x 8½. 40022-0

TEN BOOKS ON ARCHITECTURE, Vitruvius. The most important book ever written on architecture. Early Roman aesthetics, technology, classical orders, site selection, all other aspects. Morgan translation. 331pp. 5⅜ x 8½. 20645-9

THE HUMAN FIGURE IN MOTION, Eadweard Muybridge. More than 4,500 stopped-action photos, in action series, showing undraped men, women, children jumping, lying down, throwing, sitting, wrestling, carrying, etc. 390pp. 7⅞ x 10⅝. 20204-6 Clothbd.

TREES OF THE EASTERN AND CENTRAL UNITED STATES AND CANADA, William M. Harlow. Best one-volume guide to 140 trees. Full descriptions, woodlore, range, etc. Over 600 illustrations. Handy size. 288pp. 4½ x 6⅜. 20395-6

SONGS OF WESTERN BIRDS, Dr. Donald J. Borror. Complete song and call repertoire of 60 western species, including flycatchers, juncoes, cactus wrens, many more–includes fully illustrated booklet. Cassette and manual 99913-0

GROWING AND USING HERBS AND SPICES, Milo Miloradovich. Versatile handbook provides all the information needed for cultivation and use of all the herbs and spices available in North America. 4 illustrations. Index. Glossary. 236pp. 5⅜ x 8½. 25058-X

BIG BOOK OF MAZES AND LABYRINTHS, Walter Shepherd. 50 mazes and labyrinths in all–classical, solid, ripple, and more–in one great volume. Perfect inexpensive puzzler for clever youngsters. Full solutions. 112pp. 8⅛ x 11. 22951-3

PIANO TUNING, J. Cree Fischer. Clearest, best book for beginner, amateur. Simple repairs, raising dropped notes, tuning by easy method of flattened fifths. No previous skills needed. 4 illustrations. 201pp. 5⅜ x 8½. 23267-0

HINTS TO SINGERS, Lillian Nordica. Selecting the right teacher, developing confidence, overcoming stage fright, and many other important skills receive thoughtful discussion in this indispensible guide, written by a world-famous diva of four decades' experience. 96pp. 5⅜ x 8½. 40094-8

THE COMPLETE NONSENSE OF EDWARD LEAR, Edward Lear. All nonsense limericks, zany alphabets, Owl and Pussycat, songs, nonsense botany, etc., illustrated by Lear. Total of 320pp. 5⅜ x 8½. (Available in U.S. only.) 20167-8

VICTORIAN PARLOUR POETRY: An Annotated Anthology, Michael R. Turner. 117 gems by Longfellow, Tennyson, Browning, many lesser-known poets. "The Village Blacksmith," "Curfew Must Not Ring Tonight," "Only a Baby Small," dozens more, often difficult to find elsewhere. Index of poets, titles, first lines. xxiii + 325pp. 5⅝ x 8¼. 27044-0

DUBLINERS, James Joyce. Fifteen stories offer vivid, tightly focused observations of the lives of Dublin's poorer classes. At least one, "The Dead," is considered a masterpiece. Reprinted complete and unabridged from standard edition. 160pp. 5³⁄₁₆ x 8¼. 26870-5

GREAT WEIRD TALES: 14 Stories by Lovecraft, Blackwood, Machen and Others, S. T. Joshi (ed.). 14 spellbinding tales, including "The Sin Eater," by Fiona McLeod, "The Eye Above the Mantel," by Frank Belknap Long, as well as renowned works by R. H. Barlow, Lord Dunsany, Arthur Machen, W. C. Morrow and eight other masters of the genre. 256pp. 5⅜ x 8½. (Available in U.S. only.) 40436-6

THE BOOK OF THE SACRED MAGIC OF ABRAMELIN THE MAGE, translated by S. MacGregor Mathers. Medieval manuscript of ceremonial magic. Basic document in Aleister Crowley, Golden Dawn groups. 268pp. 5⅜ x 8½. 23211-5

NEW RUSSIAN-ENGLISH AND ENGLISH-RUSSIAN DICTIONARY, M. A. O'Brien. This is a remarkably handy Russian dictionary, containing a surprising amount of information, including over 70,000 entries. 366pp. 4½ x 6⅛. 20208-9

HISTORIC HOMES OF THE AMERICAN PRESIDENTS, Second, Revised Edition, Irvin Haas. A traveler's guide to American Presidential homes, most open to the public, depicting and describing homes occupied by every American President from George Washington to George Bush. With visiting hours, admission charges, travel routes. 175 photographs. Index. 160pp. 8¼ x 11. 26751-2

NEW YORK IN THE FORTIES, Andreas Feininger. 162 brilliant photographs by the well-known photographer, formerly with *Life* magazine. Commuters, shoppers, Times Square at night, much else from city at its peak. Captions by John von Hartz. 181pp. 9¼ x 10¾. 23585-8

INDIAN SIGN LANGUAGE, William Tomkins. Over 525 signs developed by Sioux and other tribes. Written instructions and diagrams. Also 290 pictographs. 111pp. 6⅛ x 9¼. 22029-X

ANATOMY: A Complete Guide for Artists, Joseph Sheppard. A master of figure drawing shows artists how to render human anatomy convincingly. Over 460 illustrations. 224pp. 8⅜ x 11¼. 27279-6

MEDIEVAL CALLIGRAPHY: Its History and Technique, Marc Drogin. Spirited history, comprehensive instruction manual covers 13 styles (ca. 4th century through 15th). Excellent photographs; directions for duplicating medieval techniques with modern tools. 224pp. 8⅜ x 11¼. 26142-5

DRIED FLOWERS: How to Prepare Them, Sarah Whitlock and Martha Rankin. Complete instructions on how to use silica gel, meal and borax, perlite aggregate, sand and borax, glycerine and water to create attractive permanent flower arrangements. 12 illustrations. 32pp. 5⅜ x 8½. 21802-3

EASY-TO-MAKE BIRD FEEDERS FOR WOODWORKERS, Scott D. Campbell. Detailed, simple-to-use guide for designing, constructing, caring for and using feeders. Text, illustrations for 12 classic and contemporary designs. 96pp. 5⅜ x 8½. 25847-5

SCOTTISH WONDER TALES FROM MYTH AND LEGEND, Donald A. Mackenzie. 16 lively tales tell of giants rumbling down mountainsides, of a magic wand that turns stone pillars into warriors, of gods and goddesses, evil hags, powerful forces and more. 240pp. 5⅜ x 8½. 29677-6

THE HISTORY OF UNDERCLOTHES, C. Willett Cunnington and Phyllis Cunnington. Fascinating, well-documented survey covering six centuries of English undergarments, enhanced with over 100 illustrations: 12th-century laced-up bodice, footed long drawers (1795), 19th-century bustles, 19th-century corsets for men, Victorian "bust improvers," much more. 272pp. 5⅝ x 8¼. 27124-2

ARTS AND CRAFTS FURNITURE: The Complete Brooks Catalog of 1912, Brooks Manufacturing Co. Photos and detailed descriptions of more than 150 now very collectible furniture designs from the Arts and Crafts movement depict davenports, settees, buffets, desks, tables, chairs, bedsteads, dressers and more, all built of solid, quarter-sawed oak. Invaluable for students and enthusiasts of antiques, Americana and the decorative arts. 80pp. 6½ x 9¼. 27471-3

WILBUR AND ORVILLE: A Biography of the Wright Brothers, Fred Howard. Definitive, crisply written study tells the full story of the brothers' lives and work. A vividly written biography, unparalleled in scope and color, that also captures the spirit of an extraordinary era. 560pp. 6⅛ x 9¼. 40297-5

THE ARTS OF THE SAILOR: Knotting, Splicing and Ropework, Hervey Garrett Smith. Indispensable shipboard reference covers tools, basic knots and useful hitches; handsewing and canvas work, more. Over 100 illustrations. Delightful reading for sea lovers. 256pp. 5⅜ x 8½. 26440-8

FRANK LLOYD WRIGHT'S FALLINGWATER: The House and Its History, Second, Revised Edition, Donald Hoffmann. A total revision–both in text and illustrations–of the standard document on Fallingwater, the boldest, most personal architectural statement of Wright's mature years, updated with valuable new material from the recently opened Frank Lloyd Wright Archives. "Fascinating"–*The New York Times.* 116 illustrations. 128pp. 9¼ x 10¾. 27430-6

PHOTOGRAPHIC SKETCHBOOK OF THE CIVIL WAR, Alexander Gardner. 100 photos taken on field during the Civil War. Famous shots of Manassas Harper's Ferry, Lincoln, Richmond, slave pens, etc. 244pp. 10⅝ x 8¼. 22731-6

FIVE ACRES AND INDEPENDENCE, Maurice G. Kains. Great back-to-the-land classic explains basics of self-sufficient farming. The one book to get. 95 illustrations. 397pp. 5⅜ x 8½. 20974-1

SONGS OF EASTERN BIRDS, Dr. Donald J. Borror. Songs and calls of 60 species most common to eastern U.S.: warblers, woodpeckers, flycatchers, thrushes, larks, many more in high-quality recording. Cassette and manual 99912-2

A MODERN HERBAL, Margaret Grieve. Much the fullest, most exact, most useful compilation of herbal material. Gigantic alphabetical encyclopedia, from aconite to zedoary, gives botanical information, medical properties, folklore, economic uses, much else. Indispensable to serious reader. 161 illustrations. 888pp. 6½ x 9¼. 2-vol. set. (Available in U.S. only.) Vol. I: 22798-7 Vol. II: 22799-5

HIDDEN TREASURE MAZE BOOK, Dave Phillips. Solve 34 challenging mazes accompanied by heroic tales of adventure. Evil dragons, people-eating plants, blood-thirsty giants, many more dangerous adversaries lurk at every twist and turn. 34 mazes, stories, solutions. 48pp. 8¼ x 11. 24566-7

LETTERS OF W. A. MOZART, Wolfgang A. Mozart. Remarkable letters show bawdy wit, humor, imagination, musical insights, contemporary musical world; includes some letters from Leopold Mozart. 276pp. 5⅜ x 8½. 22859-2

BASIC PRINCIPLES OF CLASSICAL BALLET, Agrippina Vaganova. Great Russian theoretician, teacher explains methods for teaching classical ballet. 118 illustrations. 175pp. 5⅜ x 8½. 22036-2

THE JUMPING FROG, Mark Twain. Revenge edition. The original story of The Celebrated Jumping Frog of Calaveras County, a hapless French translation, and Twain's hilarious "retranslation" from the French. 12 illustrations. 66pp. 5⅜ x 8½. 22686-7

BEST REMEMBERED POEMS, Martin Gardner (ed.). The 126 poems in this superb collection of 19th- and 20th-century British and American verse range from Shelley's "To a Skylark" to the impassioned "Renascence" of Edna St. Vincent Millay and to Edward Lear's whimsical "The Owl and the Pussycat." 224pp. 5⅜ x 8½. 27165-X

COMPLETE SONNETS, William Shakespeare. Over 150 exquisite poems deal with love, friendship, the tyranny of time, beauty's evanescence, death and other themes in language of remarkable power, precision and beauty. Glossary of archaic terms. 80pp. 5³⁄₁₆ x 8¼. 26686-9

THE BATTLES THAT CHANGED HISTORY, Fletcher Pratt. Eminent historian profiles 16 crucial conflicts, ancient to modern, that changed the course of civilization. 352pp. 5⅜ x 8½. 41129-X

THE WIT AND HUMOR OF OSCAR WILDE, Alvin Redman (ed.). More than 1,000 ripostes, paradoxes, wisecracks: Work is the curse of the drinking classes; I can resist everything except temptation; etc. 258pp. 5⅜ x 8½. 20602-5

SHAKESPEARE LEXICON AND QUOTATION DICTIONARY, Alexander Schmidt. Full definitions, locations, shades of meaning in every word in plays and poems. More than 50,000 exact quotations. 1,485pp. 6½ x 9¼. 2-vol. set.
Vol. 1: 22726-X
Vol. 2: 22727-8

SELECTED POEMS, Emily Dickinson. Over 100 best-known, best-loved poems by one of America's foremost poets, reprinted from authoritative early editions. No comparable edition at this price. Index of first lines. 64pp. 5³⁄₁₆ x 8¼. 26466-1

THE INSIDIOUS DR. FU-MANCHU, Sax Rohmer. The first of the popular mystery series introduces a pair of English detectives to their archnemesis, the diabolical Dr. Fu-Manchu. Flavorful atmosphere, fast-paced action, and colorful characters enliven this classic of the genre. 208pp. 5³⁄₁₆ x 8¼. 29898-1

THE MALLEUS MALEFICARUM OF KRAMER AND SPRENGER, translated by Montague Summers. Full text of most important witchhunter's "bible," used by both Catholics and Protestants. 278pp. 6⅝ x 10. 22802-9

SPANISH STORIES/CUENTOS ESPAÑOLES: A Dual-Language Book, Angel Flores (ed.). Unique format offers 13 great stories in Spanish by Cervantes, Borges, others. Faithful English translations on facing pages. 352pp. 5⅜ x 8½. 25399-6

GARDEN CITY, LONG ISLAND, IN EARLY PHOTOGRAPHS, 1869–1919, Mildred H. Smith. Handsome treasury of 118 vintage pictures, accompanied by carefully researched captions, document the Garden City Hotel fire (1899), the Vanderbilt Cup Race (1908), the first airmail flight departing from the Nassau Boulevard Aerodrome (1911), and much more. 96pp. 8⅞ x 11¾. 40669-5

OLD QUEENS, N.Y., IN EARLY PHOTOGRAPHS, Vincent F. Seyfried and William Asadorian. Over 160 rare photographs of Maspeth, Jamaica, Jackson Heights, and other areas. Vintage views of DeWitt Clinton mansion, 1939 World's Fair and more. Captions. 192pp. 8⅞ x 11. 26358-4

CAPTURED BY THE INDIANS: 15 Firsthand Accounts, 1750-1870, Frederick Drimmer. Astounding true historical accounts of grisly torture, bloody conflicts, relentless pursuits, miraculous escapes and more, by people who lived to tell the tale. 384pp. 5⅜ x 8½. 24901-8

THE WORLD'S GREAT SPEECHES (Fourth Enlarged Edition), Lewis Copeland, Lawrence W. Lamm, and Stephen J. McKenna. Nearly 300 speeches provide public speakers with a wealth of updated quotes and inspiration–from Pericles' funeral oration and William Jennings Bryan's "Cross of Gold Speech" to Malcolm X's powerful words on the Black Revolution and Earl of Spenser's tribute to his sister, Diana, Princess of Wales. 944pp. 5⅜ x 8⅜. 40903-1

THE BOOK OF THE SWORD, Sir Richard F. Burton. Great Victorian scholar/adventurer's eloquent, erudite history of the "queen of weapons"–from prehistory to early Roman Empire. Evolution and development of early swords, variations (sabre, broadsword, cutlass, scimitar, etc.), much more. 336pp. 6⅛ x 9¼.
25434-8

AUTOBIOGRAPHY: The Story of My Experiments with Truth, Mohandas K. Gandhi. Boyhood, legal studies, purification, the growth of the Satyagraha (nonviolent protest) movement. Critical, inspiring work of the man responsible for the freedom of India. 480pp. 5⅜ x 8½. (Available in U.S. only.) 24593-4

CELTIC MYTHS AND LEGENDS, T. W. Rolleston. Masterful retelling of Irish and Welsh stories and tales. Cuchulain, King Arthur, Deirdre, the Grail, many more. First paperback edition. 58 full-page illustrations. 512pp. 5⅜ x 8½. 26507-2

THE PRINCIPLES OF PSYCHOLOGY, William James. Famous long course complete, unabridged. Stream of thought, time perception, memory, experimental methods; great work decades ahead of its time. 94 figures. 1,391pp. 5⅜ x 8½. 2-vol. set.
Vol. I: 20381-6   Vol. II: 20382-4

THE WORLD AS WILL AND REPRESENTATION, Arthur Schopenhauer. Definitive English translation of Schopenhauer's life work, correcting more than 1,000 errors, omissions in earlier translations. Translated by E. F. J. Payne. Total of 1,269pp. 5⅜ x 8½. 2-vol. set.   Vol. 1: 21761-2   Vol. 2: 21762-0

MAGIC AND MYSTERY IN TIBET, Madame Alexandra David-Neel. Experiences among lamas, magicians, sages, sorcerers, Bonpa wizards. A true psychic discovery. 32 illustrations. 321pp. 5⅜ x 8½. (Available in U.S. only.) 22682-4

THE EGYPTIAN BOOK OF THE DEAD, E. A. Wallis Budge. Complete reproduction of Ani's papyrus, finest ever found. Full hieroglyphic text, interlinear transliteration, word-for-word translation, smooth translation. 533pp. 6½ x 9¼. 21866-X

MATHEMATICS FOR THE NONMATHEMATICIAN, Morris Kline. Detailed, college-level treatment of mathematics in cultural and historical context, with numerous exercises. Recommended Reading Lists. Tables. Numerous figures. 641pp. 5⅜ x 8½. 24823-2

PROBABILISTIC METHODS IN THE THEORY OF STRUCTURES, Isaac Elishakoff. Well-written introduction covers the elements of the theory of probability from two or more random variables, the reliability of such multivariable structures, the theory of random function, Monte Carlo methods of treating problems incapable of exact solution, and more. Examples. 502pp. 5⅜ x 8½. 40691-1

THE RIME OF THE ANCIENT MARINER, Gustave Doré, S. T. Coleridge. Doré's finest work; 34 plates capture moods, subtleties of poem. Flawless full-size reproductions printed on facing pages with authoritative text of poem. "Beautiful. Simply beautiful."—Publisher's Weekly. 77pp. 9¼ x 12. 22305-1

NORTH AMERICAN INDIAN DESIGNS FOR ARTISTS AND CRAFTSPEOPLE, Eva Wilson. Over 360 authentic copyright-free designs adapted from Navajo blankets, Hopi pottery, Sioux buffalo hides, more. Geometrics, symbolic figures, plant and animal motifs, etc. 128pp. 8⅜ x 11. (Not for sale in the United Kingdom.) 25341-4

SCULPTURE: Principles and Practice, Louis Slobodkin. Step-by-step approach to clay, plaster, metals, stone; classical and modern. 253 drawings, photos. 255pp. 8⅛ x 11. 22960-2

THE INFLUENCE OF SEA POWER UPON HISTORY, 1660–1783, A. T. Mahan. Influential classic of naval history and tactics still used as text in war colleges. First paperback edition. 4 maps. 24 battle plans. 640pp. 5⅜ x 8½. 25509-3

THE STORY OF THE TITANIC AS TOLD BY ITS SURVIVORS, Jack Winocour (ed.). What it was really like. Panic, despair, shocking inefficiency, and a little heroism. More thrilling than any fictional account. 26 illustrations. 320pp. 5⅜ x 8½.
20610-6

FAIRY AND FOLK TALES OF THE IRISH PEASANTRY, William Butler Yeats (ed.). Treasury of 64 tales from the twilight world of Celtic myth and legend: "The Soul Cages," "The Kildare Pooka," "King O'Toole and his Goose," many more. Introduction and Notes by W. B. Yeats. 352pp. 5⅜ x 8½.
26941-8

BUDDHIST MAHAYANA TEXTS, E. B. Cowell and others (eds.). Superb, accurate translations of basic documents in Mahayana Buddhism, highly important in history of religions. The Buddha-karita of Asvaghosha, Larger Sukhavativyuha, more. 448pp. 5⅜ x 8½.
25552-2

ONE TWO THREE . . . INFINITY: Facts and Speculations of Science, George Gamow. Great physicist's fascinating, readable overview of contemporary science: number theory, relativity, fourth dimension, entropy, genes, atomic structure, much more. 128 illustrations. Index. 352pp. 5⅜ x 8½.
25664-2

EXPERIMENTATION AND MEASUREMENT, W. J. Youden. Introductory manual explains laws of measurement in simple terms and offers tips for achieving accuracy and minimizing errors. Mathematics of measurement, use of instruments, experimenting with machines. 1994 edition. Foreword. Preface. Introduction. Epilogue. Selected Readings. Glossary. Index. Tables and figures. 128pp. 5⅜ x 8½.
40451-X

DALÍ ON MODERN ART: The Cuckolds of Antiquated Modern Art, Salvador Dalí. Influential painter skewers modern art and its practitioners. Outrageous evaluations of Picasso, Cézanne, Turner, more. 15 renderings of paintings discussed. 44 calligraphic decorations by Dalí. 96pp. 5⅜ x 8½. (Available in U.S. only.)
29220-7

ANTIQUE PLAYING CARDS: A Pictorial History, Henry René D'Allemagne. Over 900 elaborate, decorative images from rare playing cards (14th–20th centuries): Bacchus, death, dancing dogs, hunting scenes, royal coats of arms, players cheating, much more. 96pp. 9¼ x 12¼.
29265-7

MAKING FURNITURE MASTERPIECES: 30 Projects with Measured Drawings, Franklin H. Gottshall. Step-by-step instructions, illustrations for constructing handsome, useful pieces, among them a Sheraton desk, Chippendale chair, Spanish desk, Queen Anne table and a William and Mary dressing mirror. 224pp. 8⅛ x 11¼.
29338-6

THE FOSSIL BOOK: A Record of Prehistoric Life, Patricia V. Rich et al. Profusely illustrated definitive guide covers everything from single-celled organisms and dinosaurs to birds and mammals and the interplay between climate and man. Over 1,500 illustrations. 760pp. 7½ x 10⅛.
29371-8